American Heart Association®

Learn and Live SM

Low-Fat,
Low-Cholesterol
cookbook FOURTH EDITION

Also by the American Heart Association

American Heart Association No-Fad Diet

The New American Heart Association Cookbook, 7th Edition

American Heart Association Low-Salt Cookbook, 3rd Edition

American Heart Association Quick & Easy Cookbook

American Heart Association Meals in Minutes

American Heart Association One-Dish Meals

American Heart Association Low-Calorie Cookbook

American Heart Association Low-Fat & Luscious Desserts

American Heart Association To Your Health!

American Heart Association®

Learn and Live SM

Low-Fat, Low-Cholesterol
cookbook FOURTH EDITION

delicious recipes to help lower your cholesterol

Clarkson Potter/Publishers
NEW YORK

Published in the United States by Clarkson Potter/Publishers, an imprint of the Crown Publishing Group, a division of Random House, Inc., New York.
www.crownpublishing.com
www.clarksonpotter.com

CLARKSON POTTER is a trademark and POTTER with colophon is a registered trademark of Random House, Inc.

Originally published in hardcover by Clarkson Potter/Publishers, an imprint of the Crown Publishing Group, a division of Random House, Inc., New York, in 2008.

Your contribution to the American Heart Association supports research that helps make publications like this possible. For more information, call 1-800-AHA-USA1 (1-800-242-8721) or contact us online at www.americanheart.org.

Library of Congress Cataloging-in-Publication Data

American Heart Association's low-fat, low-cholesterol cookbook : delicious recipes to help lower your cholesterol.—4th ed.
    p. cm.
  Includes index.
  1. Low-fat diet—Recipes. 2. Low-cholesterol diet—Recipes. I. American Heart Association. II. Title: Low-fat, low-cholesterol cookbook.

  RM237.7.A44 2008
  641.5'6384—dc22   2007050010

ISBN 978-0-307-58755-8

Printed in the United States of America

Design by Dominika Dmytrowski

10   9   8   7   6   5

Cover photographs by Ben Fink

Pictured on front cover: Greek-Style Stewed Chicken *(page 163)*
Pictured on back cover: Sirloin Steak with Portobello Mushrooms
(page 184)

First Paperback Fourth Edition

contents

acknowledgments

American Heart Association Consumer Publications
>   Director: Linda S. Ball
>   Managing Editor: Deborah A. Renza
>   Senior Editor: Janice Roth Moss
>   Science Editor/Writer: Jacqueline F. Haigney
>   Assistant Editor: Roberta W. Sullivan
>   Senior Marketing Manager: Bharati Gaitonde

Recipe Developers for Fourth Edition
>   Nancy S. Hughes
>   Annie King
>   Carol Ritchie
>   Julie Shapero, R.D., L.D.

Recipe Developers for Previous Editions
>   Sherry Ferguson
>   Nancy S. Hughes
>   Laureen Mody, R.D.
>   Leni Reed, R.D.
>   Carol Ritchie
>   Linda Foley Woodrum

Nutrition Analyst
>   Tammi Hancock, R.D.

preface

At the American Heart Association, we know that managing what you eat is one of the best ways to take care of your heart. We want to help, so we bring you this updated and revised edition of the *American Heart Association Low-Fat, Low-Cholesterol Cookbook*. We have combined the American Heart Association's updated dietary and lifestyle recommendations with usable, practical advice to provide the best resource on good-for-you food and good heart health.

The *American Heart Association Low-Fat, Low-Cholesterol Cookbook, Fourth Edition,* will teach you how to make healthy food choices every day to help you lower your cholesterol level and enjoy an overall heart-healthy diet. The 200 delicious recipes—including 50 brand-new ones—show how you can savor the great flavor of food while limiting your intake of saturated fat, trans fat, and cholesterol. These three substances contribute to high low-density lipoprotein (LDL) cholesterol—a major risk factor for heart disease.

In addition to new recipes in every chapter, the cookbook offers easy-to-use strategies for healthier shopping, cooking, and dining out; information on what foods are best to eat; and ways to put together your own heart-healthy eating plan following the American Heart Association's recommendations. As the most trusted authority on heart health, the American Heart Association has also provided important health information, including the risk factors for heart disease, ways to reduce the factors you can control, and ways to lower your blood cholesterol through both diet and lifestyle.

With this newest edition of the *American Heart Association Low-Fat, Low-Cholesterol Cookbook,* we invite you to enjoy our classic favorite recipes, such as Chicken Ragout (page 156) and Strawberries Romanoff (page 328), as well as fall in love with new ones, such as Seared Tuna with Mango-Pear Salsa (page 116) and Triple-Chocolate Brownies (page 316). As the perfect companion for today's healthy cook, this book will help you put delicious food on the table and take control of your heart health.

From our kitchen to yours, eat wisely and eat well!

Rose Marie Robertson, M.D., FAHA, FACC
Chief Science Officer, American Heart Association/
American Stroke Association

"Building healthier lives, free of cardiovascular diseases and stroke"

fats, cholesterol, and heart health

Eating well is one of the joys of life. Because you want foods that both taste good and promote good health, this cookbook offers you lots of excellent choices ranging from appetizers to desserts, all high in flavor but low in saturated fat, trans fat, and cholesterol. These three substances—especially saturated fat—are the dietary villains that cause your blood levels of harmful low-density lipoprotein cholesterol (LDL, the "bad" cholesterol) to rise. That's a serious concern because high cholesterol is a major risk factor for heart disease. The more LDL cholesterol circulating in your blood, the greater your risk.

You can take three important steps to help manage your risk of heart disease. First, assess your personal situation and identify all your risk factors. Second, start reducing your LDL cholesterol level—and other risk factors—by making smart decisions about your diet and lifestyle. Third, commit to making good choices for the long term to live a longer, healthier life.

STEP 1: Know Your Risk

The first step is to assess your individual risk for heart disease. Risk factors are the behaviors and conditions that increase your chance of developing a disease. Some risk factors—aging and the medical history of your family—can't be changed. Fortunately, most risk factors *can* be changed. Lifestyle choices such as smoking and physical inactivity, as well as conditions such as high blood cholesterol, high blood pressure, overweight and obesity, and diabetes, are all factors that you *can* do something about. In fact, heart disease is largely preventable.

Before you can make changes, though, you need to identify the risk factors you can personally control. For example, your levels of total cholesterol, LDL cholesterol, and high-density lipoprotein cholesterol (HDL, the "good" cholesterol)—determined with a simple blood test—help identify your risk of heart disease. (Refer to Appendix D on page 346 for a detailed explanation of how cholesterol affects your heart health.) If you don't know your numbers for blood cholesterol, blood pressure, and blood glucose, visit your healthcare provider and find out what they are.

When your numbers are available, go through this Risk Assessment checklist. The more factors you check, the higher your risk of heart disease. (For more information, see Appendix E, page 349.) For a complete personalized risk assessment, talk with your healthcare provider.

Risk factors you *cannot* change:

☐ Age, if you're a man over 45 years or if you're a woman over 55 years

☐ Family history of premature heart disease

Risk factors you *can* change:

☐ Weight if you are overweight or obese (see the BMI chart on page 10)

☐ Waist measurement of 35 inches or more for a woman or 40 inches or more for a man

☐ Total cholesterol of 240 mg/dL or more (see the chart on page 3)

☐ LDL ("bad") cholesterol of 100 mg/dL or more

☐ HDL ("good") cholesterol less than 40 mg/dL for a man or less than 50 mg/dL for a woman

☐ Blood pressure of 130/85 mm Hg or more

☐ Triglyceride level of 150 mg/dL or more

☐ Blood glucose level of 100 mg/dL or more

☐ Less than 30 minutes of physical activity on most days

☐ Smoking or exposure to secondhand smoke

*mg/dL indicates milligrams per deciliter; mm Hg, milliliters of mercury

Understanding Cholesterol

The cholesterol measured in your blood, or serum cholesterol, is produced by your liver to meet your body's needs. The cholesterol in foods, or dietary cholesterol, comes from animal sources—meats, poultry, seafood, and fat-containing dairy products such as ice cream, whole milk, and 2%-fat milk. (Plant foods do not contain cholesterol.) Consistently eating foods high in saturated fat, trans fat, and dietary cholesterol can cause your liver to produce extra cholesterol, raising your blood cholesterol level. That's why it's important to know what you're eating and what to cut back on to keep your blood cholesterol low. Once you know your cholesterol numbers, you'll have a better idea of your level of risk.

Total Cholesterol	LDL Cholesterol	HDL Cholesterol
Desirable: less than 200 mg/dL	**Optimal (ideal):** less than 100 mg/dL*	**Major risk factor for heart disease:** less than 40 mg/dL for a man and less than 50 mg/dL for a woman
Borderline-high risk: 200 to 239 mg/dL	**Near optimal/above optimal:** 100 to 129 mg/dL	**Some protection against heart disease:** 60 mg/dL and above
High risk: 240 mg/dL and above	**Borderline-high risk:** 130 to 159 mg/dL	
	High risk: 160 to 189 mg/dL	
	Very high risk: 190 mg/dL and above	

Your other risk factors help determine what your LDL level should be. A healthy level for you may not be healthy for your friend or neighbor. If you have metabolic syndrome in addition to heart disease, your healthcare provider will assess your risk factors and decide whether an LDL goal of less than 70 is right for you, especially if your triglyceride level is 200 or higher and your HDL is less than 40.

Lowering LDL Cholesterol Lessens Risk

The main goal in treating high total cholesterol is to lower your LDL level. Reducing your LDL can slow, stop, or even reverse the buildup of plaque in your arteries that can lead to a heart attack (see Appendix D on page 346 for more information). Many variables affect the amount of cholesterol your body produces and how much of it is in the form of LDL cholesterol, HDL cholesterol, or triglycerides (other fats present in your blood). By changing some of these variables, especially your dietary habits and lifestyle choices, you can help reduce your level of blood cholesterol.

As a general rule, if you reduce your total cholesterol level by 1 percent, you reduce your heart attack risk by 2 percent. This means that if, for example, you reduce your blood cholesterol from 250 to 200 mg/dL (a 20 percent decrease), you could reduce your heart attack risk by 40 percent.

Be sure to schedule regular visits with your healthcare provider to monitor your individual situation. Depending on your cholesterol levels and your other risk factors, decide together on target goals and the best approach to reach them. How much you have to modify your diet and lifestyle depends on several things, including your other risk factors and how your body responds to changes in your diet. For many people, relatively minor changes can reduce their risk significantly. Others need to make more extensive lifestyle changes.

STEP 2: Reduce Your Risk Through Diet and Lifestyle

The second step toward managing your risk of heart disease and stroke is to make smart decisions about your diet and lifestyle. Eating well and being physically active are the best ways to start managing your LDL cholesterol and other modifiable risk factors. If your healthcare provider also prescribes cholesterol-lowering drugs, you still should modify your diet and lifestyle. These changes not only lower cholesterol but also help control many of the other risk factors for heart disease, including high blood pressure, overweight and obesity, and diabetes.

The main components of a lifestyle approach to lowering cholesterol are:

- A heart-healthy eating plan
- Physical activity
- Weight management

Follow a Heart-Healthy Diet

The more research we do, the more we understand how the foods you eat affect the levels of cholesterol in your blood. If you replace the foods in your diet that are high in saturated fat, trans fat, and cholesterol with nutritious foods that are not, you will naturally reduce your blood cholesterol levels. The recommendations here and in "Healthy Food, Healthy Heart" (pages 13–21) are designed to help you do just that.

Reduce saturated fat to 7 percent and trans fat to 1 percent of your daily calories. Saturated fat, which is found in animal products and some plant products, raises blood cholesterol more than anything else in your diet. Trans fat, found primarily in commercial products made with or fried in partially hydrogenated oils, also increases cholesterol. However, the typical American diet includes far more saturated fat than trans fat. In fact, most people currently take in an average of about 11 percent of their calories from saturated fat compared with about 2.5 percent from trans fat. When you choose foods in restaurants or for meals you prepare at home, try to limit both of these fats. See "Fats and Oils," page 19, for suggestions on how to replace harmful saturated and trans fats with helpful unsaturated oils.

Keep total fat to between 25 and 35 percent of your daily calories. It's the type of fat more than how much fat you consume that most affects your blood cholesterol level. On the other hand, all fats are high in calories (about 9 calories in each gram of fat, regardless of type, as opposed to 4 calories in proteins and carbohydrates), and eating too much of any fat can lead to adding too many

If each day you eat about...	You should limit your daily intake of		
	saturated fat to less than...	trans fat to less than...	total fat to about...
1,200 calories	9 g	1 g	33 to 47 g
1,500 calories	11 g	1.5 g	42 to 58 g
1,800 calories	13 g	2 g	50 to 70 g
2,000 calories	15 g	2 g	56 to 78 g
2,500 calories	19 g	2.5 g	70 to 97 g

calories, which causes weight gain. The range in the recommended percentage of total fat allows you to decide how much is right for you.

Reduce dietary cholesterol to less than 200 mg a day. The cholesterol in the foods you eat adds to the amount of cholesterol in your blood, but not as significantly as saturated fat. Dietary cholesterol comes exclusively from animal products, such as meats (especially organ meats), poultry, seafood, egg yolks, and dairy products containing fat, including cheeses and butter. These foods are usually high in saturated fat as well as cholesterol, so by limiting one you can help reduce the other.

See the chart on page 335 for a list of common ingredients that contain cholesterol and saturated fat. Pages 15–21, "Make Healthy Food Choices," offer practical tips on how you can choose wisely to eat less cholesterol.

Gradually increase your daily intake of soluble fiber to 10 to 25 grams. Fiber is the part of food that we cannot digest, but it plays an important role in good health. Of the two types, soluble and insoluble, only soluble fiber helps reduce LDL cholesterol. Studies show that when combined with a diet low in saturated fat and cholesterol, eating between 5 and 10 grams of soluble fiber each day may help reduce LDL cholesterol by up to 5 percent. Eating fiber-rich foods can also help you eat less by making you feel fuller. Increase your fiber intake gradually to avoid abdominal cramps or bloating.

• Whole grains, such as oatmeal and barley, are fantastic sources of fiber. Include hot or cold cereals in your routine to easily increase your daily intake.

• Eat whole fruits or vegetables instead of drinking juices. One medium orange has three times the fiber of 6 ounces of juice.

- Fiber-containing foods include apples, bananas, pears, oranges, grapefruit, strawberries, raspberries, nuts, broccoli, carrots, brussels sprouts, and legumes, such as black beans, kidney beans, lima beans, chickpeas, and lentils.

Include 2 grams of plant stanols and sterols in your diet if needed to further lower cholesterol. Studies have shown that including about 2 grams of stanols and/or sterols in your diet may help further reduce levels of LDL cholesterol. Stanols and sterols, which occur naturally in many plants, have been added to some margarines and other foods to make them readily available. (For use in commercial foods, the stanols and sterols are isolated from soybean oil and oil from tall pine trees.) Remember that foods containing stanols and/or sterols are not calorie-free. If you use these products, you may need to offset the calories by cutting back elsewhere.

If you think you might benefit from adding stanols or sterols to your diet, ask your healthcare provider whether this option should be part of your eating plan and which foods would be the best choices for you.

Consider Other Dietary Factors

Several other dietary factors have important effects on your heart health even though they do not directly relate to your cholesterol level.

Limit sodium intake. People with high cholesterol often also have high blood pressure. Eating a healthy diet, being physically active, and limiting your sodium intake to less than 2,300 milligrams per day are the first steps to managing your blood pressure. For the most benefit, your goal should be even lower. Reducing the amount of sodium in your diet helps lower your blood pressure or even prevents it from rising.

Certain people—African Americans, middle-aged and older adults, and people with high blood pressure—should aim for less than 1,500 milligrams of sodium each day.

Increase intake of omega-3 fatty acids. Research suggests that increased intake of omega-3 fatty acids—which are found in fish such as salmon, halibut, mackerel, and tuna—reduces the risk for heart attack and death from heart disease. We recommend that you eat at least two servings of fish rich in omega-3 fatty acids every week. If you already have heart disease or high blood triglyceride levels, your healthcare professional may recommend fish oil supplements to help increase your intake of omega-3 fatty acids.

Although nearly all fish and shellfish may contain mercury and other contaminants, the health risks from mercury exposure depend on the amount of seafood eaten and the levels of mercury in the fish itself. Eating a variety of fish will help minimize the possible adverse effects caused by pollutants in the environment. Women who are pregnant, planning to become pregnant, or nursing—and young children—should avoid eating potentially contaminated fish. For most people, however, the benefits of eating fish far outweigh the risks.

Use alcohol in moderation. Studies have shown that moderate intake of alcohol may reduce risk for heart disease. High alcohol intake, however, can have dangerous consequences. Alcohol also adds calories to your diet without adding nutrients. If you do drink alcohol, do so in moderation. If you don't drink, don't start.

Drinking in moderation means no more than one drink per day for women or two drinks per day for men. One drink is equal to 12 ounces of beer, 4 ounces of wine, or 1½ ounces of 80-proof distilled spirits.

Stay Active

We know that regular physical activity protects against heart disease. It increases levels of helpful HDL cholesterol and in some people reduces LDL cholesterol. It also helps you manage your weight and reduce your blood pressure. We recommend that you aim for at least 30 minutes of moderate-intensity physical activity on five days of each week or 20 minutes of vigorous activity on three days. You can break your activity into sessions of 10 minutes or more and include moderate-intensity activities you might not consider "exercise," such as gardening and housework, that add up during the day. In addition to the health benefits you'll gain from being active, you'll probably find you feel better, have more energy, and can make other lifestyle changes more easily.

Use the following chart to estimate how many calories you can burn in various activities at different intensities. Your current weight and gender affect the number of calories you use, and the more muscular you are, the more calories you burn. The numbers given are for a person of about 150 pounds. If you weigh more, you will burn more, and if you weigh less, you will burn fewer calories.

It's a good idea to talk with your healthcare provider before starting an exercise program if you haven't exercised for a long time. Likewise, if you have had a heart attack or have a medical condition (such as high blood pressure, high cholesterol, diabetes, or obesity), take prescription medication, are a smoker, are over 65, or are at risk for heart disease because of family history, it's important to discuss your situation with your healthcare professional.

Calories Burned in 30 Minutes of Physical Activity			
Moderate Intensity	Calories	Vigorous Intensity	Calories
Hiking	185	Running/jogging	295
Light gardening/yard work	165	Bicycling (more than 10 mph)	295
Dancing	165	Swimming (slow freestyle laps)	255
Golf (walking and carrying clubs)	165	Aerobics	240
Bicycling (less than 10 mph)	145	Walking (4.5 mph)	230
Walking (3.5 mph)	140	Weight lifting (active workout)	220
Weight lifting (light workout)	110	Basketball	220

Adapted from *Your Guide to Physical Activity and Your Heart,* U.S. Department of Health and Human Services, NIH Publication No. 06-5714.

Manage Your Weight

It's one thing to read about what you "should" do to stay healthy, but it's another to decide to make those recommendations a real part of your life. Recognizing the habits that keep you from effectively managing your weight will help you adopt the behaviors that lead to a longer, stronger life.

Determine how many total calories you need each day. Each of us needs an ideal number of calories to maintain a healthy weight. You can estimate how many daily calories you need based on your age, gender, and level of physical activity. (The footnotes in the chart on page 9 will give you an idea of which level is most accurate for you.) Remember that as you age, you'll need fewer calories to maintain your weight even if you stay at the same level of activity.

Maintain your calorie balance. To avoid weight gain, you should burn at least as many calories as you eat every day. Calories *in* should equal calories *out.* If you consistently take in more calories than you need for your age and level of physical activity, you will gradually gain weight. Everyone is different, but the chart on page 9 should give you an idea of what you need to maintain your individual calorie balance. For example, if you are a 35-year-old woman who is moderately active, you will usually burn about 2,000 calories a day. To maintain your calorie balance—and your current weight—you should eat no more than about 2,000 calories a day.

	Age	Sedentary	Moderately Active	Active
Female	19–30 years	2,000 calories	2,000–2,200 calories	2,400 calories
	31–50	1,800	2,000	2,200
	51+	1,600	1,800	2,000–2,200
Male	19–30	2,400	2,600–2,800	3,000
	31–50	2,200	2,400–2,600	2,800–3,000
	51+	2,000	2,200–2,400	2,400–2,800

Activity Level and Estimated Calories Burned

Sedentary means you have a lifestyle that includes only the light physical activity associated with typical day-to-day life.

Moderately active means you have a lifestyle that includes physical activity equivalent to walking about 1.5 to 3 miles per day at 3 to 4 miles per hour, in addition to the light physical activity associated with typical day-to-day life.

Active means you have a lifestyle that includes physical activity equivalent to walking more than 3 miles per day at 3 to 4 miles per hour, in addition to the light physical activity associated with typical day-to-day life.

Know when to lose weight. Being overweight or obese increases your likelihood of developing heart disease and stroke even if you have no other risk factors. Excess weight reduces levels of helpful HDL cholesterol and may raise levels of harmful LDL cholesterol. Your risk is significantly greater if you're a man with a waist measuring more than 40 inches or a woman with a waist more than 35 inches. Losing weight—even as little as 10 pounds—can help reduce your LDL cholesterol levels.

You can use the body mass index (BMI) to see whether you are overweight. This standard method classifies body weight based on your weight and height. If you fall in the overweight or obese category, think about beginning a weight-loss plan. Aim to reestablish your calorie balance to maintain a healthy weight. To find your BMI, weigh yourself without clothes or shoes. Measure your height without shoes. Find your height in the left-hand column of the chart on page 10 and see which range your weight falls into.

To calculate your exact BMI, multiply your weight in pounds by 705. Divide the product by your height in inches; divide again by your height in inches. If you have a BMI of 30 or above, you should discuss a weight-loss plan with your healthcare provider.

	Find Your Body Mass Index (BMI)		
Height	Minimal Risk (BMI Under 25)	Overweight (BMI 25.0–29.9)	Obese (BMI 30.0 and Above)
4'10"	118 lb or less	119–142 lb	143 lb or more
4'11"	123	124–147	148
5'0"	127	128–152	153
5'1"	131	132–157	158
5'2"	135	136–163	164
5'3"	140	141–168	169
5'4"	144	145–173	174
5'5"	149	150–179	180
5'6"	154	155–185	186
5'7"	158	159–190	191
5'8"	163	164–196	197
5'9"	168	169–202	203
5'10"	173	174–208	209
5'11"	178	179–214	215
6'0"	183	184–220	221
6'1"	188	189–226	227
6'2"	193	194–232	233
6'3"	199	200–239	240
6'4"	204	205–245	246

A BMI from 18.5 to 24.9 is considered healthy. A BMI from 25.0 to 29.9 is considered over-weight and indicates a moderate risk of heart and blood vessel disease. A BMI of 25 translates to about 10 percent over ideal body weight. A BMI over 30 indicates a high risk of heart and blood vessel disease.

Understand serving sizes and use portion control. Research shows that portions have increased dramatically in the last 20 years. Americans eat more at each meal than ever before. It isn't necessary, however, to count calories and measure out exact amounts every day to keep portions in line with calorie needs. Instead, learn to visualize reasonable servings of different foods.

Think in terms of the size of common objects:

- 3 ounces of cooked meat, poultry, or fish is the size of a deck of cards.
- 1½ ounces of cheese is the size of a 1½-inch cube.
- 1 medium baked potato is the size of an average fist.
- 1-cup servings are the size of a baseball.

You can use these visualizations to serve the appropriate portions at home, and when you go to a restaurant, eat only that size portion and take home the rest.

STEP 3: Commit to a Lifetime of Healthy Choices

Finally, the third step in managing risk is to commit to a lifestyle that promotes a longer, healthier life. Remember that heart disease is largely preventable. If you eat wisely, stay physically active, and follow the recommendations of your healthcare provider, chances are you will:

- Reduce your likelihood of developing high blood cholesterol if you don't have it.
- Reduce your cholesterol levels if they are high.
- Reduce your risk of developing heart disease and having a stroke.

By consistently making healthy choices throughout your life, you and your family will reap long-lasting benefits for many years to come.

healthy food, healthy heart

The best way to take care of your heart is to become familiar with the principles of good nutrition and apply them—starting in your own kitchen. Once you have the basic information at hand, you can build a heart-healthy, appealing eating plan using our recipes and creatively adapting your own.

Balance and Variety Are the Keys to Eating Well

As you plan your meals at home—and when you make food choices away from home—what matters most is to establish a balanced overall eating pattern. If one day you eat a lot of something you are trying to limit, be especially careful to eat less in the following days to get back in balance. You can satisfy your personal preferences and still be sure you get all the components of a healthy diet while limiting the less nutritious foods.

Six basic nutrition concepts make up the core of our recommendations.

- Eat at least half of your grains as whole-grain foods.
- Eat lots of different vegetables and fruits. In general, more color means more benefit.
- Include fat-free and low-fat dairy foods.
- Choose lean meats and poultry.
- Eat fish rich in omega-3 fatty acids twice a week.
- Eat most of your fats from fish, nuts, seeds, and vegetable oils.

We develop our recipes to deliver lots of flavor and good nutrition without lots of saturated fat, trans fat, cholesterol, sodium, and calories. The amounts per recipe, of course, do vary. As you look through the nutritional data that accompany the recipes, you'll see that a poultry recipe may contain 80 milligrams of cholesterol, while a vegetarian entrée has only 14 milligrams. Every recipe in this book can fit into your individual eating plan, and you can decide how to use that dish to keep your nutrient intake in balance. Unless you eat exactly the same things every day, your intake of one substance—saturated fat or sodium, for example—may go up one day and, if you make good choices, down the next, like a seesaw. Your job is to be sure that if the seesaw goes up, it comes back down. To this end, you want to avoid too much of a less nutritious food and too little of an

Sample Food Log for a Typical Work Day

	Food Choices	Number of Servings of Each Food Type						
		Grains	Vegetables, Legumes	Fruits	Dairy	Fats, Oils	Meat, Poultry	Fish
Breakfast	1 cup oat cereal with ½ cup fat-free milk; 1 banana	1		1	½			
Snack 1	1 glazed doughnut*	2				3		
Lunch	Sandwich made of 2 oz turkey breast on whole-wheat roll, ½ tomato, 1 cup shredded lettuce, 1 Tb light mayonnaise; 1 cup fat-free frozen yogurt	2	1½		1	1	2 oz	
Snack 2	1½ oz regular Cheddar cheese** with 6 whole-wheat crackers and a handful of grapes	1		1	1	1		
Dinner	3 oz broiled salmon, 1 cup broccoli, 1 cup rice pilaf, 1 cup dinner salad with 2 Tb low-fat dressing; 1 apple	2	3	1		1		3 oz
Totals		8	4½	3	2½	6	2 oz	3 oz
Goal	(Based on 2,000 calories per day)	6 to 8	3 to 5	2 to 4	2 to 3	2 to 3	< 5 oz	6 oz/week
Foods to balance in next choices	1½ oz regular Cheddar cheese: high in saturated fat					OVER GOAL: Watch intake of saturated fats		

A doughnut is high in fats and calories and is not a recommended snack, but it is included here to illustrate how such foods affect your overall eating plan.

**Remember that one serving of full-fat cheese counts as both a dairy serving and a fat serving.*

important food so that on average you are eating according to a healthy food pattern for your calorie level over a week's time.

If you are following a cholesterol-lowering eating plan (less than 200 milligrams of cholesterol each day), you will especially need to limit your portions of meat, poultry, and seafood. These animal foods are a primary source of dietary cholesterol. Like many other cookbooks, this one uses a standard portion size of 3 ounces for cooked meats, poultry, and seafood (4 ounces raw). For reference, keep in mind that restaurant portions frequently are significantly larger.

For a low-cholesterol diet, we recommend no more than an average of 5 ounces of animal protein each day. If you eat a meal that includes the standard 3-ounce portion or more, you should limit your intake of cholesterol-containing foods in the other meals you eat that day so your daily total doesn't exceed 5 ounces of animal protein. You can do that by choosing an entrée without meat and eggs, or eating less than the standard portion of meat, at the next meal. If you know you have eaten too much cholesterol on one day, aim to eat less on the following days of the week. Remember, it's all about balance.

Look at the example on page 14 of one woman's food choices for one sample day. You'll see that she does a pretty good job of choosing foods from all the food groups and using fat-free dairy products when she can. But at work, she eats a doughnut to help celebrate a birthday, and later she is served a tray of full-fat cheese in an afternoon meeting. These situations do come up, and sometimes you don't or can't make the best choice. That's okay, as long as you take stock and think about how you can return to balance.

To stay aware of your daily eating habits, keep track of your own food choices with a similar log, and take note of what you need to watch for the next few days. For example, in the sample food log you can easily see that the doughnut doubles the total amount of fat and adds harmful saturated fat. If you chose one small cookie as a treat instead of the doughnut, you could save significantly on both calories and saturated fat. After a few days of keeping a log, you'll see how your choices add up. Whether it's cutting back on one type of food or adding more of another, with a little attention you can take control and balance your overall eating plan.

Make Healthy Food Choices

You have a wide variety of foods to choose from that are low in saturated fat, trans fat, and cholesterol but high in nutrition. Use the chart on page 16 as a guide to help you choose foods and plan the amounts to serve. The range of daily servings shown here is based on a daily intake of 2,000 calories, so you'll need to adjust accordingly depending on your personal calorie balance. Determine how many calories are right for you (see "Manage Your Weight," page 8) so you'll know how many servings from each food type to include.

Concentrating on the foods recommended here will help you keep a good balance and get all the nutrients you need. It's easier, of course, if you're choosing foods you really like. Before you go shopping, write out a sample plan of what you like best from each food group and when and how you can fit those foods into your eating plan. You may find that you need to add servings in a category or two. Consider your usual eating pattern again, this time looking for ways to add what you need.

Food Type	Serving Size
Breads, Cereals, and Grains **6 or more servings per day,** adjusted to calorie needs	
Whole-grain breads and cereals, pasta (especially whole-grain), rice (brown and white), potatoes, fat-free and low-fat crackers and cookies	1 slice bread 1 cup cereal flakes ½ cup cooked rice, pasta, or potato
Vegetables and Legumes **3 to 5 servings per day**	
Fresh, frozen, or canned—without added fat, sauce, or salt	1 cup leafy or raw vegetable ½ cup cooked
Fruits **2 to 4 servings per day**	
Fresh, frozen, canned, or dried—without added sugar	1 medium piece fruit ½ cup diced fruit ¾ cup fruit juice
Dairy Products **2 to 3 servings per day**	
Fat-free or low-fat milk, buttermilk, yogurt, sour cream, cream cheese; and low-fat cheese (with no more than 3 grams of fat per ounce)	1 cup milk 1 cup yogurt 1½ ounces cheese ½ cup cottage cheese
Eggs **2 or fewer yolks per week,** including yolks in baked goods and in cooked or processed foods	
Egg whites or egg substitute as desired	¼ cup egg substitute = 1 egg
Fats and Oils **2 to 3 servings per day,** adjusted to calorie needs	
Unsaturated vegetable oils, liquid or soft margarines and vegetable oil spreads, salad dressings, nuts, and seeds	1 teaspoon soft margarine or vegetable oil 1 tablespoon regular salad dressing or 2 tablespoons low-fat dressing 1 ounce nuts or seeds
Meat, Poultry, and Seafood **5 ounces or less per day (cooked weight)**	
Lean cuts of loin, leg, round; lean ground meat; skinless poultry; fish. Strictly limit organ meats, such as brain, liver, and kidneys, as they are high in cholesterol. Shellfish, such as shrimp, can be moderately high, so eat it only occasionally.	3 ounces or less of cooked meat, poultry, and seafood

Adapted from *Your Guide to Lowering Your Cholesterol with Therapeutic Lifestyle Changes,* U.S. Department of Health and Human Services, NIH Publication No. 06-5235.

Here's an example of how to identify your food preferences and then fit those foods into your eating plan.

FOOD GROUPS: Vegetables, Legumes, and Fruits

FOODS I LIKE IN THESE CATEGORIES: (Vegetables) Broccoli, lettuce, green beans, carrots, spinach, tomatoes, potatoes; (Legumes) Kidney beans, chickpeas; (Fruits) Apples, bananas, green grapes

WHEN I CAN EAT THE FOODS I'VE CHOSEN:

Breakfast: 1 banana sliced in cereal

Lunch: 1 apple for dessert

Dinner: ½ cup steamed broccoli, 2 cups side salad (romaine, tomatoes, chickpeas, and sliced carrots)

Snacks: ½ cup grapes at work

You can also make it easier to eat more of a certain kind of food by stocking up and having that food readily available. If you know you don't eat enough vegetables, for example, keep plenty on hand at home or at work. Do as much preparation in advance as you can so they're easy to grab when you're hungry.

Even on a cholesterol-lowering eating plan, you can occasionally enjoy most of your favorite foods—as long as you plan well and make a few key substitutions. To stock your kitchen, start with a grocery list that covers good choices from all the food groups, referring to your list of favorite foods. Grocery stores are full of tempting choices, so know what you need before you go. Typically, healthful choices such as fresh produce, dairy, seafood, meats, and poultry are located at the edges, while packaged and processed foods are displayed on shelves in the interior of the store. To be sure you start filling your cart with the healthy choices first, begin your shopping trip with a sweep around the perimeter, then add the products you need from the center aisles.

Breads, Cereals, and Grains

Foods in this group are usually high in fiber and complex carbohydrates and low in saturated fat and cholesterol. Try to eat whole-grain products for at least half of your daily servings. Most commercial products are being reformulated to avoid the use of trans fat, but check their nutrition labels.

healthy hints
breads, cereals, and grains

All grains start out "whole," which means they include the entire seed, or kernel, of the plant. Refining techniques used by food manufacturers typically strip away the bran and the germ from the kernel, removing fiber and many important nutrients in the process. To find grains in their whole form, look beyond the labeling on the packaging and read the ingredient list.

CHOOSE:
Whole grains, such as wheat, corn, oats and oatmeal, brown rice, wild rice, bulgur, barley, buckwheat, quinoa.
Whole-grain breads and cereals.
Low-fat, trans-fat-free crackers and cookies.

When choosing bread, cereal, or grain products, look for those that list the whole grain as the first ingredient on the label.

Vegetables, Legumes, and Fruits

Vegetables and fruits are great examples of nutrient-rich foods. They are low in calories but provide important vitamins, minerals, fiber, and other nutrients. Legumes, especially dried beans and peas, are also rich in fiber, provide protein, and are excellent alternatives to animal proteins that contain saturated fat and cholesterol.

CHOOSE:
Vegetables, legumes, and fruits, prepared from fresh, frozen, or canned without added fat, salt, or sugar. Try a wide variety of produce, especially deeply colored vegetables and fruits, such as:
Green: spinach, kale, collard greens, mustard greens, and romaine lettuce
Red: tomatoes and tomato products and red bell peppers
Orange: carrots, sweet potatoes, pumpkins, mangoes, cantaloupes, and apricots
Also include a variety of legumes, such as green peas, black-eyed peas, chickpeas, kidney beans, navy beans, and lentils.

healthy hints
vegetables, legumes, and fruits

- Look for no-salt-added or low-sodium versions of canned vegetables and beans. Manufacturers continue to bring out new products to meet the demand for more-healthful choices.

- Fruits that are canned in water are lower in calories than fruits canned in juice or syrup. If you buy fruits canned in syrup, drain them and discard the syrup before using the fruit.

Dairy Products

Dairy foods are an important part of a healthy diet, providing calcium and protein. So many fat-free and low-fat dairy options are now available, you can easily avoid the high levels of saturated fat found in whole milk and whole-milk products. To see the difference, take a look at the nutrition labels and compare a cup of whole milk to a cup of fat-free milk. By choosing the fat-free version, you'll save about 65 calories, 4.5 grams of saturated fat, and 30 milligrams of cholesterol.

CHOOSE:

Fat-free or low-fat dairy products, such as milk, cheeses, yogurt, sour cream, and cream cheese. As often as possible, choose fat-free or low-fat cheeses, including cottage cheese, that contain less than 3 grams of fat per ounce. Keep in mind that most creamy cheeses, such as Brie and processed cheese spreads, are usually high in saturated fat.

If you buy eggs, plan to eat two or fewer egg yolks per week, including the yolks in baked goods and in cooked or processed foods. One large egg yolk contains about 212 milligrams of cholesterol, so keep this in mind when you consider your daily limit of 200 milligrams of cholesterol. Egg whites and egg substitute, on the other hand, contain no fat or cholesterol and are an excellent source of protein. To try them in recipes, use ¼ cup egg substitute or two egg whites for one whole egg.

healthy hints
dairy products

These popular products are all available as fat-free and/or low-fat:

- Milk, chocolate milk, buttermilk

- Half-and-half, sweetened condensed milk, evaporated milk, dried milk

- Yogurt (plain and flavored), frozen yogurt

- Cheeses: American, Cheddar, Colby, feta, Monterey Jack, mozzarella, ricotta, Swiss

- Cottage cheese

- Cream cheese

Fats and Oils

The main types of fat in foods are saturated fat, trans fat, and unsaturated fat. Saturated fats are found in animal products and in some plant products. Trans fat is found primarily in commercial products made with or fried in partially hydrogenated oils. These are the harmful fats. The helpful fats, polyunsaturated and monounsaturated, are found in vegetable oils, nuts, and seafood.

Percentages of Saturated and Unsaturated Fats in Commonly Used Oils and Fats			
	Saturated	Polyunsaturated	Monounsaturated
Canola oil	7%	31%	59%
Corn oil	14%	60%	25%
Olive oil	14%	10%	75%
Butter	63%	4%	30%
Coconut oil	88%	3%	7%

Values may not add up to 100 percent because of other fatty acids not represented.

- Choose products that are labeled "low-saturated-fat," which means they contain no more than 1 gram of saturated fat per serving.

- Fat-free margarines work well for cooking and for flavoring vegetables and casseroles. Because they contain water, they are not recommended for baking, however.

- Use cooking sprays—plain or flavored—in place of butter or oil on equipment such as pans, baking sheets, and casserole dishes. (Certain nonstick cookware manufacturers advise against using commercial sprays, which contain propellant. Be sure to check your warranty information.)

- Check nutrition labels for trans fat values, but be equally careful about saturated fat. Foods labeled "trans-fat-free" may contain high amounts of saturated fat instead.

One way to distinguish between the harmful and helpful types is to think in terms of consistency. Fats and oils high in saturated fat tend to become hard at room temperature. On the other hand, oils that stay liquid at room temperature are high in polyunsaturated and monounsaturated fats. When it comes to fats, remember that the more liquid, the better.

To change oils from a liquid to a solid form, such as stick margarine, manufacturers have been using the process of hydrogenation. This process creates harmful trans fat. (Many food companies and restaurants will be instituting new processes to avoid creating trans fat as the technology becomes available.) To reduce your intake of both saturated and trans fats, use liquid vegetable oil and trans-fat-free soft margarines instead of butter, stick margarine, or shortening.

CHOOSE:

Unsaturated oils, such as canola, corn, olive, safflower, soybean, sunflower; salad dressings made with vegetable oils; light mayonnaise.

Liquid or soft margarines: The first ingredient on the food label should be unsaturated liquid vegetable oil rather than hydrogenated or partially hydrogenated oil; spreads should be made with vegetable oil.

Nuts and seeds: Most nuts and any variety of seeds are high in helpful unsaturated fats. Check the food labels to compare varieties. Nuts and seeds are also high in calories, however, so adjust your intake according to your calorie needs.

Meat, Poultry, and Seafood

Many Americans eat much more protein than they need. If you are watching your cholesterol level, aim for no more than a total of 5 ounces of lean meat, skinless poultry, and seafood per day. That means you should eat only one 3-ounce portion or two smaller portions each day. The portion size used for most eating plans and in this book is 3 ounces of cooked meat, poultry, or fish.

CHOOSE:

Beef: Lean cuts, such as sirloin, round steak, rump roast; extra-lean ground beef.

Pork: Lean cuts, such as loin chops, tenderloin, and the lowest sodium available center-cut ham and Canadian bacon.

Poultry: Skinless chicken and turkey, all cuts. Dark meat is higher in saturated fat than breast meat.

Fish: At least two servings each week. Try to include oily fish high in omega-3 fatty acids, such as salmon, tuna, halibut, and mackerel.

Shellfish: Shellfish is low in saturated fat but varies in cholesterol content. Some types, such as shrimp and squid, are fairly high in cholesterol. Others, including scallops, mussels, and clams, are low. You can eat shellfish as part of a cholesterol-lowering diet, but make sure it fits within the limit of your total cholesterol for each day.

healthy hints
meats, poultry, and seafood

- Limit processed meats, such as bacon, hot dogs, bologna, salami, and sausage. They're high in saturated fat and sodium. Reduced-fat, low-fat, and/or fat-free versions are available, but watch out for high sodium. Compare labels to find the brands that are lowest in calories, saturated fat, and sodium.

- Buy canned tuna packed in water or in a vacuum-sealed pouch. Low-sodium tuna is now available as well.

The goal of these recommendations is to help you develop healthy eating habits that will last a lifetime. As you become familiar with the best ways to eat a diet low in saturated and trans fats and cholesterol, you will enjoy choosing the healthiest foods (see Appendix A: Healthy Shopping Strategies, page 333) and preparing them in the healthiest ways (see Appendix B: Healthy Cooking Strategies, page 337).

about the recipes

We hope you will be intrigued by, and excited about trying, all the delicious recipes in the following chapters. Our recipe developers have used many creative techniques to deliver the most flavorful food without using unhealthful ingredients or cooking methods. To take advantage of all this cookbook offers, spend a moment familiarizing yourself with the information that accompanies the recipes.

Using the Nutrition Analyses

With each recipe, you'll find a nutritional breakdown of the calorie count and the amounts of different nutrients. New to this edition, we've included trans fat values on all our recipes. By using this information carefully, you can choose the recipes that best meet your needs. Keep the following information in mind as you review the nutrition analyses:

- Each analysis is based on a single serving unless otherwise indicated.
- Optional ingredients and garnishes are not included in the nutrition analysis unless noted. We encourage you to be creative with garnishes, especially fruits and vegetables. If you eat them, however, you need to count them.
- Ingredients with a weight range (a 2- to 3-pound chicken, for example) are analyzed at the average weight.
- When a recipe lists two or more ingredient options, the first is used in the nutrition analysis.
- The specific amount of an ingredient listed, not the amount sometimes shown in parentheses, is analyzed. The amounts in parentheses are guidelines to help you decide how much of an ingredient to purchase to prepare that recipe. (For more information, see "Finding Ingredient Equivalents," page 25.)
- Meats are analyzed as cooked and lean, with all visible fat removed. For lean ground beef, we use 95 percent fat-free meat.
- Products in the marketplace come and go quickly, and the labeling changes as well. To avoid confusion, we use the generic terms "fat-free" for products that may be labeled either "fat-free" or "nonfat" and "low-fat" for products that may be labeled "low-fat" or "reduced-fat." The

important thing is to read labels and purchase the lowest-fat, lowest-sodium products available that will provide pleasing results.

- We use olive and canola oils for the analyses as specified in each recipe, but other unsaturated oils, such as corn, safflower, soybean, and sunflower, also are acceptable.

- Values for saturated, trans, polyunsaturated, and monounsaturated fats are rounded and may not add up to the amount listed for total fat.

- Processed foods can be very high in sodium. To keep the level of sodium in our recipes low, we call for unprocessed foods or low-sodium products when possible and add table salt sparingly for flavor. For instance, a recipe may use a can of no-salt-added tomatoes and ¼ teaspoon of table salt. The amount of sodium in the finished dish will be less than if we called for a regular can of tomatoes and no table salt.

- If meat, poultry, or seafood is marinated and the marinade is discarded, we calculate only the amount of marinade absorbed. For marinated vegetables and basting liquids, we include the total amount of the marinade in the analysis.

- If a recipe includes alcohol and is cooked, we estimate that most of the alcohol calories evaporate during the cooking time.

- The abbreviation for gram is "g"; the abbreviation for milligram is "mg."

We analyzed these recipes using the ingredients exactly as written. Many ingredients, such as herbs, spices, and vinegars, can be interchanged for greater variety without substantially changing the nutritional value of the dish. We encourage you to experiment by substituting ingredients, as long as your choices do not add saturated fat, trans fat, cholesterol, or sodium.

Likewise, the nutrition analysis won't change if you use bottled or frozen lemon, lime, or orange juice instead of fresh juice or dried instead of fresh herbs. Fresh ingredients almost always give you more flavor, however, so we have called for those in most cases.

Finding Ingredient Equivalents

To make shopping easier, we have listed commonly used ingredients and their weight and volume equivalents.

Ingredient	Measurement
Almonds	1 ounce = ¼ cup slivers
Apple	1 medium = ¾ cup chopped or 1 cup sliced
Basil leaves, fresh	⅔ ounce = ½ cup, chopped, stems removed
Bell pepper, any color	1 medium = 1 cup chopped or sliced
Carrot	1 medium = ⅓ to ½ cup chopped or sliced or ½ cup shredded
Celery	1 medium rib = ½ cup chopped or sliced
Cheese, hard, such as Parmesan	4 ounces = 1 cup grated 3½ ounces = 1 cup shredded
Cheese, semi-hard, such as Cheddar, mozzarella, or Swiss	4 ounces = 1 cup grated
Cheese, soft, such as blue, feta, or goat	1 ounce, crumbled = ¼ cup
Cucumber	1 medium = 1 cup sliced
Lemon juice	1 medium = 3 tablespoons
Lemon zest	1 medium = 2 to 3 teaspoons
Lime juice	1 medium = 1½ to 2 tablespoons
Lime zest	1 medium = 1 teaspoon
Mushrooms (button)	1 pound = 5 cups sliced or 6 cups chopped
Onions, green	8 to 9 medium = 1 cup sliced (green and white parts)
Onions, white or yellow	1 large = 1 cup chopped 1 medium = ⅔ cup chopped 1 small = ⅓ cup chopped
Orange juice	1 medium = ⅓ to ½ cup
Orange zest	1 medium = 1½ to 2 tablespoons
Strawberries	1 pint = 2 cups sliced or chopped
Tomatoes	2 large, 3 medium, or 4 small = 1½ to 2 cups chopped
Walnuts	1 ounce = ¼ cup chopped

recipes

appetizers
and
snacks

smoked salmon dip
with cucumber and herbs

SERVES 16

Creamy and cool but with a slight smoky flavor, this dip is hard to resist. Surround a bowl of it with bell pepper strips, baby carrots, jícama slices, and halved cherry tomatoes for an eye-catching presentation.

- ·1 medium cucumber, peeled and diced
- 1 cup fat-free sour cream
- 2 ounces smoked salmon (not lox), rinsed with cold water, patted dry with paper towels, and diced
- 1 tablespoon snipped fresh dillweed or 1 teaspoon dried, crumbled
- 1 teaspoon finely chopped green onion (green part only)
- 1 teaspoon grated lemon zest
- 1 tablespoon fresh lemon juice
- ¼ teaspoon paprika

In a small serving bowl, stir together all the ingredients except the paprika. Smooth the surface.

Sprinkle with the paprika. Serve immediately or cover and refrigerate for up to two days to serve chilled.

COOK'S TIP on Smoked Salmon

When shopping for smoked salmon, read the nutrition labels and choose the product with the lowest sodium. Rinsing the salmon under cold water before use helps remove some of the excess sodium.

PER SERVING

Calories 19

Total Fat 0.0 g
  Saturated Fat 0.0 g
  Trans Fat 0.0 g
  Polyunsaturated Fat 0.0 g
  Monounsaturated Fat 0.0 g
Cholesterol 3 mg
Sodium 82 mg

Carbohydrates 3 g
  Fiber 0 g
  Sugar 1 g
Protein 2 g

DIETARY EXCHANGES:
Free

roasted red bell pepper dip

Roasted red bell peppers and fresh dill really complement each other in this flavorful dip. For a festive touch, serve it in hollowed-out red, green, and/or yellow bell peppers.

> 1 cup fat-free sour cream
>
> 1 7-ounce jar roasted red bell peppers in water, rinsed and drained
>
> ¼ cup snipped fresh dillweed
>
> ¼ teaspoon garlic powder
>
> ¼ teaspoon cayenne or crushed red pepper flakes
>
> ¼ teaspoon smoked paprika
>
> ⅛ teaspoon salt
>
> 3 tablespoons dried minced onion

In a food processor or blender, process all the ingredients except the onion for 30 seconds, or until smooth. Transfer to a medium serving bowl.

Stir in the onion. Cover and refrigerate for 30 minutes, or until ready to serve. Stir before serving.

COOK'S TIP on Smoked Paprika

Smoked over wood planks, then ground into powder, sweet red bell peppers become smoked paprika and add both color and flavor to foods from soup to nuts.

PER SERVING

Calories 19
Total Fat 0.0 g
  Saturated Fat 0.0 g
  Trans Fat 0.0 g
  Polyunsaturated Fat 0.0 g
  Monounsaturated Fat 0.0 g
Cholesterol 3 mg
Sodium 47 mg

Carbohydrates 3 g
  Fiber 0 g
  Sugar 1 g
Protein 1 g
DIETARY EXCHANGES:
Free

creamy caper dip

Elegant yet so easy, this satisfying dip also makes an interesting topping for cucumber or tomato slices.

8 ounces fat-free plain yogurt

¼ cup light mayonnaise

3 tablespoons capers, rinsed and drained

2 tablespoons Dijon mustard

1 medium garlic clove, minced

1 tablespoon olive oil (extra-virgin preferred)

In a food processor or blender, process all the ingredients except the oil until smooth. Transfer to a small serving bowl.

Stir in the oil. Cover and refrigerate until ready to serve, up to 8 hours.

PER SERVING

Calories 37	Carbohydrates 3 g
Total Fat 2.5 g	Fiber 0 g
Saturated Fat 0.5 g	Sugar 2 g
Trans Fat 0.0 g	Protein 1 g
Polyunsaturated Fat 0.5 g	DIETARY EXCHANGES:
Monounsaturated Fat 1.0 g	½ Fat
Cholesterol 2 mg	
Sodium 168 mg	

fresh basil and kalamata hummus

SERVES 14

Need a quick appetizer that will wow your guests? Look no further—this is it! You can make it a day in advance if you wish, but it comes together in a flash.

1 15-ounce can no-salt-added cannellini beans, rinsed and drained

½ cup packed fresh basil leaves

½ cup fat-free sour cream

12 pitted kalamata olives

2 tablespoons olive oil (extra-virgin preferred)

1 medium garlic clove, minced

½ teaspoon salt

In a food processor or blender, process all the ingredients until smooth. Transfer to a small serving bowl.

PER SERVING	
Calories 59	Carbohydrates 6 g
Total Fat 3.0 g	Fiber 1 g
Saturated Fat 0.5 g	Sugar 1 g
Trans Fat 0.0 g	Protein 2 g
Polyunsaturated Fat 0.5 g	DIETARY EXCHANGES:
Monounsaturated Fat 2.0 g	½ Starch
Cholesterol 1 mg	½ Fat
Sodium 152 mg	

zucchini spread

SERVES 8

Serve this spread with salt-free crackers, vegetable sticks, or rounds of crusty French bread. For a change-of-pace sandwich, lightly coat the inside of a whole-wheat pita half with the spread, then stuff the pita with your favorite vegetables.

3½ cups shredded unpeeled zucchini, squeezed in paper towels to remove excess water

¼ cup finely snipped fresh parsley or cilantro

2 tablespoons red wine vinegar

1 tablespoon olive oil (extra-virgin preferred)

1 medium garlic clove, minced

¼ teaspoon salt

Pepper to taste

2 tablespoons finely chopped walnuts or pecans, dry-roasted

In a food processor or blender, process all the ingredients except the nuts until smooth. Transfer to a small serving bowl.

Fold in the nuts. Cover and refrigerate until ready to serve.

COOK'S TIP on Dry-Roasting Nuts

Don't be tempted to skip the dry-roasting step here and in many other recipes. Even though only a small amount of nuts is used, the roasting brings out a tremendous amount of flavor. Put the nuts in a single layer in a skillet. Dry-roast over medium heat for about 4 minutes, or just until fragrant, stirring frequently.

PER SERVING	
Calories 36	Carbohydrates 2 g
Total Fat 3.0 g	Fiber 1 g
Saturated Fat 0.5 g	Sugar 1 g
Trans Fat 0.0 g	Protein 1 g
Polyunsaturated Fat 1.0 g	DIETARY EXCHANGES:
Monounsaturated Fat 1.5 g	½ Fat
Cholesterol 0 mg	
Sodium 76 mg	

southwestern black bean spread

SERVES 12

Serve this zesty mixture on crisp jícama slices, toasted whole-wheat pita bread, or salt-free baked tortilla chips. For a speedy snack on the run, spread the mixture on a warm corn tortilla, wrap, and go.

1 15-ounce can no-salt-added black beans, rinsed and drained

1 4-ounce can diced green chiles, rinsed and drained

½ cup roasted red bell peppers, rinsed and drained if bottled

2 tablespoons fresh lime juice

2 medium garlic cloves, minced

1 teaspoon ground cumin

1 teaspoon onion powder

¼ teaspoon salt

½ cup fat-free sour cream

1 tablespoon fresh lime juice

1 large tomato, diced

1 small avocado, diced

In a food processor or blender, process the beans, chiles, bell peppers, 2 tablespoons lime juice, garlic, cumin, onion powder, and salt until the desired texture. Spread on a serving plate or in a shallow bowl.

In a small bowl, stir together the sour cream and 1 tablespoon lime juice. Drop by spoonfuls on the bean spread for a decorative "dolloped" look, or smooth over the surface.

Sprinkle with the tomato and avocado.

PER SERVING

Calories 58	Carbohydrates 9 g
Total Fat 1.0 g	Fiber 2 g
Saturated Fat 0.0 g	Sugar 2 g
Trans Fat 0.0 g	Protein 3 g
Polyunsaturated Fat 0.0 g	DIETARY EXCHANGES:
Monounsaturated Fat 0.5 g	½ Starch
Cholesterol 2 mg	
Sodium 100 mg	

stuffed chile peppers

SERVES 7

Jalapeños, the most popular and readily available chile peppers, make a terrific appetizer when stuffed with a creamy filling.

>   8 ounces fat-free cottage cheese, drained
>   2 tablespoons finely chopped red bell pepper
>   2 tablespoons finely chopped green onions (green part only)
>   1 medium garlic clove, minced
>   ⅛ teaspoon salt
>   14 fresh jalapeño peppers, halved lengthwise,
>   seeds and ribs discarded

In a food processor or blender, process the cottage cheese until smooth. Transfer to a small bowl.

Stir in the remaining ingredients except the jalapeños. Spoon the mixture into the jalapeño halves. (A small spoon, such as a baby spoon, works best.) Arrange on a platter. Cover and refrigerate until ready to serve.

COOK'S TIP on Hot Peppers

Hot chile peppers contain oils that can burn your skin, lips, and eyes. Wear disposable plastic gloves or wash your hands thoroughly with warm, soapy water immediately after handling hot peppers. To lessen the intensity of hot peppers, discard the seeds and ribs, as we've done here.

PER SERVING

Calories 32	Carbohydrates 4 g
Total Fat 0.0 g	Fiber 1 g
Saturated Fat 0.0 g	Sugar 2 g
Trans Fat 0.0 g	Protein 4 g
Polyunsaturated Fat 0.0 g	DIETARY EXCHANGES:
Monounsaturated Fat 0.0 g	½ Very Lean Meat
Cholesterol 1 mg	
Sodium 156 mg	

tomato bursts

SERVES 8

Fill hollowed-out cherry tomatoes with Mediterranean ingredients to create attractive bite-size appetizers for your next party.

> 2 ounces low-fat cream cheese
>
> 12 kalamata olives, finely chopped
>
> 3 tablespoons minced green onions
>
> 1 teaspoon dried basil, crumbled
>
> 1 medium garlic clove, minced
>
> ⅛ teaspoon salt
>
> 32 cherry tomatoes

In a small bowl, stir together all the ingredients except the tomatoes.

Cut a thin slice from the top of each tomato. Using a ¼-teaspoon measuring spoon, scoop out and discard the pulp. (To remove any remaining seeds or loose pulp, run the tomatoes under cold water and drain upside down on paper towels.) Fill each tomato with about 1 teaspoon cream cheese mixture. Transfer to a platter. Cover and refrigerate until ready to serve, up to 8 hours.

PER SERVING

Calories 48	Carbohydrates 4 g
Total Fat 3.5 g	Fiber 1 g
Saturated Fat 1.5 g	Sugar 2 g
Trans Fat 0.0 g	Protein 1 g
Polyunsaturated Fat 0.5 g	DIETARY EXCHANGES:
Monounsaturated Fat 1.5 g	½ Fat
Cholesterol 5 mg	
Sodium 163 mg	

sweet-spice vanilla dip
with dried plums and almonds

SERVES 8

Combine creamy vanilla yogurt with sweet spices, dried plums, and toasted almonds to make a luscious dip. Try apple slices, strawberries, pineapple chunks, and low-fat gingersnaps as dippers.

      2 tablespoons sliced almonds

         Cooking spray

      1 teaspoon light brown sugar

      ⅛ teaspoon ground nutmeg

      6 ounces fat-free vanilla yogurt

      ½ teaspoon ground cinnamon

      ⅛ teaspoon ground ginger

      3 ounces pitted dried plums (prunes)

Put the almonds in a single layer in a skillet. Dry-roast over medium heat for about 4 minutes, or just until fragrant, stirring frequently. Remove from the heat.

Lightly spray the almonds with cooking spray (being careful not to spray near a gas flame). Sprinkle with the brown sugar and nutmeg. Cook over medium heat for 1 to 2 minutes, or until the brown sugar is dissolved and slightly caramelized on the almonds, stirring constantly. Transfer to a small plate and let cool for about 5 minutes.

In a small serving bowl, stir together the yogurt, cinnamon, and ginger.

Lightly spray kitchen scissors or a knife with cooking spray to help prevent sticking. Snip or cut the plums into small pieces. Stir into the yogurt mixture.

If serving immediately, sprinkle with the almonds. If serving chilled, cover and refrigerate for up to four days without the almonds. Store the almonds in an airtight container at room temperature. Just before serving, sprinkle the almonds over the dip.

PER SERVING

Calories 55	Carbohydrates 11 g
Total Fat 1.0 g	Fiber 1 g
Saturated Fat 0.0 g	Sugar 8 g
Trans Fat 0.0 g	Protein 2 g
Polyunsaturated Fat 0.0 g	DIETARY EXCHANGES:
Monounsaturated Fat 0.5 g	½ Other Carbohydrate
Cholesterol 0 mg	
Sodium 16 mg	

nectarine-plum chutney

SERVES 6

To serve this sweet-and-sour chutney as an appetizer, pour it over a block of fat-free or low-fat cream cheese and spread on salt-free crackers. You can also serve the chutney as a condiment with curried dishes or use it to perk up almost any entrée, from meat loaf to grilled chicken.

3 small plums, diced

1 medium nectarine, diced

1 medium Granny Smith apple, peeled and diced

⅓ cup sugar

¼ small onion, diced

¼ medium red bell pepper, diced

¼ cup cider vinegar

2 tablespoons golden raisins

1 teaspoon grated orange zest

⅛ teaspoon salt

⅛ teaspoon ground nutmeg

In a medium stainless steel, enameled steel, or nonstick saucepan, stir together all the ingredients. Cook over medium-high heat for 3 to 4 minutes, or until the sugar dissolves, stirring occasionally. Reduce the heat and simmer for 40 to 45 minutes, or until the fruit is tender, stirring occasionally. Let cool. Transfer to a serving bowl. Cover and refrigerate until ready to serve.

PER SERVING

Calories 95	Carbohydrates 24 g
Total Fat 0.0 g	Fiber 2 g
Saturated Fat 0.0 g	Sugar 21 g
Trans Fat 0.0 g	Protein 1 g
Polyunsaturated Fat 0.0 g	DIETARY EXCHANGES:
Monounsaturated Fat 0.0 g	1 Fruit
Cholesterol 0 mg	½ Other Carbohydrate
Sodium 50 mg	

crab spring rolls
with peanut dipping sauce

SERVES 10

These golden-brown, crisp spring rolls are a treat in themselves—the sauce is a rich-tasting, fragrant bonus! Experiment with lean cooked chicken or beef instead of crab for variety.

Cooking spray

Spring Rolls

4 cups shredded cabbage

1 medium carrot, shredded

2 medium green onions, thinly sliced

4 ounces imitation crab meat, finely chopped or shredded

2 teaspoons plain rice vinegar

1 teaspoon soy sauce (lowest sodium available)

10 spring roll wrappers (8 × 8 inches)

White of 1 large egg, lightly beaten

Dipping Sauce

3 tablespoons low-fat peanut butter (lowest sodium available)

3 tablespoons plain rice vinegar

2 tablespoons soy sauce (lowest sodium available)

2 tablespoons water

½ teaspoon toasted sesame oil

1 medium green onion (green part only), thinly sliced

Lightly spray a large skillet with cooking spray. Cook the cabbage over medium-high heat for 1 to 2 minutes, stirring occasionally.

PER SERVING	
Calories 83	Carbohydrates 11 g
Total Fat 2.0 g	Fiber 2 g
Saturated Fat 0.5 g	Sugar 2 g
Trans Fat 0.0 g	Protein 5 g
Polyunsaturated Fat 0.5 g	DIETARY EXCHANGES:
Monounsaturated Fat 1.0 g	½ Other Carbohydrate
Cholesterol 6 mg	½ Lean Meat
Sodium 148 mg	

Stir in the carrot and green onions. Cook for 1 minute, stirring occasionally.

Stir in the crab meat, 2 teaspoons vinegar, and 1 teaspoon soy sauce. Cook for 30 seconds, or until the crab meat is warmed through. Transfer to a large bowl. Cover and refrigerate for at least 30 minutes.

Preheat the oven to 400° F.

To assemble the spring rolls, place a wrapper on a flat surface with one point of the wrapper pointing toward you. Spoon about ⅓ cup filling along the center of the wrapper. Bring the bottom point of the wrapper over the filling. Lightly brush the two side points of the wrapper with egg white. Bring the side points to the center of the wrapper (it will look like an unsealed envelope). Starting from the bottom, roll the wrapper up to the top point so the filling is enclosed. Lightly brush the top point with egg white and press to seal. Place with the seam side down on a baking sheet. Repeat with the remaining wrappers and filling. Lightly spray the spring rolls with cooking spray.

Bake for 25 to 30 minutes, or until the wrappers turn light golden brown.

Meanwhile, in a medium serving bowl, whisk together all the dipping sauce ingredients except the green onion. Sprinkle with the green onion. Serve with the spring rolls.

COOK'S TIPS

❉ You can assemble these spring rolls and cover and refrigerate them for up to 8 hours before baking or freeze for up to two months. (Do not thaw before baking.) The dipping sauce will keep for up to two days in the refrigerator, the filling for up to four days.

❉ Find spring roll wrappers in the Asian section of your grocery store or substitute egg roll wrappers.

toasted ravioli
with italian salsa

SERVES 10

These tempting ravioli (traditionally deep-fried but baked in this recipe) boast an interesting fusion twist—a salsa flavored with herbs common to the Italian kitchen.

Ravioli

1 pound frozen beef ravioli
(about 30 pieces; lowest sodium available)

Cooking spray

¼ cup light Italian salad dressing

½ cup plain dry bread crumbs

1½ teaspoons Italian seasoning, crumbled

Italian Salsa

1 14.5-ounce can no-salt-added tomatoes, undrained

½ small red onion, quartered

1 hot banana pepper or ½ small green bell pepper,
seeds and ribs discarded

1 tablespoon chopped fresh oregano or 1 teaspoon dried, crumbled

1 tablespoon chopped fresh basil or 1 teaspoon dried, crumbled

1 medium garlic clove, halved

1 teaspoon balsamic or red wine vinegar

¼ teaspoon sugar

Prepare the ravioli using the package directions, omitting the salt and oil. Drain in a colander. Let cool for at least 10 minutes.

Lightly spray two baking sheets with cooking spray.

PER SERVING	
Calories 133	Carbohydrates 23 g
Total Fat 2.5 g	Fiber 2 g
Saturated Fat 1.0 g	Sugar 4 g
Trans Fat 0.0 g	Protein 5 g
Polyunsaturated Fat 0.5 g	DIETARY EXCHANGES:
Monounsaturated Fat 0.0 g	1½ Starch
Cholesterol 7 mg	
Sodium 231 mg	

Using a pastry or basting brush, lightly coat the top of each ravioli with the salad dressing. Transfer to the baking sheets.

In a small bowl, combine the bread crumbs and Italian seasoning. Sprinkle over the ravioli. (The ravioli can be covered and refrigerated for up to 8 hours at this point.)

In a food processor or blender, process the salsa ingredients for 15 to 20 seconds. (The salsa can be refrigerated in an airtight container for up to four days at this point.)

Preheat the oven to 400° F.

Lightly spray the tops of the ravioli with cooking spray.

Bake for 9 to 11 minutes, or until cooked through.

To serve, drizzle the salsa over the ravioli or use the salsa for dipping.

canapés with roasted garlic, artichoke, and chèvre spread

SERVES 18

Good planning is the secret to easy entertaining! Make the spread for these canapés up to three days in advance for quick assembly shortly before your guests arrive.

> 6 medium garlic cloves, unpeeled
>
> 6 7-inch pita breads (whole-wheat preferred)
>
> 1 14-ounce can artichoke hearts, rinsed, drained, and chopped
>
> ½ cup light mayonnaise
>
> 2 ounces soft goat cheese (chèvre)
>
> ⅛ teaspoon white pepper
>
> 2 tablespoons thinly sliced green onions (green part only)
>
> 18 cherry tomatoes, halved lengthwise

Preheat the oven to 350° F.

Put the garlic in a garlic roaster or small ovenproof pan and place on the bottom oven rack. Bake for 5 minutes.

Meanwhile, cut each pita into sixths. (Don't separate the bottoms from the tops.) Put the pitas in a single layer on a baking sheet.

After the garlic has baked, leave it in place in the oven and put the baking sheet with the pitas on the middle oven rack. Bake for 10 minutes. Transfer the garlic and pitas to cooling racks and let cool for 10 minutes. (Leave the oven on.)

Discard the stem ends of the garlic. Squeeze the garlic onto a cutting board, discarding the peel. Mince the garlic. Transfer to a medium bowl.

Stir in the artichokes, mayonnaise, goat cheese, and pepper.

PER SERVING

Calories 95	Carbohydrates 16 g
Total Fat 2.5 g	Fiber 2 g
Saturated Fat 1.0 g	Sugar 2 g
Trans Fat 0.0 g	Protein 3 g
Polyunsaturated Fat 1.0 g	DIETARY EXCHANGES:
Monounsaturated Fat 0.5 g	1 Starch
Cholesterol 3 mg	½ Fat
Sodium 229 mg	

To assemble, spread about 1 teaspoon artichoke mixture on each pita wedge. Sprinkle with the green onions. Press a cherry tomato half with the cut side up into the artichoke mixture. Place in a single layer on the baking sheet.

Bake for 5 minutes. Serve immediately.

COOK'S TIP on Roasted Garlic

Add roasted and peeled garlic cloves to your favorite spaghetti sauce or stew, mashed potatoes, or cold pasta salad. Puree roasted and peeled garlic and brush it on toast, corn on the cob, or pizza dough before you add the sauce and toppings.

orange-ginger chicken skewers

SERVES 10

Fruit and gingerroot provide the tangy flavor for these standout appetizers.

Cooking spray
12 ounces boneless, skinless chicken breasts
½ cup barbecue sauce (lowest sodium available)
¼ cup all-fruit blackberry spread
2 teaspoons grated orange zest
1 teaspoon grated peeled gingerroot

Soak twenty 6- to 8-inch wooden skewers in cold water for at least 10 minutes to keep them from charring, or use metal skewers.

Lightly spray a broiler pan and rack with cooking spray. Preheat the broiler.

Meanwhile, discard all visible fat from the chicken. Cut the chicken into 40 thin strips. Thread 2 strips onto each skewer in an "s" shape.

In a small bowl, whisk together the remaining ingredients until smooth. (If the spread is too lumpy, microwave on high for 30 seconds, or until smooth, stirring halfway through.) Divide the sauce as follows: one-half in a small bowl for the basting sauce, one-fourth in the original bowl for the finishing sauce, and the remaining one-fourth in a small serving bowl for the dipping sauce.

Baste the chicken with about half the basting sauce. Wash the basting brush (to avoid spreading harmful bacteria).

Broil the chicken about 4 inches from the heat for 2 minutes. Turn over and baste with the remaining basting sauce. Broil for 2 minutes, or until the chicken is no longer pink in the center. Wash the basting brush and baste the chicken with the finishing sauce.

Place the skewers on a platter. Serve with the reserved dipping sauce.

PER SERVING

Calories 78	Carbohydrates 9 g
Total Fat 0.5 g	Fiber 0 g
Saturated Fat 0.0 g	Sugar 8 g
Trans Fat 0.0 g	Protein 8 g
Polyunsaturated Fat 0.0 g	DIETARY EXCHANGES:
Monounsaturated Fat 0.0 g	½ Other Carbohydrate
Cholesterol 20 mg	1 Very Lean Meat
Sodium 106 mg	

zesty potato skins

SERVES 8

These filled potato skins are perfect for entertaining or snacking. Spiced with southwestern flair, they're a great alternative to the usual chips and dip.

6 medium red potatoes (about 1¼ pounds total), baked

Cooking spray

½ teaspoon garlic powder

½ teaspoon chili powder

½ teaspoon ground cumin

⅛ teaspoon pepper

8 ounces fat-free cottage cheese, undrained

½ teaspoon grated lime zest

1½ tablespoons fresh lime juice

1 tablespoon green onions (green part only), finely chopped

¼ teaspoon chili powder

4 large black olives, each cut into 6 slices

Preheat the oven to 450° F.

Cut each potato in half. Scoop out the centers, leaving about ¼ inch of potato around the inside. Cut each half in half. Lightly spray the pulp side with cooking spray.

In a small bowl, stir together the garlic powder, ½ teaspoon chili powder, the cumin, and pepper. Sprinkle on the pulp side. Place with the skin side down on a baking sheet.

Bake for 15 to 20 minutes, or until lightly browned.

Meanwhile, in a food processor or blender, process the remaining ingredients except the olives until smooth. Spoon about 1 teaspoon mixture into each baked potato skin. Top each piece with an olive slice.

PER SERVING

Calories 64
Total Fat 0.5 g
  Saturated Fat 0.0 g
  Trans Fat 0.0 g
  Polyunsaturated Fat 0.0 g
  Monounsaturated Fat 0.0 g
Cholesterol 1 mg
Sodium 125 mg

Carbohydrates 11 g
  Fiber 1 g
  Sugar 2 g
Protein 4 g

DIETARY EXCHANGES:
1 Starch

soups

summertime soup

Serve this chilled creation in pretty bowls at your next summertime brunch—its refreshing taste will delight your guests.

1 small cantaloupe, cubed	⅓ cup port wine
2 large mangoes, cubed	2 tablespoons orange liqueur
2 medium peaches, cubed	1 tablespoon fresh lime juice
16 ounces strawberries, hulled	1½ teaspoons raspberry vinegar
½ cup fat-free plain yogurt	
⅓ cup frozen orange juice concentrate	½ cup fat-free plain yogurt, well chilled

In a food processor or blender, process all the ingredients except the second ½ cup yogurt until thick and creamy. Pour into a large bowl. Cover and put in the freezer for about 20 minutes.

To serve, ladle the soup into six soup bowls. Top each serving with 1 heaping tablespoon remaining yogurt. Serve immediately.

COOK'S TIP on Cutting Mangoes

If you do not have a special tool for cutting mangoes, place a mango on its flattest side. Slice off about the top half of the mango. (You won't be able to cut the fruit exactly in half because of the large pit.) Turn the mango over, pit side down. Slice off the top part of the second side. (If you prefer, hold the mango upright and slice off one side, then the other.) Remove the peel from the 3 pieces. Trim any remaining fruit from the pit. Cut the flesh into the desired pieces.

PER SERVING

Calories 192	Carbohydrates 40 g
Total Fat 0.5 g	Fiber 4 g
Saturated Fat 0.0 g	Sugar 34 g
Trans Fat 0.0 g	Protein 5 g
Polyunsaturated Fat 0.0 g	DIETARY EXCHANGES:
Monounsaturated Fat 0.0 g	2 Fruit
Cholesterol 1 mg	½ Other Carbohydrate
Sodium 47 mg	

light and lemony spinach soup

An intriguing flavor combination, quick preparation, and a very low calorie count make this recipe an outstanding choice anytime you're hungry for soup.

2 cups fat-free, low-sodium chicken broth

2 teaspoons fresh lemon juice

¼ teaspoon dried thyme, crumbled

⅛ teaspoon salt

4 spinach or other green leaves, such as escarole,
   torn into bite-size pieces

1 medium green onion (green part only), thinly sliced

In a small saucepan, bring the broth, lemon juice, thyme, and salt to a boil over high heat.

To serve, put the spinach in two soup bowls. Ladle the hot soup over the spinach. Sprinkle with the green onion. Serve immediately.

PER SERVING

Calories 21	Carbohydrates 2 g
Total Fat 0.0 g	Fiber 1 g
Saturated Fat 0.0 g	Sugar 1 g
Trans Fat 0.0 g	Protein 3 g
Polyunsaturated Fat 0.0 g	DIETARY EXCHANGES:
Monounsaturated Fat 0.0 g	Free
Cholesterol 0 mg	
Sodium 224 mg	

silky winter-squash soup

SERVES 4

Chase away a winter chill with this soothing soup of roasted acorn squash and aromatic vegetables, pureed until as smooth as silk.

1 1-pound acorn squash, cut in half vertically, seeds and strings discarded

1 medium onion, halved

2 medium ribs of celery, cut into 2-inch pieces

½ cup baby carrots

Olive oil spray

4 medium garlic cloves, unpeeled

3 cups fat-free, low-sodium chicken broth, divided use

¼ cup fat-free half-and-half

¼ teaspoon ground cumin

⅛ teaspoon salt

¼ teaspoon pepper

Preheat the oven to 350° F.

Put the squash and onion with the cut sides up in a nonstick 13 × 9 × 2-inch baking pan. Add the celery and carrots. Lightly spray the vegetables with olive oil spray.

Bake for 45 minutes, or until the vegetables are almost done (just past tender-crisp). Add the garlic cloves. Bake for 15 minutes, or until the vegetables are tender when pierced with the tip of a sharp knife. Transfer the pan to a cooling rack. Let cool for 10 minutes.

Using a spoon, scoop the flesh from the squash, discarding the skin. Peel the garlic, discarding the skin. Put the squash and garlic in a food processor or blender. Add the onion, celery, carrots, and 1 cup chicken broth. Process for

PER SERVING	
Calories 82	Carbohydrates 18 g
Total Fat 0.5 g	Fiber 3 g
Saturated Fat 0.0 g	Sugar 6 g
Trans Fat 0.0 g	Protein 4 g
Polyunsaturated Fat 0.0 g	DIETARY EXCHANGES:
Monounsaturated Fat 0.0 g	1 Starch
Cholesterol 0 mg	
Sodium 160 mg	

1 to 2 minutes, or until smooth, scraping the sides of the work bowl occasionally. Transfer to a medium saucepan.

Stir in the remaining ingredients, including 2 cups broth. Bring to a simmer over medium-high heat, stirring occasionally. Reduce the heat and simmer for 5 to 6 minutes, or until the flavors have blended and the soup is heated through, stirring occasionally.

COOK'S TIP on Defatting Broth

To defat homemade or canned broth, refrigerate it to allow the fat to harden. (Leave commercially prepared broth in the unopened can.) Remove and discard the fat before using the broth.

rustic tomato soup

Nothing warms you up on a frigid day like a steaming bowl of soup. This one gets a fiber boost from beans and multigrain macaroni.

1 teaspoon olive oil

1 small onion, chopped

1 medium rib of celery, chopped

2 medium garlic cloves, minced

2 cups water

1 14.5-ounce can no-salt-added diced tomatoes, undrained

1 8-ounce can no-salt-added tomato sauce

1½ tablespoons Worcestershire sauce (lowest sodium available)

2 teaspoons sodium-free instant powdered chicken bouillon

2 teaspoons sugar

1½ teaspoons dried oregano, crumbled

½ teaspoon dried basil, crumbled

½ teaspoon pepper

⅔ cup dried multigrain or whole-wheat elbow macaroni

1 15-ounce can no-salt-added chickpeas or cannellini beans, rinsed and drained

½ cup fat-free half-and-half

2 tablespoons shredded or grated Parmesan cheese

In a medium saucepan, heat the oil over medium heat, swirling to coat the bottom. Cook the onion and celery for 3 minutes, or until soft but not brown, stirring frequently.

Stir in the garlic. Cook for 30 seconds.

PER SERVING

Calories 171	Carbohydrates 32 g
Total Fat 2.0 g	Fiber 6 g
Saturated Fat 0.5 g	Sugar 9 g
Trans Fat 0.0 g	Protein 8 g
Polyunsaturated Fat 0.0 g	DIETARY EXCHANGES:
Monounsaturated Fat 0.5 g	1½ Starch
Cholesterol 1 mg	2 Vegetable
Sodium 116 mg	

In a food processor or blender, process the onion mixture, water, tomatoes with liquid, tomato sauce, and Worcestershire sauce for about 20 seconds, or until almost smooth, scraping the sides once with a rubber scraper. Return the mixture to the pan.

Stir in the powdered bouillon, sugar, oregano, basil, and pepper. Bring to a boil over medium-high heat.

Stir in the macaroni. Reduce the heat and simmer for 8 to 10 minutes, or until the macaroni is tender, stirring occasionally.

Stir in the chickpeas. Cook for 1 minute. Remove from the heat.

Stir in the half-and-half.

To serve, ladle the soup into six soup bowls. Sprinkle with the Parmesan.

broccoli-cheese soup

SERVES 4

This soup has all the creaminess you expect from a classic broccoli-cheese soup, but so much less saturated fat and cholesterol.

2½ cups fat-free, low-sodium chicken broth

6 ounces chopped fresh broccoli (about 2 cups) or 1 10-ounce package frozen chopped broccoli, thawed

1 medium carrot, chopped

1 medium rib of celery, chopped

¼ teaspoon salt

¼ teaspoon pepper

⅛ teaspoon ground nutmeg

1 cup fat-free half-and-half

3 tablespoons all-purpose flour

3 slices (about ¾ ounce each) low-fat sharp Cheddar cheese, torn into pieces, or ½ cup shredded low-fat sharp Cheddar cheese

In a large saucepan, stir together the broth, broccoli, carrot, celery, salt, pepper, and nutmeg. Bring to a simmer over medium-high heat. Reduce the heat and simmer, covered, for 6 to 8 minutes, or until the vegetables are tender.

In a small bowl, whisk together the half-and-half and flour. Stir into the saucepan. Simmer for 1 to 2 minutes, or until thickened, stirring occasionally.

Add the cheese. Remove from the heat. Stir until the cheese is melted.

COOK'S TIP

One of the best ways to reheat this soup and keep it from being scorched is to use a double boiler. Pour the soup into the top pan of the double boiler and heat over simmering water. If you don't have a double boiler, place a medium stainless steel bowl over a pan of simmering water. In either case, be sure the water in the bottom pan doesn't touch the top container.

PER SERVING	
Calories 119	Carbohydrates 18 g
Total Fat 1.5 g	Fiber 2 g
Saturated Fat 0.5 g	Sugar 6 g
Trans Fat 0.0 g	Protein 11 g
Polyunsaturated Fat 0.0 g	DIETARY EXCHANGES:
Monounsaturated Fat 0.5 g	1 Vegetable
Cholesterol 3 mg	1 Other Carbohydrate
Sodium 375 mg	1 Very Lean Meat

country-style vegetable soup

A great anytime dish, this hearty soup contains an abundance of fresh vegetables.

- 1 pound white or red potatoes, chopped
- 4 large carrots, chopped
- 3 medium ribs of celery with leaves, chopped
- 2 medium zucchini, chopped
- 1 medium onion, chopped
- ¼ cup snipped fresh parsley
- 2 bay leaves
- ¼ teaspoon salt
- Pepper to taste
- 6 cups fat-free, low-sodium chicken broth
- ¾ cup shredded low-fat Cheddar cheese

In a large, heavy saucepan or Dutch oven, stir together the potatoes, carrots, celery, zucchini, onion, parsley, bay leaves, salt, and pepper.

Stir in the broth. Bring to a boil over high heat. Reduce the heat and simmer, covered, for 45 minutes to 1 hour, or until the vegetables are very tender. Discard the bay leaves.

To serve, ladle the soup into 10 soup bowls. Sprinkle with the Cheddar.

COOK'S TIP

If you like the crunch of celery, don't add it to the soup until about 10 minutes before serving.

PER SERVING	
Calories 83	Carbohydrates 14 g
Total Fat 1.0 g	Fiber 2 g
Saturated Fat 0.5 g	Sugar 4 g
Trans Fat 0.0 g	Protein 5 g
Polyunsaturated Fat 0.0 g	DIETARY EXCHANGES:
Monounsaturated Fat 0.0 g	1 Starch
Cholesterol 2 mg	1 Vegetable
Sodium 183 mg	

creamy wild rice and wheat berry soup

SERVES 4

Adding a variety of whole grains to your diet is easier than you may think. This soup provides two—wild rice (actually the seed of an annual marsh grass, but it counts as a grain) and wheat berries.

¼ cup wild rice	½ teaspoon curry powder
¼ cup wheat berries	¼ teaspoon pepper
2 cups water	1 12-ounce can fat-free evaporated milk
1 cup fat-free, low-sodium chicken broth	2 tablespoons dry sherry (optional)
1 large onion, chopped	4 very thin lemon slices (optional)
2 medium ribs of celery, chopped	2 tablespoons snipped fresh parsley (optional)
2 medium garlic cloves, minced	

Put the wild rice and wheat berries in a colander. Rinse and drain. Transfer to a large saucepan.

Add the water, broth, onion, celery, garlic, curry powder, and pepper to the pan. Bring to a boil over high heat. Reduce the heat and simmer, covered, for 1 hour, or until the wild rice is tender.

Stir in the milk and sherry. Simmer until heated through.

To serve, ladle the soup into four soup bowls. Garnish with the lemon slices and parsley.

COOK'S TIP

If you can't find wheat berries, you can substitute millet or increase the wild rice to ½ cup.

PER SERVING

Calories 173	Carbohydrates 33 g
Total Fat 0.5 g	Fiber 4 g
Saturated Fat 0.0 g	Sugar 13 g
Trans Fat 0.0 g	Protein 11 g
Polyunsaturated Fat 0.0 g	DIETARY EXCHANGES:
Monounsaturated Fat 0.0 g	1 Starch
Cholesterol 3 mg	1 Fat-Free Milk
Sodium 136 mg	

chunky barley soup

SERVES 4

For a modern spin on an ancient grain, try quick-cooking barley teamed with chunky vegetables and topped with a zesty sour cream garnish.

¼ cup fat-free sour cream

½ teaspoon bottled white horseradish

⅛ teaspoon dried basil, crumbled

1 teaspoon olive oil

1 medium rib of celery, chopped

½ medium red bell pepper, chopped

½ medium onion, chopped

½ cup frozen whole-kernel corn, thawed

½ teaspoon ground cumin

¼ teaspoon salt

¼ teaspoon pepper

3½ cups fat-free, low-sodium chicken broth

⅓ cup uncooked quick-cooking barley

In a small bowl, stir together the sour cream, horseradish, and basil. Cover with plastic wrap and refrigerate until needed.

In a medium saucepan, heat the oil over medium-high heat, swirling to coat the bottom. Cook the celery, bell pepper, and onion for 3 to 4 minutes, or until tender, stirring occasionally.

Stir in the corn, cumin, salt, and pepper. Cook for 1 minute, or until the cumin is fragrant.

Stir in the broth and barley. Bring to a simmer. Reduce the heat and simmer, covered, for 10 minutes, or until the barley is tender.

To serve, ladle the soup into four soup bowls. Garnish each serving with a dollop of the sour cream mixture.

PER SERVING	
Calories 127	Carbohydrates 24 g
Total Fat 1.5 g	Fiber 4 g
Saturated Fat 0.0 g	Sugar 4 g
Trans Fat 0.0 g	Protein 6 g
Polyunsaturated Fat 0.5 g	DIETARY EXCHANGES:
Monounsaturated Fat 1.0 g	1½ Starch
Cholesterol 3 mg	
Sodium 225 mg	

hot-and-sour soup
with exotic mushrooms

SERVES 8

Make the most of the variety of fresh mushrooms available at your local market. Their earthy flavors enhance this tangy, peppery soup. Even though the recipe title touts exotic mushrooms, you can use some domestic ones, too, if you wish.

4 cups fat-free, low-sodium chicken broth

1 pound mixed mushrooms, such as enoki, oyster, portobello, shiitake, wood ear, and button, larger mushrooms cut into ¼-inch slices

2 boneless center-cut pork chops (about 4 ounces each), all visible fat discarded, cut into 2 × ¼-inch strips

¼ cup cider vinegar

1½ tablespoons soy sauce (lowest sodium available)

2 teaspoons toasted sesame oil

1 teaspoon sugar

¼ to ½ teaspoon pepper

3 tablespoons cornstarch

¼ cup water

6 ounces fresh snow peas, ends trimmed

1 8-ounce can sliced water chestnuts, rinsed and drained

¼ cup egg substitute, lightly beaten

In a medium saucepan, bring the broth, mushrooms, pork, vinegar, soy sauce, sesame oil, sugar, and pepper to a boil over high heat, stirring occasionally. Reduce the heat and simmer for 10 minutes, or until the mushrooms are tender and the pork is no longer pink in the center, stirring occasionally.

PER SERVING

Calories 106	Carbohydrates 9 g
Total Fat 3.0 g	Fiber 2 g
Saturated Fat 1.0 g	Sugar 3 g
Trans Fat 0.0 g	Protein 10 g
Polyunsaturated Fat 0.5 g	DIETARY EXCHANGES:
Monounsaturated Fat 1.0 g	½ Other Carbohydrate
Cholesterol 17 mg	1 Lean Meat
Sodium 138 mg	

Put the cornstarch in a cup. Add the water, stirring to dissolve. Stir into the soup. Increase the heat to medium high and cook for 2 to 3 minutes, or until thickened, stirring occasionally.

Stir in the snow peas and water chestnuts. Cook for 1 to 2 minutes, or until the snow peas are tender-crisp, stirring occasionally.

Slowly drizzle the egg substitute into the soup. Cook for 1 minute, or until the egg is cooked through, stirring constantly but gently. Remove from the heat and serve immediately.

COOK'S TIP on Dried Mushrooms

Can't find your favorite fresh mushroom? Feel free to substitute dried mushrooms. Cover them with warm water and soak for 20 to 30 minutes, or until softened. Drain, squeeze out any excess water, and proceed with the recipe. Keep in mind that 1 ounce of dried mushrooms equals about 1 cup of rehydrated mushrooms.

COOK'S TIP on Sesame Oil

Toasted sesame oil, also called Asian sesame oil, is darker, stronger, and more fragrant than other sesame oil. Toasted sesame oil is widely used in Asian and Indian foods. Because it is so flavorful, you get a lot of taste for just a little fat.

gumbo
with greens and ham

SERVES 8

Gumbo typically starts with a high-fat roux that is cooked until it browns. We eliminate the fat but still brown the flour to give this southern soup an authentic Cajun taste.

½ cup all-purpose flour

1¼ cups uncooked brown rice

Cooking spray

2 medium onions, chopped

2 medium ribs of celery, chopped

1 medium yellow or green bell pepper, chopped

1 medium red bell pepper, chopped

6 medium garlic cloves, minced

6 ounces fresh collard greens, mustard greens, kale, or spinach, coarsely chopped

3 cups water

2 cups chopped lower-sodium, low-fat ham, all visible fat discarded

1½ cups sliced fresh or frozen okra

2 bunches watercress, coarsely chopped

1 bunch fresh parsley, coarsely snipped

¼ to ½ teaspoon pepper

⅛ to ¼ teaspoon cayenne

¼ teaspoon red hot-pepper sauce

PER SERVING

Calories 222
Total Fat 2.5 g
  Saturated Fat 0.5 g
  Trans Fat 0.0 g
  Polyunsaturated Fat 0.5 g
  Monounsaturated Fat 1.0 g
Cholesterol 15 mg
Sodium 349 mg

Carbohydrates 39 g
  Fiber 5 g
  Sugar 5 g
Protein 12 g

DIETARY EXCHANGES:
2 Starch
2 Vegetable
1 Very Lean Meat

Heat a Dutch oven or soup pot over medium-high heat. Cook the flour for 5 minutes, stirring occasionally. Reduce the heat to medium and cook for 5 to 7 minutes, or until evenly browned, stirring constantly. Transfer to a small bowl or plate. Allow the pot to cool.

Prepare the rice using the package directions, omitting the salt and margarine.

Meanwhile, lightly spray the cooled pot with cooking spray. Cook the onions, celery, bell peppers, and garlic over medium heat for 15 minutes, stirring occasionally.

Stir in the browned flour and remaining ingredients except the rice. Increase the heat to high and bring to a boil. Reduce the heat and simmer, covered, for 30 minutes.

To serve, spoon the rice into eight soup bowls. Ladle the gumbo over the rice.

chicken and spinach enchilada soup

SERVES 4

Chock-full of chicken and spinach, this entrée soup captures the essence of enchiladas without the fuss. Serve steaming bowls of this soup with warmed corn muffins or corn tortillas on the side.

2 teaspoons olive oil

1 pound boneless, skinless chicken breasts, all visible fat discarded, cut into ¾-inch cubes

½ medium onion, chopped

2 cups fat-free, low-sodium chicken broth

1½ cups fat-free milk

1 10.5-ounce can low-fat condensed cream of chicken soup (lowest sodium available)

1 10-ounce package frozen chopped spinach, thawed and squeezed dry

½ teaspoon chili powder

½ teaspoon ground cumin

¼ cup shredded low-fat Cheddar cheese

In a large nonstick saucepan, heat the oil over medium-high heat, swirling to coat the bottom. Cook the chicken for 6 to 8 minutes, or until no longer pink in the center, stirring occasionally.

Stir in the onion. Cook for 1 to 2 minutes, or until the onion is tender-crisp, stirring occasionally.

Stir in the remaining ingredients except the Cheddar. Bring to a boil over high heat, stirring occasionally. Reduce the heat and simmer for 6 to 8 minutes, so the flavors blend, stirring occasionally.

To serve, ladle the soup into four soup bowls. Sprinkle with the Cheddar.

PER SERVING

Calories 268	Carbohydrates 17 g
Total Fat 6.0 g	Fiber 3 g
Saturated Fat 1.5 g	Sugar 7 g
Trans Fat 0.0 g	Protein 37 g
Polyunsaturated Fat 1.0 g	DIETARY EXCHANGES:
Monounsaturated Fat 2.5 g	1 Other Carbohydrate
Cholesterol 74 mg	5 Lean Meat
Sodium 508 mg	

triple-pepper and white bean soup with rotini

When it's cold or rainy, try this meal in a bowl. Serve with a green salad on the side.

> 2 cups low-sodium vegetable broth
>
> 8 ounces frozen red and green bell pepper and onion stir-fry mixture
>
> 1 medium zucchini, halved lengthwise, then sliced crosswise
>
> 1 cup quartered cherry tomatoes
>
> 1 tablespoon dried basil, crumbled
>
> 1/8 teaspoon crushed red pepper flakes
>
> 6 ounces dried rotini (whole-wheat preferred)
>
> 1 15-ounce can no-salt-added navy beans, rinsed and drained
>
> 1 tablespoon olive oil (extra-virgin preferred)
>
> 1/4 teaspoon salt

In a Dutch oven, bring the broth to a boil over high heat. Stir in the bell pepper and onion stir-fry, zucchini, tomatoes, basil, and red pepper flakes. Return to a boil. Reduce the heat and simmer, covered, for 20 minutes.

Meanwhile, prepare the pasta using the package directions, omitting the salt and oil. Drain well in a colander.

Stir the beans into the bell pepper mixture. Cook for 5 minutes, or until heated through. Remove from the heat.

Stir in the olive oil and salt.

To serve, spoon the pasta into four soup bowls. Ladle the soup over the pasta.

PER SERVING

Calories 313	Carbohydrates 58 g
Total Fat 4.5 g	Fiber 10 g
Saturated Fat 0.5 g	Sugar 9 g
Trans Fat 0.0 g	Protein 14 g
Polyunsaturated Fat 0.5 g	DIETARY EXCHANGES:
Monounsaturated Fat 2.5 g	3 Starch
Cholesterol 0 mg	2 Vegetable
Sodium 187 mg	1/2 Very Lean Meat

salads
and
dressings

salad
with creamy mustard vinaigrette

SERVES 8 (Plus heaping ¼ cup dressing remaining)

In addition to providing iron and protein, tofu makes the dressing for this simple salad creamy and rich. You'll have enough to use half here and save the rest for another salad.

Dressing

4 ounces light firm tofu, well drained

½ cup light vinaigrette dressing

2 tablespoons water

½ teaspoon honey

½ teaspoon Dijon mustard

Salad

1 head leaf lettuce or about 8 ounces mixed salad greens, torn into bite-size pieces

3 dried apricot halves, slivered

1 tablespoon plus 1 teaspoon unsalted shelled sunflower seeds, very lightly dry-roasted

In a food processor or blender, process the dressing ingredients until creamy.

In a large serving bowl, toss the lettuce with ¼ cup plus 1 tablespoon dressing. (Pour the remaining dressing into a jar with a tight-fitting lid and refrigerate for later use.) Sprinkle with the apricots and sunflower seeds.

PER SERVING	
Calories 34	Carbohydrates 6 g
Total Fat 1.5 g	Fiber 1 g
Saturated Fat 0.0 g	Sugar 2 g
Trans Fat 0.0 g	Protein 2 g
Polyunsaturated Fat 1.0 g	DIETARY EXCHANGES:
Monounsaturated Fat 0.5 g	½ Other Carbohydrate
Cholesterol 0 mg	½ Fat
Sodium 212 mg	

boston citrus salad

SERVES 6

Delicate, pale green Boston lettuce is the perfect backdrop for juicy citrus fruit. The orange-flower water gives an aromatic touch to this salad.

> 1 large head Boston, butter, or Bibb lettuce
>
> 2 large oranges
>
> 2 medium grapefruit
>
> 1½ tablespoons fresh lemon juice
>
> 1½ tablespoons honey
>
> ½ teaspoon orange-flower water or orange liqueur (optional)
>
> 3 tablespoons slivered almonds, dry-roasted

Tear the lettuce leaves into bite-size pieces. Put in a large bowl.

Peel the oranges. Cut crosswise into ¼-inch slices. Cut the slices into quarters. Transfer the oranges to a medium bowl and any juice to a small bowl.

Peel and section the grapefruit. Cut into bite-size pieces. Add the grapefruit to the oranges and the grapefruit juice to the orange juice. Drain the fruit, adding any accumulated juice to the juice mixture.

Stir the lemon juice, honey, and orange-flower water into the juice mixture. Pour over the lettuce. Toss to coat.

To serve, arrange the lettuce on six plates. Top each serving with orange and grapefruit pieces. Sprinkle with the almonds.

COOK'S TIP on Orange-Flower Water

Orange-flower water, found at Middle Eastern markets, most gourmet grocery stores, and some supermarkets, is wonderful in many cakes, cookies, puddings, and beverages.

PER SERVING	
Calories 97	Carbohydrates 20 g
Total Fat 2.0 g	Fiber 3 g
Saturated Fat 0.0 g	Sugar 17 g
Trans Fat 0.0 g	Protein 2 g
Polyunsaturated Fat 0.5 g	DIETARY EXCHANGES:
Monounsaturated Fat 1.0 g	1 Fruit
Cholesterol 0 mg	½ Other Carbohydrate
Sodium 2 mg	½ Fat

green bean and toasted pecan salad

SERVES 4

This pretty combination is a refreshing break from the usual lettuce salads or slaws.

12 ounces fresh green beans, trimmed

2 to 4 tablespoons thinly sliced red onion

1½ tablespoons white balsamic vinegar

2¼ teaspoons sugar

⅛ teaspoon salt

2 tablespoons finely chopped pecans, dry-roasted

2 tablespoons crumbled blue cheese

In a medium saucepan, steam the green beans for 4 minutes, or just until tender-crisp. Transfer to a colander and rinse with cold water to stop the cooking process. Let cool to room temperature. Dry on paper towels.

Meanwhile, in a medium serving bowl, stir together the onion, vinegar, sugar, and salt.

Add the green beans, tossing to combine.

Sprinkle with the pecans and blue cheese.

warm mushroom salad

SERVES 4

Balsamic vinegar gives mushrooms a deep, rich flavor. If you wish, you can use meaty-textured portobello mushrooms and serve this salad as part of a meatless meal.

¼ cup port, sweet red wine, or frozen unsweetened apple juice concentrate

3 to 3½ tablespoons balsamic vinegar or plain rice vinegar

2 tablespoons water

3 medium garlic cloves, finely minced

12 ounces button or portobello mushrooms, cut into ¼-inch slices

1 teaspoon olive oil (extra-virgin preferred)

⅛ teaspoon pepper, or to taste

4 Boston lettuce leaves

1 teaspoon snipped fresh parsley

In a medium nonstick skillet, heat the port, vinegar, water, and garlic over medium-high heat until small bubbles begin to form.

Stir in the mushrooms. Cook for 8 to 10 minutes, or until all the liquid has evaporated, stirring frequently.

Stir in the oil and pepper.

To serve, place the lettuce leaves on four plates. Spoon the mushrooms over the lettuce. Sprinkle with the parsley. Serve immediately so the mushrooms will be warm.

PER SERVING

Calories 68	Carbohydrates 9 g
Total Fat 1.5 g	Fiber 1 g
Saturated Fat 0.0 g	Sugar 5 g
Trans Fat 0.0 g	Protein 3 g
Polyunsaturated Fat 0.5 g	DIETARY EXCHANGES:
Monounsaturated Fat 1.0 g	½ Other Carbohydrate
Cholesterol 0 mg	½ Fat
Sodium 10 mg	

jícama and grapefruit salad
with ancho-honey dressing

SERVES 4

Ancho peppers are dried poblano peppers. Wrinkled and dark reddish brown, they add a medium-hot boost to this salad dressing.

Dressing

½ cup water

2 ancho chiles, halved lengthwise, seeds and ribs discarded

2 medium garlic cloves, quartered

2 tablespoons white wine vinegar

2 tablespoons honey

1 tablespoon canola or corn oil

1 tablespoon fresh lime juice

Salad

1 pound jícama, peeled and cut into matchstick-size pieces

½ cup chopped red onion

¼ cup snipped fresh cilantro

1 large red or pink grapefruit

In a small saucepan, bring the water, chiles, and garlic to a boil over high heat. Reduce the heat and simmer for 10 minutes. Transfer to a food processor or blender and process until smooth.

Add the remaining dressing ingredients. Process until smooth.

PER SERVING

Calories 171	Carbohydrates 33 g
Total Fat 4.5 g	Fiber 9 g
Saturated Fat 0.5 g	Sugar 18 g
Trans Fat 0.0 g	Protein 3 g
Polyunsaturated Fat 1.5 g	DIETARY EXCHANGES:
Monounsaturated Fat 2.0 g	½ Fruit
Cholesterol 0 mg	3 Vegetable
Sodium 11 mg	½ Other Carbohydrate
	1 Fat

In a medium serving bowl, combine the jícama, onion, and cilantro. Pour the dressing over the mixture, tossing to coat. Cover and refrigerate for 2 to 24 hours so the flavors blend.

Shortly before serving, peel and section the grapefruit. Drain well. Gently stir the grapefruit sections into the salad.

COOK'S TIP on Jícama

Also called Mexican potato, jícama is a root vegetable with a thin brown skin and crunchy cream-colored flesh. It has a sweet, nutty flavor and can be eaten raw or cooked. Use jícama as you would carrot and celery sticks, or chop or shred jícama to add to a fresh green salad. Choose bulbs that are firm and free of blemishes. Store whole jícama, unwrapped, in the refrigerator for up to five days. Peel the skin just before using. Wrap leftover jícama in plastic wrap and store for two to three days in the refrigerator.

cucumber-melon salad
with raspberry vinegar

SERVES 4

Expand your taste horizons by trying this unusual combination of ingredients. Turn the salad into a relish by finely chopping all the ingredients except the lettuce.

> 1 medium cucumber
> ½ large cantaloupe
> 1 bunch of radishes
> ¼ cup raspberry vinegar
>   Pepper (optional)
> 4 large lettuce leaves

Remove strips of peel from part of the cucumber, leaving some of the dark green to add color. Cut the cucumber into bite-size pieces. Peel the cantaloupe, discarding the seeds and rind. Cut the cantaloupe into cubes or use a melon baller to scoop out small ball-size pieces. Thinly slice the radishes.

In a medium bowl, combine the cucumber, cantaloupe, radishes, and vinegar. Toss to coat.

Sprinkle with pepper. Cover and refrigerate for 30 minutes to 1 hour, or until chilled.

To serve, place the lettuce leaves on four plates. Spoon the salad over the lettuce.

PER SERVING

Calories 47
Total Fat 0.5 g
  Saturated Fat 0.0 g
  Trans Fat 0.0 g
  Polyunsaturated Fat 0.0 g
  Monounsaturated Fat 0.0 g
Cholesterol 0 mg
Sodium 24 mg
Carbohydrates 10 g
  Fiber 2 g
  Sugar 8 g
Protein 1 g
DIETARY EXCHANGES:
1 Fruit

fresh fruit salad
with poppy seed and yogurt dressing

As you select a variety of fresh fruit for this salad, look for pleasing combinations of color, texture, and taste.

    3 medium oranges
    3 cups bite-size pieces assorted fresh fruit
    1 cup fat-free lemon yogurt
    ¼ teaspoon poppy seeds
    6 fresh sprigs of mint or edible flowers (optional)

Cut each orange in half crosswise. Cut and discard a thin slice from the bottom of each half so the halves will sit upright. Remove the flesh from each orange half, being careful to avoid the bitter pith. Coarsely chop the flesh. Transfer to a large bowl.

Gently stir in the remaining fruit.

Place each orange "bowl" on a small plate. Spoon the fruit mixture into the orange bowls, letting any extra fruit cascade onto the plate.

In a small bowl, whisk together the yogurt and poppy seeds. Pour over the fruit. Top each serving with a sprig of mint or a flower.

PER SERVING

Calories 97	Carbohydrates 22 g
Total Fat 0.5 g	Fiber 3 g
Saturated Fat 0.0 g	Sugar 19 g
Trans Fat 0.0 g	Protein 3 g
Polyunsaturated Fat 0.0 g	DIETARY EXCHANGES:
Monounsaturated Fat 0.0 g	1 Fruit
Cholesterol 1 mg	½ Other Carbohydrate
Sodium 29 mg	

citrus rice salad

Orange and honey add a sweet tang to this salad.

Salad

¾ cup fresh orange juice

¼ cup water

1 cup instant brown rice

1 10.5-ounce can mandarin
oranges in water or juice,
drained

⅓ cup dried cranberries

¼ cup chopped red onion

½ medium rib of celery, chopped

2 tablespoons finely snipped
fresh parsley

2 tablespoons chopped fresh
basil

Dressing

⅓ cup fresh orange juice

1 tablespoon balsamic vinegar

2 teaspoons canola or corn oil

2 teaspoons honey

In a small saucepan, bring the ¾ cup orange juice and the water to a boil.

Stir in the rice. Reduce the heat and simmer, covered, for 5 minutes. Remove from the heat and stir. Let stand, covered, for 5 minutes.

Meanwhile, in a medium serving bowl, stir together the remaining salad ingredients.

In a small bowl, whisk together the dressing ingredients.

Stir the rice into the salad. Pour the dressing over the salad, tossing gently to coat. Serve at room temperature or cover and refrigerate for up to 24 hours to serve chilled.

PER SERVING

Calories 140	Carbohydrates 29 g
Total Fat 2.0 g	Fiber 2 g
Saturated Fat 0.0 g	Sugar 15 g
Trans Fat 0.0 g	Protein 2 g
Polyunsaturated Fat 0.5 g	DIETARY EXCHANGES:
Monounsaturated Fat 1.0 g	1 Starch
Cholesterol 0 mg	1 Fruit
Sodium 10 mg	

lemon-curried black-eyed pea salad

SERVES 8

This colorful salad comes together in a snap, thanks to a base of canned ingredients, and fresh vegetables and lemon make the flavor sparkle.

Salad

- 1 15-ounce can no-salt-added black-eyed peas, rinsed and drained
- 1 11-ounce can no-salt-added whole-kernel corn, rinsed and drained
- ½ cup chopped red onion
- ½ cup thinly sliced celery
- 1 teaspoon finely shredded lemon zest

Dressing

- 2 tablespoons fresh lemon juice
- 1 tablespoon water
- 1 teaspoon olive oil
- 1 medium garlic clove, minced
- ½ teaspoon curry powder
- ½ teaspoon Dijon mustard
- ⅛ teaspoon pepper

In a medium serving bowl, stir together the salad ingredients.

In a small bowl, whisk together the dressing ingredients. Pour over the salad, stirring to coat. Cover and refrigerate for 1 to 24 hours so the flavors blend.

COOK'S TIP

Look for canned no-salt-added "fresh" black-eyed peas. They will offer more flavor than those made from dried peas. If you want to use dried black-eyed peas, soak 1 cup peas overnight in enough water to cover. Drain. In a medium saucepan, bring the peas and 3 cups fresh water to a boil over high heat. Reduce the heat and simmer, covered, for 50 to 60 minutes, or just until the peas are tender. Drain well in a colander and continue with the recipe.

PER SERVING

Calories 89
Total Fat 1.0 g
  Saturated Fat 0.0 g
  Trans Fat 0.0 g
  Polyunsaturated Fat 0.0 g
  Monounsaturated Fat 0.5 g
Cholesterol 0 mg
Sodium 119 mg

Carbohydrates 18 g
  Fiber 3 g
  Sugar 4 g
Protein 4 g
DIETARY EXCHANGES:
1 Starch

stacked slaw, asian style

SERVES 8

Topped with baked wonton strips for extra crunch, this slaw makes a lovely presentation.

Cooking spray

8 wonton wrappers

¼ teaspoon five-spice powder or no-salt-added all-purpose seasoning

2 tablespoons all-fruit apricot spread

2 tablespoons fresh orange juice

1 tablespoon cider vinegar

2 teaspoons canola or corn oil

1 teaspoon toasted sesame oil

2 cups shredded green cabbage

1 cup shredded red cabbage

1 medium carrot, shredded

6 medium radishes, thinly sliced

2 medium green onions, thinly sliced

Preheat the oven to 400° F. Lightly spray a baking sheet with cooking spray.

Cut the wonton wrappers into strips ¼ inch wide. Arrange the strips in a single layer on the baking sheet (they don't have to be perfectly straight; a slight twist or bend looks interesting). Lightly spray the tops with cooking spray.

Sprinkle the strips with the five-spice powder.

Bake for 5 to 6 minutes, or until golden brown. Transfer the baking sheet to a cooling rack and let the strips cool for 5 to 10 minutes.

PER SERVING

Calories 65	Carbohydrates 11 g
Total Fat 2.0 g	Fiber 1 g
Saturated Fat 0.0 g	Sugar 4 g
Trans Fat 0.0 g	Protein 1 g
Polyunsaturated Fat 0.5 g	DIETARY EXCHANGES:
Monounsaturated Fat 1.0 g	½ Other Carbohydrate
Cholesterol 1 mg	½ Fat
Sodium 60 mg	

In a medium bowl, whisk together the fruit spread, orange juice, vinegar, and oils.

Add the remaining ingredients, tossing to coat.

To serve, mound the slaw on eight plates. Sprinkle with the wonton strips.

COOK'S TIP

A package of wonton wrappers will provide more than you need for this recipe. Separate the extras into batches of 8 so you'll be ready to make this recipe again, then freeze them in plastic freezer bags or other airtight containers for up to four months. You can also cut all the wrappers into strips, bake, and store in an airtight container at room temperature for up to five days.

COOK'S TIP on Five-Spice Powder

You can usually find five-spice powder in the spice section of your grocery store and in Asian markets. If you prefer, you can easily make your own. Simply combine equal amounts of cinnamon, cloves, fennel seed, star anise, and Szechuan peppercorns, all in ground form. If Szechuan peppercorns aren't readily available, substitute black pepper; if you can't find star anise, you can leave it out.

tabbouleh

SERVES 6

Make this dish well in advance—the flavors improve with age. Serve it at room temperature or chilled, by itself, on a leaf of lettuce, or as stuffing for hollowed-out tomatoes, zucchini halves, or bell peppers.

2 cups water

2 cups low-sodium vegetable broth

1 cup uncooked bulgur

¼ cup fresh lemon juice

1 tablespoon olive oil (extra-virgin preferred)

2 medium tomatoes, finely chopped

3 medium green onions, finely chopped

¼ cup finely chopped fresh mint or 1 tablespoon dried, crumbled

¼ cup snipped fresh parsley

Pepper to taste

In a medium saucepan, bring the water and broth to a boil over high heat.

Put the bulgur in a large heatproof bowl. Stir in the boiling broth mixture. Cover and let stand for 1 hour, or until most of the liquid is absorbed. Drain well in a colander. Squeeze out the excess moisture with your hands or by putting the bulgur in cheesecloth or a dish towel, gathering the ends together, and squeezing. Return the bulgur to the large bowl.

In a small bowl, whisk together the lemon juice and oil. Pour over the bulgur.

PER SERVING

Calories 124	Carbohydrates 23 g
Total Fat 2.5 g	Fiber 6 g
Saturated Fat 0.5 g	Sugar 2 g
Trans Fat 0.0 g	Protein 4 g
Polyunsaturated Fat 0.5 g	DIETARY EXCHANGES:
Monounsaturated Fat 1.5 g	1½ Starch
Cholesterol 0 mg	½ Fat
Sodium 31 mg	

Gently stir in the remaining ingredients. Cover and refrigerate for at least 1 hour so the flavors blend. Serve chilled or let the salad return to room temperature before serving.

COOK'S TIP on Bulgur

Bulgur is a form of whole wheat that's been cleaned, soaked, dried, and cracked into fine, medium, or coarse grains. Nutritious and versatile, bulgur is available at most supermarkets and health food stores.

seafood pasta salad

SERVES 6

As a change from the tuna listed here, try canned or vacuum-packed salmon or a cooked fish of your choice. To add nutrients and make the salad look fancier, line a bowl or platter with romaine leaves, spoon the salad over the lettuce, and top with tomato wedges.

10 ounces dried small or medium pasta shells (whole-wheat preferred)

2 6-ounce cans low-sodium tuna in water, drained and flaked

1 medium red, green, or yellow bell pepper, chopped

1 cup frozen green peas, thawed

1 small red onion, finely chopped

4 or 5 medium radishes, finely chopped

¼ cup chopped fresh basil or 1 tablespoon plus 1 teaspoon dried, crumbled

¼ cup snipped fresh parsley

½ cup light Italian salad dressing

½ teaspoon Dijon mustard

Prepare the pasta using the package directions, omitting the salt and oil. Drain well in a colander. Transfer to a large serving bowl.

Stir the tuna, bell pepper, peas, onion, radishes, basil, and parsley into the pasta.

In a small bowl, whisk together the salad dressing and mustard. Stir gently into the pasta mixture. Serve at room temperature or cover and refrigerate for several hours so the flavors blend.

PER SERVING

Calories 304	Carbohydrates 42 g
Total Fat 6.5 g	Fiber 8 g
Saturated Fat 1.0 g	Sugar 5 g
Trans Fat 0.0 g	Protein 22 g
Polyunsaturated Fat 3.0 g	DIETARY EXCHANGES:
Monounsaturated Fat 1.5 g	3 Starch
Cholesterol 24 mg	2 Very Lean Meat
Sodium 337 mg	

herbed chicken salad

Like the Tabouleh on page 80, this salad is excellent on lettuce and as a stuffing for tomatoes, bell peppers, or zucchini.

Chicken Salad

2 cups diced boneless cooked chicken breast, cooked without salt, skin and all visible fat discarded

¼ cup fat-free plain yogurt

¼ cup light mayonnaise

2 medium green onions, thinly sliced

1 small carrot, grated

2 medium radishes, grated

3 tablespoons chopped celery

2 tablespoons chopped green bell pepper

2 tablespoons snipped fresh parsley

1½ tablespoons tarragon vinegar, or 1½ tablespoons plain rice vinegar or white wine vinegar plus ⅛ teaspoon dried tarragon, crumbled

1 teaspoon Italian seasoning, crumbled

1 teaspoon Worcestershire sauce (lowest sodium available)

¼ teaspoon pepper, or to taste

❋ ❋

6 large lettuce leaves, such as romaine

1 8-ounce can mandarin oranges in water or juice, drained

In a large bowl, stir together the chicken salad ingredients. Cover and refrigerate for at least 1 hour so the flavors blend.

To serve, place the lettuce leaves on six plates. Spoon the chicken salad over the lettuce. Top with the mandarin oranges.

PER SERVING

Calories 146	Carbohydrates 8 g
Total Fat 5.5 g	Fiber 1 g
Saturated Fat 1.5 g	Sugar 5 g
Trans Fat 0.0 g	Protein 16 g
Polyunsaturated Fat 2.5 g	DIETARY EXCHANGES:
Monounsaturated Fat 1.5 g	½ Other Carbohydrate
Cholesterol 43 mg	2 Lean Meat
Sodium 135 mg	

roasted potato and chicken
salad with greek dressing

SERVES 6

Warm from the oven, roasted potatoes are tossed with a colorful mix of chicken, green beans, roasted bell peppers, kalamata olives, and a lemony—but not too lemony—dressing.

Salad

Olive oil spray

1 pound small red potatoes (about 6), unpeeled, cut into ¾-inch cubes

1½ pounds fresh or frozen green beans, trimmed if fresh

2 cups diced boneless cooked chicken breast, cooked without salt, skin and all visible fat discarded

½ cup roasted red bell peppers, drained and rinsed if bottled, coarsely chopped

½ cup kalamata olives, coarsely chopped

½ teaspoon salt

Dressing

2 tablespoons white wine vinegar

2 tablespoons fresh lemon juice

2 medium garlic cloves, minced

2 teaspoons light brown sugar

2 teaspoons olive oil

1 teaspoon grated lemon zest

½ teaspoon dried oregano, crumbled

⅛ teaspoon pepper (optional)

PER SERVING

Calories 224	Carbohydrates 24 g
Total Fat 6.5 g	Fiber 5 g
Saturated Fat 1.0 g	Sugar 4 g
Trans Fat 0.0 g	Protein 18 g
Polyunsaturated Fat 1.0 g	DIETARY EXCHANGES:
Monounsaturated Fat 4.0 g	1 Starch
Cholesterol 40 mg	2 Vegetable
Sodium 452 mg	2 Lean Meat

Preheat the oven to 400° F. Lightly spray a baking sheet with olive oil spray.

Put the potatoes in a single layer on the baking sheet. Lightly spray the potatoes with olive oil spray.

Bake for 35 to 40 minutes, or until the potatoes are golden brown and tender when pierced with the tip of a sharp knife.

Meanwhile, in a large saucepan, bring the green beans and enough water to cover to a boil over high heat. Reduce the heat to medium high and cook for 6 to 8 minutes, or until tender, stirring occasionally. Drain well in a colander. Pat dry with paper towels. Transfer to a large serving bowl.

Gently stir in the potatoes, chicken, bell pepper, olives, and salt.

In a small bowl, whisk together the dressing ingredients. Pour over the salad. Toss to coat. Serve warm or cover and refrigerate until needed to serve chilled.

artichoke-rotini salad
with chicken

SERVES 4

Get double the flavor boost from the artichokes in this one-dish meal by using them in both the lively dressing and the salad.

4 ounces dried rotini (whole-wheat preferred)

1 14-ounce can artichokes, drained, with ¼ cup liquid reserved, divided use

¼ cup fresh lemon juice

2 tablespoons dried basil, crumbled

2 medium garlic cloves, minced

¼ teaspoon crushed red pepper flakes

2 cups diced boneless cooked chicken breast, cooked without salt, skin and all visible fat discarded

1 medium red bell pepper, cut into thin strips about 2 inches long

2 tablespoons olive oil (extra-virgin preferred)

¼ teaspoon salt

4 large lettuce leaves

Prepare the pasta using the package directions, omitting the salt and oil. Transfer to a colander and run under cold water to cool completely. Drain well.

Meanwhile, in a food processor or blender, process half the artichokes, the reserved artichoke liquid, and the lemon juice, basil, garlic, and red pepper flakes until smooth.

Coarsely chop the remaining artichokes. Transfer to a medium bowl.

To assemble, stir the chicken and bell pepper into the chopped artichokes. Stir in the pasta. Pour in the dressing, tossing gently to coat. Gently stir in the olive oil and salt. Place the lettuce leaves on four plates. Spoon the salad over the lettuce. Serve immediately for peak flavor.

PER SERVING

Calories 323	Carbohydrates 31 g
Total Fat 10.5 g	Fiber 6 g
Saturated Fat 2.0 g	Sugar 4 g
Trans Fat 0.0 g	Protein 28 g
Polyunsaturated Fat 1.5 g	DIETARY EXCHANGES:
Monounsaturated Fat 6.0 g	1½ Starch
Cholesterol 60 mg	1 Vegetable
Sodium 382 mg	3 Lean Meat

crispy tortilla salad

SERVES 6

You can bake the tortillas and, if you wish, make your own salsa for this crisp, light vegetarian entrée in advance, then assemble the salad just before serving.

6 6-inch corn tortillas

Cooking spray

½ teaspoon chili powder

6 cups shredded romaine (about 12 ounces)

1 19-ounce can no-salt-added kidney beans, rinsed and drained

½ cup grated fat-free mozzarella cheese

½ cup grated fat-free Cheddar cheese

3 medium tomatoes (2 red and 1 yellow preferred), chopped

6 tablespoons salsa

Preheat the oven to 350° F.

Lightly spray both sides of each tortilla with cooking spray. Sprinkle the top side with chili powder. Place in a single layer on a baking sheet.

Bake for 10 to 15 minutes, or until crisp and lightly browned.

To assemble, break the tortillas into bite-size pieces. Sprinkle on six plates. Top each serving with the remaining ingredients in the order listed.

PER SERVING	
Calories 166	Carbohydrates 28 g
Total Fat 0.5 g	Fiber 7 g
Saturated Fat 0.0 g	Sugar 5 g
Trans Fat 0.0 g	Protein 14 g
Polyunsaturated Fat 0.5 g	DIETARY EXCHANGES:
Monounsaturated Fat 0.0 g	1½ Starch
Cholesterol 3 mg	½ Other Carbohydrate
Sodium 303 mg	1½ Very Lean Meat

ham and rice salad

Team this pretty entrée salad with fresh fruit and crusty whole-grain bread.

Salad

1 cup uncooked brown rice

1 cup fat-free, low-sodium chicken broth

6 ounces lower-sodium, low-fat ham, all visible fat discarded, cut into ¼-inch cubes

1 cup fresh or frozen whole-kernel corn, thawed if frozen

1 cup frozen green peas, thawed

4 medium green onions, thinly sliced

1 medium red, yellow, or green bell pepper, finely chopped

4 or 5 medium radishes, finely chopped

¼ cup snipped fresh parsley

1 tablespoon fresh dillweed or 1 teaspoon dried, crumbled

Dressing

½ cup light Italian salad dressing

½ teaspoon Dijon mustard

❉ ❉ ❉

8 lettuce leaves, preferably red leaf

Fresh mint or parsley sprigs (optional)

Prepare the rice using the package directions, substituting the broth for 1 cup of the water and omitting the salt. Pour the rice onto a large baking sheet and let cool. Transfer to a large bowl.

PER SERVING	
Calories 179	Carbohydrates 28 g
Total Fat 4.5 g	Fiber 4 g
Saturated Fat 1.0 g	Sugar 4 g
Trans Fat 0.0 g	Protein 8 g
Polyunsaturated Fat 2.0 g	DIETARY EXCHANGES:
Monounsaturated Fat 1.5 g	2 Starch
Cholesterol 9 mg	½ Lean Meat
Sodium 422 mg	

Stir in the remaining salad ingredients.

In a small bowl, whisk together the salad dressing and mustard. Pour over the salad, stirring to coat.

Serve at room temperature or cover and refrigerate to serve chilled. At serving time, place the lettuce leaves on eight plates. Put a scoop of salad on each lettuce leaf. Garnish with the sprigs.

creamy herb dressing

MAKES ABOUT 1¼ CUPS; 2 tablespoons per serving

Serve this dressing cold or hot. It can be used as a dip or on poultry, baked potatoes, or cold seafood. It keeps well when covered and refrigerated.

½ cup fat-free plain yogurt

½ cup fat-free sour cream

1 medium green onion, minced

2 tablespoons finely snipped fresh parsley or cilantro

½ teaspoon salt-free lemon-herb seasoning

½ teaspoon honey or sugar

¼ teaspoon Italian seasoning, crumbled (optional)

In a small bowl, whisk together the yogurt and sour cream.

Whisk in the remaining ingredients.

To serve cold, cover and refrigerate until ready to use. To serve heated, pour into a small saucepan and warm over medium heat, gently stirring until heated through. Do not boil.

PER SERVING

Calories 21	Carbohydrates 4 g
Total Fat 0.0 g	Fiber 0 g
Saturated Fat 0.0 g	Sugar 2 g
Trans Fat 0.0 g	Protein 2 g
Polyunsaturated Fat 0.0 g	DIETARY EXCHANGES:
Monounsaturated Fat 0.0 g	Free
Cholesterol 2 mg	
Sodium 20 mg	

tomatillo-avocado dressing

MAKES ABOUT 1 CUP; 2 tablespoons per serving

You can use this guacamole-like recipe as a salad dressing, condiment, or dip. The flavor of the avocado is enhanced by the broiled tomatillos, which look like small green tomatoes enclosed in thin, papery husks.

Cooking spray

6 tomatillos

1 medium avocado, chopped (about 1 cup)

1 medium green onion, chopped

2 medium garlic cloves, minced

½ fresh jalapeño pepper, seeds and ribs discarded, chopped

1 teaspoon sugar

1 teaspoon fresh lemon juice

½ teaspoon ground cumin

½ teaspoon chili powder

¼ teaspoon salt

⅛ teaspoon pepper

Preheat the broiler. Lightly spray the broiler pan and rack with cooking spray.

Discard the husks of the tomatillos. Rinse the tomatillos in cold water. Cut each in half. Place with the skin side up in the broiler pan.

Broil 4 to 6 inches from the heat for 5 minutes. Turn over and broil for 2 to 3 minutes, or until slightly tender. Transfer to a covered container and refrigerate for at least 10 minutes to cool.

In a food processor or blender, process all the ingredients for 1 minute, or until smooth.

PER SERVING

Calories 56	Carbohydrates 5 g
Total Fat 4.0 g	Fiber 3 g
Saturated Fat 0.5 g	Sugar 2 g
Trans Fat 0.0 g	Protein 1 g
Polyunsaturated Fat 0.5 g	DIETARY EXCHANGES:
Monounsaturated Fat 2.5 g	1 Vegetable
Cholesterol 0 mg	1 Fat
Sodium 77 mg	

gazpacho dressing

MAKES ABOUT ¾ CUP; 2 tablespoons per serving

Replacing the cilantro with other herbs, such as parsley, mint, oregano, and tarragon, or with salt-free herb seasoning will give you a range of flavored salad dressings.

6 ounces low-sodium mixed-vegetable juice or low-sodium tomato juice

1 tablespoon very finely chopped onion, any variety

1 tablespoon very finely chopped celery

1 tablespoon very finely chopped bell pepper, any color

1 tablespoon grated carrot

1 tablespoon finely snipped fresh cilantro or 1 teaspoon dried, crumbled

1 teaspoon fresh lemon juice

½ teaspoon sugar

¼ teaspoon red hot-pepper sauce or ½ teaspoon Worcestershire sauce (lowest sodium available)

Pepper to taste

In a small bowl, whisk together all the ingredients. Cover and refrigerate for at least 2 hours so the flavors blend.

PER SERVING	
Calories 9	Carbohydrates 2 g
Total Fat 0.0 g	Fiber 0 g
Saturated Fat 0.0 g	Sugar 2 g
Trans Fat 0.0 g	Protein 0 g
Polyunsaturated Fat 0.0 g	DIETARY EXCHANGES:
Monounsaturated Fat 0.0 g	Free
Cholesterol 0 mg	
Sodium 20 mg	

parmesan-peppercorn ranch dressing

MAKES ABOUT 1 CUP; 2 tablespoons per serving

Cool and creamy, this dressing puts the finishing touch on your favorite salad greens. Pack some in a small airtight container along with some raw vegetables for lunchtime dipping.

¾ cup low-fat buttermilk

¼ cup fat-free sour cream

2 tablespoons light mayonnaise

2 tablespoons shredded or grated Parmesan cheese

½ teaspoon dried parsley, crumbled

½ teaspoon dried chives

¼ teaspoon dried oregano, crumbled

¼ teaspoon garlic powder

⅛ teaspoon salt

⅛ teaspoon pepper (coarsely ground preferred)

In a medium bowl, whisk together all the ingredients. Cover and refrigerate for 30 minutes before serving.

PER SERVING

Calories 35
Total Fat 2.0 g
 Saturated Fat 0.5 g
 Trans Fat 0.0 g
 Polyunsaturated Fat 0.5 g
 Monounsaturated Fat 0.5 g
Cholesterol 4 mg
Sodium 117 mg

Carbohydrates 3 g
 Fiber 0 g
 Sugar 2 g
Protein 2 g
DIETARY EXCHANGES:
 ½ Fat

feta cheese vinaigrette
with dijon mustard

MAKES ABOUT 1 CUP; 2 tablespoons per serving

Why bother with a salad dressing that has to be cooked? Because it is delicious enough to make the little bit of extra time well worthwhile. Also, the recipe makes eight servings and keeps well for up to five days, so you'll probably have plenty left over. This zesty, tangy vinaigrette is especially good over crisp romaine.

 1 tablespoon cornstarch

 ¾ cup water

 ¼ cup crumbled low-fat feta cheese

 2 tablespoons white wine vinegar

 1 tablespoon plus 1 teaspoon olive oil (extra-virgin preferred)

 1 tablespoon Dijon mustard

 2 teaspoons honey

 1 medium garlic clove, minced

 ⅛ teaspoon salt

 ⅛ teaspoon pepper

Put the cornstarch in a small saucepan. Add the water, stirring to dissolve. Bring to a boil over high heat, stirring occasionally. Cook for 2 to 3 minutes, or until thick and bubbly. Transfer to a medium bowl. Cover and refrigerate for at least 15 minutes.

Stir in the remaining ingredients. Serve or pour into a jar with a tight-fitting lid and store, refrigerated.

PER SERVING	
Calories 40	Carbohydrates 3 g
Total Fat 3.0 g	Fiber 0 g
Saturated Fat 0.5 g	Sugar 2 g
Trans Fat 0.0 g	Protein 1 g
Polyunsaturated Fat 0.5 g	DIETARY EXCHANGES:
Monounsaturated Fat 1.5 g	½ Fat
Cholesterol 1 mg	
Sodium 123 mg	

creamy artichoke dressing

MAKES ABOUT ¾ CUP; 2 tablespoons per serving

Try this silky-smooth dressing over salad greens tossed with the extra half-can of artichokes.

½ 14-ounce can artichoke hearts, undrained

2 tablespoons fat-free, low-sodium chicken broth

2 tablespoons fresh lemon juice

1 tablespoon olive oil (extra-virgin preferred)

2 medium garlic cloves, minced

½ teaspoon Dijon mustard

¼ teaspoon pepper

Pour off 1 tablespoon liquid from the artichokes and reserve. In a colander, rinse and drain the artichokes. Transfer to a food processor or blender.

Add the remaining ingredients, including the 1 tablespoon artichoke liquid, and process until very smooth. Transfer to a jar with a tight-fitting lid and refrigerate until ready to serve.

PER SERVING

Calories 31
Total Fat 2.5 g
  Saturated Fat 0.5 g
  Trans Fat 0.0 g
  Polyunsaturated Fat 0.0 g
  Monounsaturated Fat 1.5 g
Cholesterol 0 mg
Sodium 69 mg

Carbohydrates 2 g
  Fiber 0 g
  Sugar 0 g
Protein 1 g

DIETARY EXCHANGES:
½ Fat

seafood

crisp catfish
with creole sauce

SERVES 4

This catfish boasts a quick marinade of spicy buttermilk, a crisp coating, and a horseradish-spiked Creole sauce.

¼ cup low-fat buttermilk

⅛ teaspoon cayenne

4 catfish fillets (about 4 ounces each)

Creole Sauce

⅓ cup no-salt-added tomato sauce

1 medium rib of celery, finely chopped

1 medium green onion, thinly sliced

1 teaspoon bottled white horseradish

1 teaspoon fresh lemon juice

¼ teaspoon salt

❊ ❊ ❊

Cooking spray

1½ cups cornflake cereal

⅓ cup yellow cornmeal

In a large resealable plastic bag, combine the buttermilk and cayenne. Rinse the fish and pat dry with paper towels. Add the fish to the buttermilk mixture. Seal the bag and turn gently to coat. Refrigerate for 15 minutes to 1 hour, turning occasionally.

Meanwhile, in a small bowl, stir together the sauce ingredients. Cover and refrigerate until ready to use, up to four days.

PER SERVING

Calories 199	Carbohydrates 21 g
Total Fat 3.5 g	Fiber 2 g
Saturated Fat 1.0 g	Sugar 3 g
Trans Fat 0.0 g	Protein 21 g
Polyunsaturated Fat 1.0 g	DIETARY EXCHANGES:
Monounsaturated Fat 1.0 g	1½ Starch
Cholesterol 66 mg	3 Very Lean Meat
Sodium 286 mg	

Preheat the oven to 425° F. Lightly spray a baking sheet with cooking spray.

Put the cereal in a large resealable plastic bag. Seal the bag and use a rolling pin to crush the cereal into fine crumbs. Pour into a medium shallow bowl.

Stir in the cornmeal.

Set the plastic bag with the fish, bowl with the crumb mixture, and baking sheet in a row, assembly-line fashion. Drain the fish, discarding the marinade. Coat the fish with the cornflake mixture, shaking off the excess. Place on the baking sheet. Lightly spray the top side of the fish with cooking spray.

Bake for 10 to 12 minutes, or until the fish flakes easily when tested with a fork.

Meanwhile, remove the sauce from the refrigerator if you want to serve it at room temperature instead of chilled. Spoon the sauce over the fish.

grilled catfish
with mustard-lemon sauce

SERVES 4

Use the creamy mustard sauce in this recipe for an easy way to dress up other fish dishes or chicken. You can substitute honey mustard for the Dijon mustard if you prefer a sweeter sauce.

    Cooking spray

    4 catfish fillets (about 4 ounces each)

    ½ teaspoon pepper

Sauce

    2 medium garlic cloves, minced

    1 tablespoon all-purpose flour

    1¼ cups fat-free evaporated milk

    1 tablespoon Dijon mustard

    2 teaspoons finely grated lemon zest

    1 teaspoon chopped fresh basil, thyme, dillweed, parsley, or oregano or ½ teaspoon dried herb, crumbled

    Fresh herbs for garnish (optional)

Lightly spray the grill rack with cooking spray. Preheat the grill on medium-high.

Rinse the fish and pat dry with paper towels. Sprinkle both sides of the fish with the pepper.

Grill the fish for 5 minutes on each side, or until it flakes easily when tested with a fork.

Meanwhile, lightly spray a small saucepan or skillet with cooking spray. Cook the garlic over medium heat for 2 minutes, stirring occasionally.

PER SERVING	
Calories 186	Carbohydrates 12 g
Total Fat 3.5 g	Fiber 0 g
Saturated Fat 1.0 g	Sugar 10 g
Trans Fat 0.0 g	Protein 25 g
Polyunsaturated Fat 1.0 g	DIETARY EXCHANGES:
Monounsaturated Fat 1.0 g	1 Fat-Free Milk
Cholesterol 69 mg	3 Very Lean Meat
Sodium 218 mg	

Stir in the flour.

Pour in the milk all at once, whisking constantly. Whisk in the mustard and lemon zest. Cook for 3 to 5 minutes, or until thickened and bubbly, whisking constantly.

Whisk in the 1 teaspoon chopped herb. Cook for 1 minute, whisking constantly.

To serve, transfer the fish to four plates. Spoon the sauce over the fish. Garnish with the fresh herbs.

lemony crumb-topped catfish

SERVES 4

Press the blender button to make fresh bread crumbs, sprinkle them on fish fillets, bake, and serve. That's all it takes to get a healthy, great-tasting entrée on the table.

Cooking spray

4 catfish or other mild, thin fish fillets (about 4 ounces each)

½ medium lemon

3 slices reduced-calorie whole-grain bread, coarsely torn

2 tablespoons snipped fresh parsley

1 tablespoon shredded or grated Parmesan cheese

1 teaspoon grated lemon zest

1 teaspoon dried oregano, crumbled

⅛ teaspoon cayenne

⅛ teaspoon salt

2 tablespoons olive oil

1 medium lemon, quartered (optional)

Preheat the oven to 400° F. Line a baking sheet with aluminum foil. Lightly spray with cooking spray.

Rinse the fish and pat dry with paper towels. Place on the baking sheet. Squeeze the lemon over the fish.

In a food processor, process the bread, pulsing to make coarse crumbs. Transfer to a medium bowl.

Stir in the parsley, Parmesan, lemon zest, oregano, cayenne, and salt.

Stir in the oil. Sprinkle over the fish.

Bake for 12 to 15 minutes, or until the fish flakes easily when tested with a fork.

Serve with the lemon wedges.

PER SERVING

Calories 206
Total Fat 10.5 g
  Saturated Fat 2.0 g
  Trans Fat 0.0 g
  Polyunsaturated Fat 1.5 g
  Monounsaturated Fat 6.0 g
Cholesterol 67 mg
Sodium 230 mg

Carbohydrates 8 g
  Fiber 3 g
  Sugar 1 g
Protein 21 g

DIETARY EXCHANGES:
½ Starch
3 Lean Meat

---

halibut kebabs

Kebabs are an easy-to-prepare and fun way to enjoy mild halibut. For a simple but festive meal, serve with brown rice or whole-wheat pita bread and steamed zucchini.

Marinade

¼ cup fresh lemon juice

¼ cup olive oil

3 medium shallots, thinly sliced

1 teaspoon Italian seasoning, crumbled

½ teaspoon dried thyme, crumbled

❋ ❋ ❋

1 pound halibut steak (about 1 inch thick)

Cooking spray

½ large red onion, cut lengthwise into thirds

1 medium lemon, quartered

In a large resealable plastic bag, combine the marinade ingredients.

Rinse the fish and pat dry with paper towels. Discard the skin. Cut the fish into 16 cubes. Add to the marinade. Seal the bag and turn gently to coat. Refrigerate for 15 minutes to 1 hour, turning occasionally.

Meanwhile, soak 4 long wooden skewers in cold water for at least 10 minutes to keep them from charring, or use metal skewers.

Preheat the broiler. Lightly spray a broiler pan and rack with cooking spray.

Remove the fish from the bag and discard the marinade.

Separate the onion into single layers until you have 20 pieces. Alternating onion and fish, thread each skewer with 5 pieces of onion and 4 pieces of fish.

Broil the kebabs about 4 inches from the heat for 2 to 2½ minutes on each side, or until the fish flakes easily when tested with a fork.

Garnish with the lemon.

PER SERVING

Calories 132	Carbohydrates 2 g
Total Fat 2.5 g	Fiber 0 g
Saturated Fat 0.5 g	Sugar 1 g
Trans Fat 0.0 g	Protein 24 g
Polyunsaturated Fat 1.0 g	DIETARY EXCHANGES:
Monounsaturated Fat 1.0 g	3 Very Lean Meat
Cholesterol 36 mg	
Sodium 62 mg	

grilled cod
with artichoke-horseradish sauce

SERVES 4

Strong horseradish and mild artichokes mingle in a creamy sauce that complements grilled or broiled fish.

Cooking spray

1 tablespoon light tub margarine

½ cup chopped shallots or onion

2 medium garlic cloves, minced

2 tablespoons all-purpose flour

⅛ teaspoon salt

⅛ teaspoon pepper

1 12-ounce can fat-free evaporated milk

1 14-ounce can quartered artichoke hearts, rinsed and drained, or 1 9-ounce package frozen artichoke hearts, thawed, drained, and quartered

1 to 2 tablespoons grated fresh or prepared white horseradish

1 tablespoon chopped fresh oregano or 1 teaspoon dried, crumbled

4 small or 2 medium cod fillets or halibut steaks (about 1 pound total)

If grilling the fish, lightly spray the grill rack with cooking spray. Preheat the grill on medium high. If broiling, lightly spray the broiler pan and rack with cooking spray. Preheat the broiler.

In a medium saucepan, melt the margarine over medium heat. Cook the shallots and garlic for 5 minutes, or until the shallots are soft, stirring occasionally.

Stir in the flour, salt, and pepper.

PER SERVING	
Calories 227	Carbohydrates 22 g
Total Fat 2.0 g	Fiber 1 g
Saturated Fat 0.5 g	Sugar 11 g
Trans Fat 0.0 g	Protein 29 g
Polyunsaturated Fat 0.5 g	DIETARY EXCHANGES:
Monounsaturated Fat 1.0 g	1 Fat-Free Milk
Cholesterol 52 mg	1½ Vegetable
Sodium 420 mg	3 Very Lean Meat

Pour in the milk all at once, whisking constantly. Cook for 5 to 10 minutes, or until the sauce is thickened and bubbly, whisking constantly. Continue cooking for 1 minute, whisking constantly.

Stir in the artichokes, horseradish, and oregano. Cook for 3 to 5 minutes, or until heated through, stirring constantly. Cover and keep warm.

Rinse the fish and pat dry with paper towels.

Grill the fish or broil about 4 inches from the heat for 7 minutes. Turn over and grill or broil for 5 to 7 minutes, or until it flakes easily when tested with a fork.

To serve, spoon the sauce over the fish.

poached fish
in asian broth

SERVES 4

Packed with spices and other seasonings, this broth gives the fish a delicate flavor. The grated carrot confetti makes the dish pretty enough for company.

Broth

   3 cups fat-free, low-sodium chicken broth

   2 tablespoons dry sherry

   2 tablespoons soy sauce (lowest sodium available)

   2 lemon slices

   3 thin slices peeled gingerroot

   ⅛ teaspoon cayenne

   ✻ ✻ ✻

   1 pound orange roughy or other mild, thick fish fillets

   5 or 6 medium green onions (green part only), cut into 1-inch pieces

   1 medium red bell pepper, cut into 1 × ¼-inch strips

   1 medium rib of celery, cut into 1 × ¼-inch strips

   ½ teaspoon toasted sesame oil

   1 medium carrot, grated

   Pepper to taste

In a nonaluminum fish poacher, wok, or large skillet, stir together the broth ingredients. Bring to a boil over high heat.

Meanwhile, rinse the fish and pat dry with paper towels.

Reduce the heat to low and put the fish in the broth. Add a small amount of water, if needed, barely covering the fish. Adjust the heat if necessary and

PER SERVING	
Calories 139	Carbohydrates 7 g
Total Fat 1.5 g	Fiber 3 g
Saturated Fat 0.0 g	Sugar 4 g
Trans Fat 0.0 g	Protein 21 g
Polyunsaturated Fat 0.5 g	DIETARY EXCHANGES:
Monounsaturated Fat 0.5 g	1 Vegetable
Cholesterol 68 mg	3 Very Lean Meat
Sodium 351 mg	

simmer the fish for about 10 minutes per inch of thickness at the thickest point, or just until it flakes easily when tested with a fork. Do not overcook. Cut the fish into 4 pieces. Using slotted spatulas, transfer each piece to a separate soup bowl.

Return the liquid to a boil. Stir in the green onions, bell pepper, and celery. Cook for 2 to 3 minutes, or until the bell pepper and celery are tender-crisp. Discard the lemon and gingerroot.

To serve, use a slotted spoon to transfer the vegetables to the soup bowls. Stir the sesame oil into the broth. Pour into the soup bowls. Sprinkle each serving with the grated carrot and pepper.

mesquite-grilled red snapper
with gingered black bean salsa

SERVES 4

Chunks of mesquite wood give this grilled snapper recipe its distinctive smoky taste.
If your grill doesn't use charcoal or you prefer to broil your fish, you won't get the
mesquite essence, but the fish will still be very good.

Cooking spray

Gingered Black Bean Salsa

¼ cup chopped onion

¼ cup chopped carrot

1 to 2 fresh jalapeño peppers, seeds and ribs discarded, chopped

2 tablespoons finely chopped peeled gingerroot

2 to 3 medium garlic cloves, minced

1 15-ounce can no-salt-added black beans, drained reserving
   3 tablespoons liquid, then rinsed

¼ teaspoon salt

1 medium tomato, seeds discarded, chopped

❉ ❉ ❉

1 pound red snapper fillets (about ½ inch thick)

At least 1 hour before cooking, soak 4 to 6 mesquite wood chunks in enough
water to cover.

Lightly spray the grill rack or broiler pan and rack with cooking spray. Light
the charcoal grill and let the coals get medium hot, preheat the grill on medium
high, or preheat the broiler.

PER SERVING

Calories 224	Carbohydrates 21 g
Total Fat 1.5 g	Fiber 5 g
Saturated Fat 0.5 g	Sugar 5 g
Trans Fat 0.0 g	Protein 30 g
Polyunsaturated Fat 0.5 g	DIETARY EXCHANGES:
Monounsaturated Fat 0.5 g	1 Starch
Cholesterol 42 mg	1 Vegetable
Sodium 227 mg	3½ Very Lean Meat

Meanwhile, lightly spray a medium saucepan with cooking spray. Cook the onion, carrot, jalapeños, gingerroot, and garlic over medium-low heat for 5 minutes, or until the onion is soft.

Stir in the beans, reserved bean liquid, and salt. Cook for 1 to 2 minutes, or until heated through.

Stir in the tomato. Set aside.

Rinse the fish and pat dry with paper towels.

If using charcoal, drain the wood chunks and put them directly on the medium-hot coals. Grill the fish (directly over the coals if using charcoal) for 5 minutes. Turn over and grill for 5 to 7 minutes, or until it flakes easily when tested with a fork. Or broil the fish about 4 inches from the heat for 5 minutes. Turn over and broil for 5 to 7 minutes, or until it flakes easily when tested with a fork.

Serve the fish with the salsa.

mediterranean grilled salmon

SERVES 6

The heady aroma of fresh herbs and the zing of lemon turn this salmon into a feast for the senses. Serve with crusty whole-grain bread and grilled or broiled asparagus.

Marinade

1 medium Italian plum tomato, finely chopped

2 tablespoons red wine vinegar

1 tablespoon chopped fresh rosemary or 1 teaspoon dried, crushed

1 tablespoon chopped fresh sage or 1 teaspoon dried

2 teaspoons olive oil

1 teaspoon grated lemon zest

¼ teaspoon pepper

✳ ✳ ✳

6 salmon fillets (about 4 ounces each)

Cooking spray

In a large resealable plastic bag, combine the marinade ingredients. Rinse the fish and pat dry with paper towels. Add the fish to the marinade. Seal the bag and turn gently to coat. Refrigerate for 30 minutes to 2 hours, turning occasionally.

Meanwhile, if grilling the fish, lightly spray the grill rack with cooking spray. Preheat the grill on medium high. If broiling, lightly spray the broiler pan with cooking spray. Preheat the broiler.

Remove the fish from the bag and discard the marinade.

Grill the fish or broil about 4 inches from the heat for 5 to 6 minutes. Turn over and grill or broil for 4 to 5 minutes, or until the fish flakes easily when tested with a fork.

PER SERVING

Calories 132	Carbohydrates 0 g
Total Fat 4.0 g	Fiber 0 g
Saturated Fat 0.5 g	Sugar 0 g
Trans Fat 0.0 g	Protein 23 g
Polyunsaturated Fat 1.5 g	DIETARY EXCHANGES:
Monounsaturated Fat 1.0 g	3 Lean Meat
Cholesterol 59 mg	
Sodium 76 mg	

broiled salmon
with pesto and olives

SERVES 4

An aromatic paste of fresh basil flecked with olives and pine nuts makes this salmon entrée very elegant, yet incredibly easy to prepare.

    Cooking spray
    1 cup loosely packed fresh basil leaves
    2 tablespoons pine nuts
    2 tablespoons sliced black olives
    1 tablespoon light mayonnaise
    2 medium garlic cloves, minced
    2 teaspoons olive oil
    1 teaspoon grated orange zest
    2 tablespoons fresh orange juice
    4 salmon fillets (about 4 ounces each)

Preheat the broiler. Lightly spray a broiler-safe baking sheet with cooking spray.

In a food processor or blender, process the remaining ingredients except the fish for 15 to 20 seconds, or until slightly chunky.

Rinse the fish, pat dry with paper towels, and place on the baking sheet. Using a pastry brush or spoon, spread the basil mixture over both sides of the fish.

Broil the fish about 4 inches from the heat for 4 to 5 minutes on each side, or until it flakes easily when tested with a fork.

PER SERVING

Calories 197	Carbohydrates 3 g
Total Fat 10.0 g	Fiber 1 g
Saturated Fat 1.5 g	Sugar 1 g
Trans Fat 0.0 g	Protein 24 g
Polyunsaturated Fat 3.5 g	DIETARY EXCHANGES:
Monounsaturated Fat 4.0 g	3 Lean Meat
Cholesterol 60 mg	
Sodium 142 mg	

skillet salmon
with broccoli and rice

SERVES 4

This dish combines the ease of quick-cooking brown rice and salmon in a pouch with the bright taste of fresh vegetables, fresh basil, and a hint of lemon.

1 teaspoon olive oil

2 medium garlic cloves, minced

12 ounces fresh broccoli florets

1½ cups fat-free, low-sodium chicken broth

1 teaspoon grated lemon zest

¼ teaspoon pepper

1 cup uncooked quick-cooking brown rice

12 ounces salmon from vacuum-sealed pouches, flaked

1 cup cherry tomatoes, halved

¼ cup fresh basil leaves, coarsely chopped

In a large deep skillet, heat the oil over medium heat, swirling to coat the bottom. Cook the garlic for 10 to 15 seconds. Watch carefully so it doesn't burn.

Stir in the broccoli. Increase the heat to medium high and cook for 2 to 3 minutes, or until tender-crisp, stirring occasionally.

Stir in the broth, lemon zest, and pepper. Bring to a simmer, stirring occasionally.

Stir in the rice. Reduce the heat and simmer, covered, for 5 minutes. Remove from the heat. Let stand, still covered, for 5 minutes, or until the rice is tender and all the liquid is absorbed.

Stir in the salmon, tomatoes, and basil.

COOK'S TIP

If you buy two vacuum-packed pouches of salmon, each about 7 ounces, you'll have enough left over to top a salad for tomorrow's lunch.

PER SERVING	
Calories 234	Carbohydrates 26 g
Total Fat 5.5 g	Fiber 4 g
Saturated Fat 1.5 g	Sugar 3 g
Trans Fat 0.0 g	Protein 21 g
Polyunsaturated Fat 1.5 g	DIETARY EXCHANGES:
Monounsaturated Fat 1.5 g	1 Starch
Cholesterol 30 mg	2 Vegetable
Sodium 486 mg	2½ Lean Meat

salmon and rotini
with chipotle cream

SERVES 4

The chipotle pepper gives this recipe a smoky blast of heat.

> 6 ounces dried whole-grain rotini
>
> 12 ounces fresh green beans, trimmed and halved
>
> ½ cup fat-free sour cream
>
> ¼ cup light mayonnaise
>
> ½ to 1 chipotle pepper canned in adobo sauce, minced, 2 teaspoons sauce reserved
>
> ¼ teaspoon garlic powder
>
> ¼ teaspoon ground cumin
>
> 1 7.1-ounce vacuum-sealed pouch salmon, flaked
>
> 2 to 3 tablespoons snipped fresh cilantro

Prepare the pasta using the package directions, omitting the salt and oil. Three minutes before the end of the cooking time, stir in the green beans. Drain well in a colander.

Meanwhile, in a large shallow bowl, stir together the sour cream, mayonnaise, chipotle pepper, reserved adobo sauce, garlic powder, and cumin.

Gently stir in the pasta and beans.

Sprinkle with the salmon and cilantro. Do not stir.

PER SERVING

Calories 318	Carbohydrates 45 g
Total Fat 8.0 g	Fiber 8 g
Saturated Fat 2.0 g	Sugar 5 g
Trans Fat 0.0 g	Protein 19 g
Polyunsaturated Fat 3.5 g	DIETARY EXCHANGES:
Monounsaturated Fat 1.5 g	2½ Starch
Cholesterol 28 mg	1 Vegetable
Sodium 501 mg	1½ Lean Meat

trout amandine
with orange-dijon sauce

SERVES 4

An old favorite, trout amandine, gets a modern makeover with a yogurt sauce enhanced with orange marmalade and Dijon mustard.

⅓ cup fat-free plain yogurt

1 tablespoon all-fruit orange marmalade

1 tablespoon Dijon mustard

4 trout fillets with skin (about 4½ ounces each)

½ teaspoon salt-free lemon pepper

3 tablespoons all-purpose flour

2 teaspoons olive oil

2 tablespoons sliced almonds

In a small bowl, whisk together the yogurt, marmalade, and mustard. Cover and refrigerate until needed.

Rinse the fish and pat dry with paper towels. Sprinkle the flesh side of the fish with the lemon pepper.

Put the flour in a medium shallow bowl. Lightly coat the flesh side of the fish, shaking off the excess. Transfer to a plate.

Using a pastry brush, brush the oil over the flesh side. Sprinkle with the almonds. Press them lightly into the oil to adhere.

Heat a large nonstick skillet over medium-high heat. Starting with the almond side down, cook the fish for 3 to 4 minutes on each side, or until it flakes easily when tested with a fork.

Meanwhile, remove the sauce from the refrigerator if you want to serve it at room temperature instead of chilled.

PER SERVING	
Calories 220	Carbohydrates 10 g
Total Fat 8.0 g	Fiber 1 g
Saturated Fat 1.5 g	Sugar 4 g
Trans Fat 0.0 g	Protein 26 g
Polyunsaturated Fat 2.0 g	DIETARY EXCHANGES:
Monounsaturated Fat 4.0 g	½ Other Carbohydrate
Cholesterol 67 mg	3 Lean Meat
Sodium 128 mg	

To serve, place the fish with the skin side up on a platter. Let cool for 1 minute. Using tongs, carefully peel off the skin. Turn so the almond-coated side faces up. Spoon the sauce over the fish.

COOK'S TIP on Trout

If your favorite seafood counter has only whole trout, look for one with clear eyes (not cloudy) and no fishy aroma. Ask for it to be "pan-dressed"—cleaned, trimmed, filleted, and ready to go in the pan.

seared tuna
with mango-pear salsa

SERVES 4

The unexpected combination of mango and pear works deliciously as a salsa here, or chop the fruit in slightly larger pieces and serve it as a salad with other entrées.

Mango-Pear Salsa

1 medium mango, chopped

½ firm pear, peeled if desired and chopped

1 medium fresh jalapeño pepper, ribs and seeds discarded, finely chopped

2 tablespoons finely chopped red onion

2 tablespoons snipped fresh cilantro

1 to 2 teaspoons grated peeled gingerroot

½ teaspoon grated lemon zest

1 tablespoon fresh lemon juice

✴ ✴ ✴

1 teaspoon chili powder

½ teaspoon pepper (coarsely ground preferred)

¼ teaspoon salt

1 1-pound tuna steak, about 1 inch thick

2 teaspoons canola or corn oil

PER SERVING	
Calories 203	Carbohydrates 17 g
Total Fat 4.0 g	Fiber 3 g
Saturated Fat 0.5 g	Sugar 12 g
Trans Fat 0.0 g	Protein 26 g
Polyunsaturated Fat 1.0 g	DIETARY EXCHANGES:
Monounsaturated Fat 1.5 g	1 Fruit
Cholesterol 53 mg	3 Lean Meat
Sodium 196 mg	

In a medium bowl, gently stir together the salsa ingredients. Set aside.

In a small bowl, stir together the chili powder, pepper, and salt.

Rinse the fish and pat dry with paper towels. Sprinkle the chili powder mixture over both sides of the fish. Using your fingertips, firmly press the mixture into the fish so it will adhere.

In a large nonstick skillet, heat the oil over medium-high heat, swirling to coat the bottom. Cook the fish for 4 minutes on each side, or until it flakes easily when tested with a fork and is cooked as desired. Cut into 4 pieces.

Serve with the salsa on the side.

jamaican jerk tuna steaks

For a tropical meal that is sure to please, serve jerk-seasoned tuna steaks over brown rice cooked with pineapple chunks.

8 ounces canned pineapple chunks in their own juice, drained and juice reserved

2 ounces diced pimientos, rinsed and drained

2 medium green onions, thinly sliced

¾ cup uncooked quick-cooking brown rice

Cooking spray

1 1-pound tuna steak, about ¾ inch thick

1 tablespoon olive oil

¼ teaspoon dried thyme, crumbled

¼ teaspoon ground allspice

¼ teaspoon ground ginger

¼ teaspoon garlic powder

Add enough water to the reserved pineapple juice to measure ½ cup. Put the pineapple and juice mixture in a small saucepan.

Stir in the pimientos and green onions. Bring to a simmer over medium-high heat.

Stir in the brown rice. Reduce the heat and simmer, covered, for 10 minutes, or until the rice is tender and the liquid is absorbed.

Meanwhile, lightly spray the grill rack with cooking spray. Preheat the grill on medium high.

Rinse the fish and pat dry with paper towels. Cut the fish into 4 pieces. Brush the oil over both sides.

In a small bowl, stir together the thyme, allspice, ginger, and garlic powder. Sprinkle on both sides of the fish.

Grill for 3 to 5 minutes on each side, or until the desired doneness.

To serve, spoon the rice mixture onto four plates. Top with the fish.

PER SERVING	
Calories 254	Carbohydrates 24 g
Total Fat 5.0 g	Fiber 2 g
Saturated Fat 1.0 g	Sugar 9 g
Trans Fat 0.0 g	Protein 27 g
Polyunsaturated Fat 1.0 g	DIETARY EXCHANGES:
Monounsaturated Fat 3.0 g	1 Starch
Cholesterol 53 mg	½ Fruit
Sodium 51 mg	3 Lean Meat

tuna-pasta casserole

SERVES 6

This heart-healthy version of an old standby will please everyone in your family.

8 ounces dried linguine, vermicelli, spaghetti, or other thin pasta (whole-wheat preferred)

Cooking spray

1 teaspoon canola or corn oil

1 small onion, chopped

1 medium garlic clove, minced

2 6-ounce cans low-sodium tuna in water, drained and flaked

½ cup finely chopped carrot

⅓ cup finely chopped green bell pepper

¼ cup finely snipped fresh parsley

¼ teaspoon paprika

8 ounces fat-free cottage cheese

½ cup fat-free sour cream

½ cup fat-free plain yogurt

½ cup plain dry bread crumbs, toasted

¼ cup shredded or grated Parmesan cheese

Prepare the pasta using the package directions, omitting the salt and oil. Drain well in a colander.

Meanwhile, preheat the oven to 350° F. Lightly spray an 11 × 9 × 2-inch casserole dish with cooking spray.

In a small nonstick skillet, heat the oil over medium-high heat, swirling to coat the bottom. Cook the onion and garlic for 2 to 3 minutes, or until the onion is soft, stirring frequently.

In a large bowl, stir together the onion mixture, tuna, carrot, bell pepper, parsley, and paprika.

In a small bowl, stir together the cottage cheese, sour cream, and yogurt. Stir with the pasta into the tuna mixture. Spoon into the casserole dish.

In a small bowl, combine the bread crumbs and Parmesan. Sprinkle over the casserole.

Bake for 30 to 45 minutes, or until the top is lightly browned.

PER SERVING	
Calories 343	Carbohydrates 46 g
Total Fat 4.5 g	Fiber 2 g
Saturated Fat 1.5 g	Sugar 8 g
Trans Fat 0.0 g	Protein 28 g
Polyunsaturated Fat 1.5 g	DIETARY EXCHANGES:
Monounsaturated Fat 1.5 g	2½ Starch
Cholesterol 32 mg	½ Other Carbohydrate
Sodium 339 mg	3 Very Lean Meat

tilapia piccata

Lemon and capers enhance the mild flavor of tilapia. The finished dish is especially tasty over whole-wheat pasta. Buon appetito!

1 tablespoon all-purpose flour

1 teaspoon sodium-free instant powdered chicken bouillon

¾ cup water

¼ cup dry white wine (regular or nonalcoholic)

1 tablespoon fresh lemon juice

1 tablespoon capers, rinsed and drained

⅓ cup all-purpose flour

⅛ teaspoon salt

⅛ teaspoon pepper

4 tilapia or other mild, thin fish fillets (about 4 ounces each)

1 tablespoon olive oil

Cooking spray

2 teaspoons light tub margarine

1 medium lemon, quartered

In a small bowl, stir together 1 tablespoon flour and the bouillon. Gradually pour in the water, whisking until smooth. Whisk in the wine and lemon juice. Stir in the capers. Set aside.

On a plate, stir together the ⅓ cup flour, salt, and pepper.

Rinse the fish and pat dry with paper towels. Coat a fillet with the flour mixture, gently shaking off the excess. Transfer to another plate. Repeat with the remaining fish.

PER SERVING

Calories 205	Carbohydrates 11 g
Total Fat 6.0 g	Fiber 0 g
Saturated Fat 1.0 g	Sugar 0 g
Trans Fat 0.0 g	Protein 24 g
Polyunsaturated Fat 1.0 g	DIETARY EXCHANGES:
Monounsaturated Fat 3.5 g	½ Starch
Cholesterol 57 mg	3 Lean Meat
Sodium 208 mg	

In a large nonstick skillet, heat the oil over medium-high heat, swirling to coat the bottom. Cook the fish for 3 minutes. Remove the pan from the heat. Lightly spray the top of the fish with cooking spray. Turn over. Cook for 2 to 3 minutes, or until the fish flakes easily when tested with a fork. Transfer the fish to a third plate.

Pour the bouillon mixture into the skillet. Bring to a boil over medium-high heat, stirring constantly. Reduce the heat and simmer for 3 to 5 minutes, or until slightly thickened, stirring often.

With the heat on low, stir in the margarine until melted. Return the fish to the skillet. Spoon the sauce over the fish. Simmer for 1 to 2 minutes, or until the fish and sauce are heated through.

To serve, transfer the fish to four plates. Spoon the sauce over the fish. Garnish with the lemon wedges.

tilapia tacos
with fresh salsa

SERVES 4

A dusting of cornmeal gives these lime-marinated tilapia fillets a nice crust when browned, and homemade salsa adds a touch of heat.

2 tilapia or other mild, thin fish fillets (about 4 ounces each)

1 tablespoon fresh lime juice

½ teaspoon chili powder

½ teaspoon garlic powder

½ teaspoon onion powder

¼ teaspoon salt

2 small Italian plum tomatoes

1 small fresh jalapeño pepper, seeds and ribs discarded, diced

1 medium green onion, thickly sliced

2 tablespoons fresh cilantro

3 tablespoons yellow cornmeal

2 teaspoons olive oil

8 6-inch corn tortillas

Rinse the fish and pat dry with paper towels. Put the fish in a large shallow casserole dish. Sprinkle the lime juice on both sides of the fish.

In a small bowl, stir together the chili powder, garlic powder, onion powder, and salt. Rub over both sides of the fish. Cover and refrigerate for 15 minutes to 1 hour.

Meanwhile, in a food processor or blender, process the tomatoes, jalapeño, green onion, and cilantro for 10 to 15 seconds, or until finely chopped. Transfer to a small bowl. Cover and refrigerate until needed.

PER SERVING	
Calories 173	Carbohydrates 21 g
Total Fat 4.0 g	Fiber 3 g
Saturated Fat 1.0 g	Sugar 2 g
Trans Fat 0.0 g	Protein 14 g
Polyunsaturated Fat 1.0 g	DIETARY EXCHANGES:
Monounsaturated Fat 2.0 g	1½ Starch
Cholesterol 28 mg	1½ Lean Meat
Sodium 227 mg	

Put the cornmeal in a medium shallow bowl.

Remove the fish from the marinade, discarding any remaining marinade. Lightly coat the fish in the cornmeal, shaking off the excess. Transfer to a plate.

In a large nonstick skillet, heat the oil over medium-high heat, swirling to coat the bottom. Cook the fish for 4 to 5 minutes on each side, or until it flakes easily when tested with a fork. Transfer to a cutting board. Quarter each fillet.

Warm the tortillas using the package directions.

To assemble, place 1 piece of fish in the center of each tortilla. Spoon the salsa over the fish. Fold each tortilla in half.

tilapia with roasted red bell peppers and olives

SERVES 4

You can count on evenly sized tilapia fillets and an array of red, yellow, and green to make a picture-perfect presentation in this dish.

Cooking spray

4 tilapia or other mild, thin fish fillets (about 4 ounces each)

¼ teaspoon pepper

Paprika to taste

¾ cup diced roasted red bell peppers, rinsed and drained if bottled

12 medium pimiento-stuffed green olives, chopped

2 tablespoons minced green onions

2 tablespoons finely snipped fresh parsley

2 teaspoons olive oil (extra-virgin preferred)

1½ teaspoons dried basil, crumbled

2 medium lemons, quartered

Preheat the oven to 350° F.

Lightly spray a baking sheet with cooking spray. Rinse the fish, pat dry with paper towels, and place on the baking sheet. Lightly spray the fish with cooking spray. Sprinkle with the pepper and paprika.

Bake for 10 to 12 minutes, or until the fish flakes easily when tested with a fork.

Meanwhile, in a small bowl, stir together the remaining ingredients except the lemons.

To serve, squeeze a lemon wedge over each fillet. Top with the bell pepper mixture. Serve with the remaining lemon wedges.

PER SERVING

Calories 163	Carbohydrates 4 g
Total Fat 6.0 g	Fiber 0 g
Saturated Fat 1.0 g	Sugar 1 g
Trans Fat 0.0 g	Protein 23 g
Polyunsaturated Fat 1.5 g	DIETARY EXCHANGES:
Monounsaturated Fat 3.0 g	3 Lean Meat
Cholesterol 57 mg	
Sodium 343 mg	

rosemary-dijon fish fillets

SERVES 4

Even after the busiest day, you can serve dinner with a flair by preparing this incredibly easy entrée. The sauce gives a punch of flavor and a light caramel color to the fish.

1 teaspoon olive oil

4 grouper, sole, tilapia, or other mild, thin fish fillets (about 4 ounces each)

1 medium lime, quartered

1 tablespoon olive oil

1 tablespoon plus 1 teaspoon Dijon mustard

¼ teaspoon dried rosemary, crushed

¼ teaspoon salt

⅛ teaspoon pepper

1 tablespoon water

Preheat the oven to 400° F. Spread 1 teaspoon oil over a rimmed nonstick baking sheet.

Rinse the fish and pat dry with paper towels. Place the fish on the baking sheet so the fillets are about 2 inches apart.

Squeeze the lime over the fish. Brush with 1 tablespoon oil. With a clean brush, brush with the mustard. Sprinkle with the rosemary, salt, and pepper.

Bake for 10 to 12 minutes, or until the fish flakes easily when tested with a fork. Using a slotted spatula, transfer to four plates.

Pour the water into the baking sheet, stirring to dislodge any clinging bits of topping. Drizzle over the fish.

PER SERVING

Calories 154	Carbohydrates 2 g
Total Fat 6.0 g	Fiber 0 g
Saturated Fat 1.0 g	Sugar 1 g
Trans Fat 0.0 g	Protein 22 g
Polyunsaturated Fat 1.0 g	DIETARY EXCHANGES:
Monounsaturated Fat 3.5 g	3 Lean Meat
Cholesterol 42 mg	
Sodium 308 mg	

fish fillets
with broiled-veggie rice

The brown rice in this dish picks up a whisper of smokiness from the broiled vegetables.

1 medium red bell pepper, cut into ¼-inch strips

1 medium yellow summer squash, cut into ¼-inch rounds

1 medium onion, cut into ¼-inch strips

2 teaspoons olive oil (extra-virgin preferred)

½ cup quick-cooking brown rice

2 tablespoons chopped fresh basil or snipped fresh parsley

1 teaspoon grated lemon zest

¼ teaspoon salt

Cooking spray

4 sole, tilapia, or other mild, thin fish fillets (about 4 ounces each)

2 teaspoons olive oil (extra-virgin preferred)

1 teaspoon seafood seasoning (lowest sodium available)

⅛ teaspoon salt

2 tablespoons fresh lemon juice

2 teaspoons olive oil (extra-virgin preferred)

Preheat the broiler.

Line a baking sheet with aluminum foil. Put the bell pepper, squash, and onion on the baking sheet. Pour 2 teaspoons oil over the vegetables and toss gently to coat. Arrange the vegetables in a single layer.

PER SERVING	
Calories 233	Carbohydrates 16 g
Total Fat 8.5 g	Fiber 3 g
Saturated Fat 1.5 g	Sugar 5 g
Trans Fat 0.0 g	Protein 24 g
Polyunsaturated Fat 1.0 g	DIETARY EXCHANGES:
Monounsaturated Fat 5.0 g	½ Starch
Cholesterol 54 mg	1 Vegetable
Sodium 465 mg	3 Lean Meat

Broil at least 4 inches from the heat for 9 to 10 minutes, or until richly browned on the edges. Keeping the cooked vegetables on the aluminum foil, remove them from the baking sheet and pour onto a cutting board. Coarsely chop.

Meanwhile, prepare the rice using the package directions, omitting the salt and margarine.

Stir the broiled vegetables, basil, lemon zest, and ¼ teaspoon salt into the cooked rice. Cover to keep warm.

Line the baking sheet with another sheet of aluminum foil. Lightly spray with cooking spray.

Rinse the fish and pat dry with paper towels. Place the fish in a single layer on the baking sheet. Spoon ½ teaspoon oil over each fillet. Sprinkle with the seafood seasoning and ⅛ teaspoon salt.

Broil about 4 inches from the heat for 5 minutes, or until the fish flakes easily when tested with a fork.

To serve, spoon the vegetable-rice mixture onto the center of a platter. Arrange the fish around the mixture. Spoon the lemon juice over the fish, then drizzle with the remaining 2 teaspoons oil.

fish with mustard sauce over steamed spinach

SERVES 4

Golden mustard sauce, white fish, and dark green spinach make a picture-perfect dish that is incredibly easy to prepare.

4 sole, flounder, or other mild, thin fish fillets (about 4 ounces each)

¼ cup light ranch salad dressing

3 tablespoons fat-free plain yogurt

1½ tablespoons prepared mustard

8 ounces fresh spinach leaves

Preheat the oven to 400° F.

Rinse the fish and pat dry with paper towels. Place in a single layer in a 12   8   2-inch or 13   9   2-inch glass baking dish.

In a small bowl, whisk together the salad dressing, yogurt, and mustard. Spoon over the fish.

Bake for 8 to 10 minutes, or until the fish flakes easily when tested with a fork.

Heat a large nonstick skillet over medium-high heat. Cook the spinach for 30 seconds, or just until wilted, stirring constantly.

To serve, spoon a thin layer of spinach onto four plates. Top with the baked fish.

PER SERVING

Calories 159
Total Fat 4.5 g
  Saturated Fat 0.5 g
  Trans Fat 0.0 g
  Polyunsaturated Fat 1.0 g
  Monounsaturated Fat 1.0 g
Cholesterol 58 mg
Sodium 349 mg

Carbohydrates 6 g
  Fiber 2 g
  Sugar 2 g
Protein 24 g

DIETARY EXCHANGES:
½ Other Carbohydrate
3 Lean Meat

cajun red scallops

SERVES 4

The secret to perfectly cooked, tender scallops is in the timing—as soon as they become opaque, pull them off the heat.

6 ounces dried no-yolk egg
noodles

1 pound sea scallops

½ teaspoon paprika

½ teaspoon salt-free Cajun or
Creole seasoning blend

3 tablespoons light tub
margarine

1 teaspoon Dijon mustard

1 teaspoon grated lemon zest

¼ teaspoon salt

1 teaspoon olive oil

2 tablespoons finely snipped
fresh parsley

1 medium lemon, quartered

Prepare the noodles using the package directions, omitting the salt and margarine. Drain well in a colander. Transfer to a platter and cover to keep warm.

Meanwhile, rinse the scallops and pat dry with paper towels. Transfer to a plate.

In a small bowl, stir together the paprika and seasoning blend. Sprinkle evenly over the scallops to coat.

In the same bowl, stir together the margarine, mustard, lemon zest, and salt.

In a large nonstick skillet, heat the oil over medium-high heat, swirling to coat the bottom. Cook the scallops for 3 minutes. Turn over and cook for 2 minutes, or just until opaque in the center when you cut into one. Remove from the heat.

Using a rubber scraper, stir the margarine mixture into the scallops until completely blended, scraping the bottom and sides of the skillet to dislodge any browned bits.

Spoon the scallops over the noodles. Sprinkle with the parsley. Serve with the lemon wedges.

PER SERVING	
Calories 301	Carbohydrates 35 g
Total Fat 6.0 g	Fiber 2 g
Saturated Fat 0.5 g	Sugar 2 g
Trans Fat 0.0 g	Protein 24 g
Polyunsaturated Fat 1.0 g	DIETARY EXCHANGES:
Monounsaturated Fat 2.5 g	2½ Starch
Cholesterol 37 mg	3 Very Lean Meat
Sodium 443 mg	

mussels
with yogurt-caper sauce

SERVES 6

A tangy yogurt sauce seasoned with green onions, capers, and lemon complements the sweetness of tender mussels. Serve this distinctive dish with crusty whole-wheat bread to soak up the aromatic cooking liquid.

Yogurt Sauce

¾ cup fat-free plain yogurt

1 tablespoon finely chopped green onions (green part only)

1 tablespoon capers, rinsed and drained

1 teaspoon grated lemon zest

¼ teaspoon sugar

   ✽ ✽ ✽

2 pounds raw mussels in shells

1 cup dry white wine (regular or nonalcoholic), dry vermouth, or water

1 small lemon, thinly sliced crosswise

2 tablespoons coarsely chopped fresh basil or 2 teaspoons dried, crumbled

2 medium garlic cloves, minced

In a small bowl, stir together the yogurt sauce ingredients. Cover and refrigerate until ready to serve.

Scrub the mussels under cold running water. With fingertips or kitchen scissors, remove any black, stringy beards.

In a stockpot, bring the remaining ingredients to a boil over high heat. Stir in the mussels. Reduce the heat and simmer, covered, for 6 to 8 minutes, or until

---

PER SERVING

Calories 147	Carbohydrates 8 g
Total Fat 2.5 g	Fiber 0 g
Saturated Fat 0.5 g	Sugar 3 g
Trans Fat 0.0 g	Protein 15 g
Polyunsaturated Fat 0.5 g	DIETARY EXCHANGES:
Monounsaturated Fat 0.5 g	½ Other Carbohydrate
Cholesterol 32 mg	2½ Very Lean Meat
Sodium 390 mg	

the shells open. Using tongs or a slotted spoon, discard any mussels that have not opened. Transfer the mussels with the cooking liquid to a serving bowl. Serve the yogurt sauce on the side.

COOK'S TIP on Fresh Mussels

Use these rules of thumb when preparing fresh mussels: Be sure the mussels have no offensive odor, and do not use mussels with broken or cracked shells. If possible, cook mussels the day you buy them; do not wait longer than the next day. When choosing fresh mussels, look for those with closed shells. If the shell is open, give it a light tap to be sure it will close tightly. If it doesn't close, discard it. The reverse holds once the mussels are cooked! The shells open if the mussels were fresh. Discard any mussels that did not open when cooked.

seafood and lemon risotto

Creamy lemony rice joins scallops and shrimp in this hearty entrée, made colorful by snow peas and red bell pepper. This recipe uses a streamlined preparation method that lets you stir less than in most other risotto recipes.

Cooking spray

1 medium leek, sliced

2 medium garlic cloves, minced

1 cup uncooked arborio rice

2 cups fat-free, low-sodium chicken broth, divided use

1 cup dry white wine (regular or nonalcoholic)

8 ounces raw medium shrimp in shells

8 ounces bay scallops

3 ounces fresh snow pea pods, trimmed and halved crosswise

½ medium red bell pepper, chopped

3 tablespoons shredded or grated Parmesan cheese

2 tablespoons chopped fresh basil or 2 teaspoons dried, crumbled

1½ to 2 tablespoons finely shredded lemon zest

3 tablespoons shredded or grated Parmesan cheese

Lightly spray a medium saucepan with cooking spray. Cook the leek slices and garlic over medium-low heat for 5 minutes, or until the leeks are soft.

Stir in the rice. Cook for 5 minutes, stirring often.

Stir in 1½ cups broth. Increase the heat to high and bring to a boil, stirring occasionally. Reduce the heat and simmer for 5 minutes, stirring occasionally.

Pour in the remaining ½ cup broth and the wine. Increase the heat to

---

PER SERVING

Calories 364	Carbohydrates 47 g
Total Fat 3.5 g	Fiber 4 g
Saturated Fat 1.5 g	Sugar 2 g
Trans Fat 0.0 g	Protein 27 g
Polyunsaturated Fat 0.5 g	DIETARY EXCHANGES:
Monounsaturated Fat 1.0 g	2½ Starch
Cholesterol 98 mg	1 Vegetable
Sodium 342 mg	3 Very Lean Meat

medium and cook for 5 to 8 minutes, stirring constantly (a small amount of liquid should remain).

Meanwhile, peel the shrimp. Rinse the shrimp and scallops and pat dry with paper towels. Stir with the pea pods and bell pepper into the rice mixture. Cook for 5 minutes, or until the liquid is almost absorbed, stirring constantly. (The rice should be just tender and slightly creamy.)

Stir in 3 tablespoons Parmesan, basil, and lemon zest.

Spoon the mixture onto four plates. Sprinkle with the remaining 3 tablespoons Parmesan.

COOK'S TIP on Risotto

For proper consistency, carefully regulate the cooking temperature so the risotto boils lightly, not vigorously. If the liquid is absorbed before the rice reaches the just-tender stage, add more broth, wine, or water, a little at a time. Arborio rice is usually used in risottos, but you can substitute a medium-grain rice if you prefer. It won't be quite as creamy, however.

poultry

asian grilled chicken

SERVES 6

An oil-free marinade gives this chicken its deliciously different barbecue taste.

Marinade

¼ cup soy sauce (lowest sodium available)

¼ cup honey

3 tablespoons red wine vinegar

2 tablespoons finely snipped fresh parsley

2 teaspoons grated peeled gingerroot or 1 teaspoon ground ginger

½ teaspoon pepper

1 medium garlic clove, minced

✳ ✳ ✳

3 skinless chicken breast halves with bone (about 12 ounces each)

Cooking spray

In a small bowl, whisk together the marinade ingredients. Pour into a large resealable plastic bag.

Discard all visible fat from the chicken. Add the chicken to the marinade. Seal the bag and turn to coat. Refrigerate for at least 2 hours, turning occasionally.

To grill the chicken, lightly spray a grill rack with cooking spray. Preheat the grill on high. Grill the chicken for 30 to 45 minutes, or until no longer pink in the center, brushing the pieces with marinade and turning them frequently. To protect against harmful bacteria, be sure to wash the basting brush between basting

---

PER SERVING

Calories 167	Carbohydrates 4 g
Total Fat 1.5 g	Fiber 0 g
Saturated Fat 0.5 g	Sugar 3 g
Trans Fat 0.0 g	Protein 32 g
Polyunsaturated Fat 0.5 g	DIETARY EXCHANGES:
Monounsaturated Fat 0.5 g	4 Very Lean Meat
Cholesterol 79 mg	
Sodium 349 mg	

steps until the chicken surface turns white. (Washing the brush is not necessary after this point.) Cut each breast in half before serving.

COOK'S TIP

To broil the chicken, follow the instructions above except preheat the broiler and lightly spray a broiler-safe baking sheet with cooking spray. Broil about 5 inches from the heat for 25 to 30 minutes, basting as directed.

COOK'S TIP on Skinning Poultry

You can dramatically reduce the amount of fat and cholesterol in poultry by discarding the skin. Because of its slippery nature, poultry skin can be a challenge to remove, however. Hold a piece of poultry on a flat surface (a plastic cutting board is recommended), grasp the skin with a double thickness of paper towels, and pull firmly. Discard the skin and the paper towels. Use a knife or kitchen scissors to trim any remaining visible fat.

crispy oven-fried chicken

SERVES 6

This spicy, heart-friendly alternative to traditional fried chicken surprises your taste buds with a pleasant touch of ginger.

Cooking spray (butter flavor preferred)

1 teaspoon ground ginger, or to taste

1 teaspoon paprika

¼ teaspoon salt

Pepper to taste

3 skinless chicken breasts with bone (about 12 ounces each)

4 cups wheat-flake or cornflake cereal, lightly crushed

1 medium garlic clove, crushed (optional)

Preheat the oven to 350° F. Lightly spray a baking sheet with cooking spray.

In a small bowl, combine the ginger, paprika, salt, and pepper.

Discard all visible fat from the chicken. Sprinkle the ginger mixture on both sides.

In a pie pan or on a piece of aluminum foil, stir together the cereal and garlic. Roll the chicken in the mixture to coat.

Lightly spray the chicken on all sides with the cooking spray. Place on the baking sheet.

Bake for 45 minutes to 1 hour, or until the chicken is golden brown, tender, and no longer pink in the center. (The timing depends on the thickness of the chicken.) Cut each breast in half before serving.

PER SERVING

Calories 225	Carbohydrates 17 g
Total Fat 2.5 g	Fiber 2 g
Saturated Fat 0.5 g	Sugar 3 g
Trans Fat 0.0 g	Protein 34 g
Polyunsaturated Fat 0.5 g	DIETARY EXCHANGES:
Monounsaturated Fat 0.5 g	1 Starch
Cholesterol 79 mg	4 Very Lean Meat
Sodium 326 mg	

chicken
with spicy black pepper sauce

SERVES 4

A very simple, barely cooked sauce is the secret to this lively dish.

½ teaspoon pepper (coarsely ground preferred)

¼ teaspoon garlic powder

⅛ teaspoon salt

4 boneless, skinless chicken breast halves (about 4 ounces each)

1 teaspoon olive oil

1 tablespoon soy sauce (lowest sodium available)

1 tablespoon steak sauce (lowest sodium available)

1 tablespoon Worcestershire sauce (lowest sodium available)

1 tablespoon olive oil

2 teaspoons fresh lime juice

1 medium Italian plum tomato, finely chopped (optional)

In a small bowl, stir together the pepper, garlic powder, and salt.

Discard all the visible fat from the chicken. Sprinkle the pepper mixture over both sides, pressing firmly so the mixture adheres.

In a large nonstick skillet, heat 1 teaspoon oil over medium heat, swirling to coat the bottom. Cook the chicken with the smooth side down for 5 minutes. Turn over and cook for 4 minutes, or until no longer pink in the center. Transfer to four plates.

In the same skillet, stir together the remaining ingredients except the tomato. Increase the heat to medium high and bring just to a boil, scraping the bottom and sides of the skillet to dislodge any browned bits. Remove from the heat.

To serve, spoon the sauce over the chicken. Sprinkle with the tomato.

PER SERVING

Calories 173	Carbohydrates 2 g
Total Fat 6.0 g	Fiber 0 g
Saturated Fat 1.0 g	Sugar 1 g
Trans Fat 0.0 g	Protein 27 g
Polyunsaturated Fat 1.0 g	DIETARY EXCHANGES:
Monounsaturated Fat 3.5 g	3 Lean Meat
Cholesterol 66 mg	
Sodium 272 mg	

creamy chicken curry

SERVES 6

This intricately flavored dish brings the warmth and intensity of Indian cuisine to your table. Serve over basmati rice so you can savor all the deep orange, cilantro-flecked sauce.

1 pound boneless, skinless chicken breasts

2 tablespoons canola or corn oil

1 medium onion, finely chopped

2 teaspoons garlic powder

1 6-ounce can no-salt-added tomato paste

2 teaspoons ground cumin

1½ teaspoons ground coriander

½ teaspoon ground turmeric

½ teaspoon cayenne

1 cup fat-free sour cream

¾ teaspoon salt

1 medium fresh jalapeño pepper, ribs and seeds discarded

1 tablespoon minced peeled gingerroot

½ cup finely snipped fresh cilantro

1 teaspoon garam masala (optional)

Discard all visible fat from the chicken. Cut the chicken into bite-size pieces. Set aside.

In a large skillet, heat the oil over medium-high heat, swirling to coat the bottom. Cook the onion for 3 to 4 minutes, or until soft, stirring occasionally.

Stir in the garlic powder. Cook for 1 minute, stirring constantly.

Stir in the tomato paste, cumin, coriander, turmeric, and cayenne. Cook for 1 minute, stirring occasionally.

PER SERVING	
Calories 203	Carbohydrates 15 g
Total Fat 6.0 g	Fiber 2 g
Saturated Fat 0.5 g	Sugar 8 g
Trans Fat 0.0 g	Protein 22 g
Polyunsaturated Fat 1.5 g	DIETARY EXCHANGES:
Monounsaturated Fat 3.0 g	1 Other Carbohydrate
Cholesterol 50 mg	2½ Lean Meat
Sodium 400 mg	

Stir in the chicken, sour cream, and salt. If the mixture seems dry, gradually stir in a little water as needed. Bring to a boil. Reduce the heat and simmer for 15 minutes, stirring occasionally.

Stir in the jalapeño and gingerroot. Cook for 10 minutes, or until the chicken is no longer pink in the center.

Sprinkle with the cilantro and garam masala just before serving.

COOK'S TIP on Garam Masala

Dry-roasted spices are ground together to make the distinctive blend known as garam masala. It may include 10 to 12 different spices, such as cumin, coriander, cloves, cardamom, black pepper, and mace, and is usually added to food near the end of cooking or right before the dish is served to enhance the complexity of flavor.

thai chicken
with basil and vegetables

SERVES 4

Fragrant fresh basil complements the chicken and vibrant vegetables in this all-in-one meal. Because this dish cooks quickly, have your ingredients gathered and prepped before you start stir-frying.

Sauce

2 tablespoons fat-free, low-sodium chicken broth or water

2 teaspoons sugar

2 teaspoons fish sauce

1 teaspoon soy sauce (lowest sodium available)

✻ ✻ ✻

1 teaspoon canola or corn oil

2 medium garlic cloves, minced

1 serrano chile, ribs and seeds discarded, chopped (optional)

1 pound boneless, skinless chicken breasts, all visible fat discarded, cut into thin slices

2 cups broccoli florets

2 medium carrots, cut into matchstick-size pieces

4 medium green onions, cut into 1-inch pieces

¼ cup firmly packed fresh basil leaves

2 cups hot cooked rice (jasmine or brown preferred)

In a small bowl, stir together the sauce ingredients. Set aside.

In a wok or large skillet, heat the oil over medium-high heat, swirling to coat the bottom. Cook the garlic and serrano chile for 10 to 15 seconds.

PER SERVING	
Calories 288	Carbohydrates 33 g
Total Fat 3.0 g	Fiber 3 g
Saturated Fat 0.5 g	Sugar 6 g
Trans Fat 0.0 g	Protein 30 g
Polyunsaturated Fat 1.0 g	DIETARY EXCHANGES:
Monounsaturated Fat 1.0 g	1½ Starch
Cholesterol 66 mg	2 Vegetable
Sodium 382 mg	3 Very Lean Meat

Stir in the chicken. Cook for 3 to 4 minutes, or until the chicken is no longer pink in the center, stirring constantly.

Stir in the broccoli, carrots, and green onions. Cook for 2 to 3 minutes, or until the vegetables are tender-crisp, stirring constantly.

Stir in the reserved sauce and the basil. Cook for 1 minute, or until the mixture is warmed through, stirring constantly.

Serve over the rice.

COOK'S TIP on Jasmine Rice

Expand your taste horizons by preparing jasmine rice from Thailand to accompany this dish. Jasmine rice is classified as an aromatic rice because of its perfumy fragrance and nuttiness.

COOK'S TIP on Fish Sauce

Pungent and salty, fish sauce imparts a rich flavor to many Asian dishes. A little goes a long way, so you may want to purchase only a small bottle. Store fish sauce in a cool place for up to six months.

chicken fajitas

Before rolling up the tortillas, add shredded lettuce, chopped tomatoes, salsa, and a dollop of fat-free sour cream if you wish.

Marinade

3 tablespoons Worcestershire sauce (lowest sodium available)

1½ tablespoons fresh lemon or lime juice

1 tablespoon water

1 teaspoon canola or corn oil

1 medium garlic clove, minced

½ teaspoon pepper, or to taste

* * *

1 pound boneless, skinless chicken breasts

1 large onion

1 large green bell pepper

1 teaspoon canola or corn oil

8 6-inch corn tortillas

Cooking spray

1 teaspoon canola or corn oil

In a large resealable plastic bag, combine the marinade ingredients.

Discard all visible fat from the chicken. Cut the chicken lengthwise into ⅜-inch strips. Add to the marinade. Seal the bag and turn to coat. Refrigerate for 10 to 20 minutes, turning at least once.

Meanwhile, preheat the oven to 350° F.

PER SERVING

Calories 240	Carbohydrates 20 g
Total Fat 4.5 g	Fiber 3 g
Saturated Fat 0.5 g	Sugar 5 g
Trans Fat 0.0 g	Protein 29 g
Polyunsaturated Fat 1.5 g	DIETARY EXCHANGES:
Monounsaturated Fat 2.0 g	1 Starch
Cholesterol 66 mg	1 Vegetable
Sodium 137 mg	3 Very Lean Meat

Cut the onion and bell pepper into ⅛-inch strips. Put in a small bowl.

Stir 1 teaspoon oil into the onion mixture.

When the chicken has marinated, wrap the tortillas in aluminum foil and heat in the oven for 8 to 10 minutes.

Meanwhile, lightly spray a large skillet with cooking spray. Put the remaining 1 teaspoon oil in the skillet, swirling to coat the bottom. Heat over medium-high heat. Remove the chicken from the marinade, discarding the marinade. Cook the chicken for 4 minutes, stirring occasionally.

Add the onion and bell pepper. Cook for 5 minutes, or until the onion is slightly brown and the chicken is no longer pink in the center, stirring constantly.

To serve, spread the chicken mixture on the tortillas. Roll the tortillas around the filling, jelly-roll style.

chicken-vegetable stir-fry

SERVES 6

A bed of steamed brown rice or yolk-free noodles pairs nicely with this stir-fry. Add some pizzazz by using a mixture of colorful bell peppers.

> 1 pound boneless, skinless chicken breasts
>
> 1½ tablespoons soy sauce (lowest sodium available)
>
> 1 tablespoon grated peeled gingerroot or 1 teaspoon ground ginger
>
> 1 teaspoon canola or corn oil
>
> 2 medium green, red, or yellow bell peppers, or any combination, cut into 1-inch strips
>
> 4 medium green onions, cut into 1-inch pieces
>
> ¾ cup fresh pineapple chunks plus ¼ cup canned pineapple juice, or ¾ cup pineapple chunks canned in their own juice, ¼ cup juice reserved
>
> 1½ tablespoons cornstarch
>
> ⅔ cup fat-free, low-sodium chicken broth
>
> 1 tablespoon sesame seeds, dry-roasted

Discard all visible fat from the chicken. Cut into 1-inch cubes.

In a large resealable plastic bag, combine the chicken, soy sauce, and ginger-root. Seal the bag and turn to coat. Refrigerate for 30 to 45 minutes, turning occasionally.

In a large nonstick skillet or wok, heat the oil over high heat, swirling to coat the bottom. Cook the chicken mixture for 2 minutes, stirring constantly. Using a slotted spoon, transfer the chicken to a plate, leaving the marinade in the skillet.

Stir in the bell peppers and green onions. Cook for 1 minute, stirring constantly.

PER SERVING

Calories 141	Carbohydrates 9 g
Total Fat 3.0 g	Fiber 2 g
Saturated Fat 0.5 g	Sugar 5 g
Trans Fat 0.0 g	Protein 19 g
Polyunsaturated Fat 1.0 g	DIETARY EXCHANGES:
Monounsaturated Fat 1.0 g	½ Other Carbohydrate
Cholesterol 44 mg	2½ Very Lean Meat
Sodium 160 mg	

Stir in the pineapple (reserve the juice for later) and chicken. Cook for 2 to 3 minutes, or until the vegetables are tender-crisp, stirring constantly.

Put the cornstarch in a small bowl. Pour in the broth and reserved pineapple juice, whisking to dissolve. Stir into the chicken mixture. Bring to a boil and cook for 1 minute, or until thickened and smooth, stirring occasionally.

To serve, spoon the mixture onto six plates. Sprinkle with the sesame seeds.

brunswick stew

SERVES 6

You don't have to live in Brunswick County, Virginia, to enjoy this variation of its famous stew.

1 pound boneless, skinless chicken breasts

Cooking spray

1 teaspoon olive oil

1 medium onion, chopped

3 cups fat-free, low-sodium chicken broth

2 cups fresh or frozen whole-kernel corn

1½ cups fresh or frozen baby lima beans

1½ cups chopped tomatoes

1 6-ounce can no-salt-added tomato paste

3 tablespoons fresh lemon juice

1 tablespoon Worcestershire sauce (lowest sodium available)

Discard all visible fat from the chicken. Cut into 1-inch cubes.

Lightly spray a deep skillet or Dutch oven with cooking spray. Put the oil in the skillet, swirling to coat the bottom. Heat over medium-high heat. Cook the onion for 3 minutes, or until soft, stirring occasionally.

Stir in the remaining ingredients, including the chicken. Reduce the heat and simmer, covered, for 1 hour.

PER SERVING	
Calories 238	Carbohydrates 30 g
Total Fat 2.5 g	Fiber 6 g
Saturated Fat 0.5 g	Sugar 9 g
Trans Fat 0.0 g	Protein 25 g
Polyunsaturated Fat 0.5 g	DIETARY EXCHANGES:
Monounsaturated Fat 1.0 g	1½ Starch
Cholesterol 44 mg	2 Vegetable
Sodium 241 mg	3 Very Lean Meat

chicken
with mushroom-sherry sauce

Adding a splash of dry sherry after reducing the sauce provides a delectable explosion of flavor.

4 boneless, skinless chicken breast halves (about 4 ounces each)

¼ teaspoon salt

¼ teaspoon pepper

1 tablespoon olive oil

8 ounces sliced button mushrooms

1 medium onion, thinly sliced

¼ teaspoon dried thyme, crumbled

¼ teaspoon salt

½ cup dry sherry, divided use

Discard all visible fat from the chicken. Sprinkle both sides with ¼ teaspoon salt and the pepper.

In a large nonstick skillet, heat the oil over medium heat, swirling to coat the bottom. Cook the chicken with the smooth side down for 5 minutes. Turn over and cook for 4 minutes, or until no longer pink in the center. Transfer to a platter. Cover to keep warm.

In the same skillet, stir together the remaining ingredients except the sherry. Cook for 4 minutes, or until the onion is soft, stirring frequently.

Stir in ⅓ cup sherry. Increase the heat to high and boil for 1 minute, or until the liquid has almost evaporated, stirring occasionally. Remove from the heat.

Stir in the remaining 2 tablespoons plus 2 teaspoons sherry. Spoon over the chicken.

PER SERVING

Calories 203	Carbohydrates 6 g
Total Fat 5.0 g	Fiber 3 g
Saturated Fat 1.0 g	Sugar 1 g
Trans Fat 0.0 g	Protein 29 g
Polyunsaturated Fat 1.0 g	DIETARY EXCHANGES:
Monounsaturated Fat 3.0 g	1 Vegetable
Cholesterol 66 mg	3 Lean Meat
Sodium 371 mg	

chicken breasts stuffed
with ricotta and goat cheese

SERVES 4

This impressive dish is a snap to make and classy enough to serve for very special occasions. The tomato sauce keeps the chicken breasts moist.

Cooking spray

Stuffing

7 ounces fat-free ricotta cheese

2 ounces soft goat cheese (chèvre)

2 tablespoons snipped fresh parsley or 2 teaspoons dried, crumbled

1 tablespoon finely chopped green onions (green part only)

Sauce

1 8-ounce can no-salt-added tomato sauce

2 teaspoons Italian seasoning

1½ teaspoons chopped fresh oregano or ½ teaspoon dried, crumbled

1 medium garlic clove, minced

¼ teaspoon salt

⅛ teaspoon pepper

❊ ❊ ❊

4 boneless, skinless chicken breast halves (about 4 ounces each)

Preheat the oven to 350° F. Lightly spray an 8-inch square glass baking dish with cooking spray.

In a small bowl, stir together the stuffing ingredients.

In another small bowl, stir together the sauce ingredients.

PER SERVING	
Calories 234	Carbohydrates 7 g
Total Fat 6.5 g	Fiber 4 g
Saturated Fat 3.5 g	Sugar 1 g
Trans Fat 0.0 g	Protein 34 g
Polyunsaturated Fat 0.5 g	DIETARY EXCHANGES:
Monounsaturated Fat 1.5 g	1 Vegetable
Cholesterol 84 mg	4 Lean Meat
Sodium 323 mg	

Discard all visible fat from the chicken. Put a chicken breast half with the smooth side up between two pieces of plastic wrap. Using the smooth side of a meat mallet or a heavy pan, lightly flatten the breast to a thickness of ¼ inch, being careful not to tear the meat. Repeat with the remaining chicken.

To assemble, spoon about one-fourth of the stuffing down the center of each breast. Starting with the short end, roll up jelly-roll style. Place with the seam side down in the dish. Spoon the sauce over the breasts.

Bake, covered, for 40 to 45 minutes, or until the chicken is no longer pink in the center.

cheese-herb chicken medallions

Although just about any fresh vegetable can be used to garnish this family favorite, carrots add a wonderful splash of color. Chilling the mozzarella beforehand keeps it from oozing when baking.

 Cooking spray

 6 boneless, skinless chicken breast halves (about 4 ounces each)

 1 tablespoon finely chopped green onions (green part only)

 1 tablespoon finely chopped fresh basil or 1 teaspoon dried, crumbled

 ¼ teaspoon paprika

 Pepper to taste

 ¾ cup shredded part-skim mozzarella cheese, chilled

 2 medium carrots (optional)

Preheat the oven to 400° F. Lightly spray a medium baking dish with cooking spray.

Discard all visible fat from the chicken. Sprinkle each breast with the green onion, basil, paprika, and pepper.

Form the cheese into 6 loose balls. Place one in the center of each breast. Roll the chicken around the cheese, making sure the ends are tucked in. Tie each breast with kitchen twine to hold the cheese in place. Put the breasts in the baking dish.

Bake for 15 to 20 minutes, or until the chicken is no longer pink in the center. Let cool for 10 minutes.

PER SERVING	
Calories 161	Carbohydrates 1 g
Total Fat 3.5 g	Fiber 0 g
Saturated Fat 2.0 g	Sugar 0 g
Trans Fat 0.0 g	Protein 30 g
Polyunsaturated Fat 0.5 g	DIETARY EXCHANGES:
Monounsaturated Fat 1.0 g	3½ Very Lean Meat
Cholesterol 75 mg	
Sodium 162 mg	

Meanwhile, using a vegetable peeler, pare the carrots lengthwise into long, thin strips. Soak in ice water for at least 10 minutes. Drain well and pat dry with paper towels.

To serve, arrange a bed of carrot curls on a platter. Cut each breast into ½-inch medallions. Place on the carrots.

COOK'S TIP on Dried Herbs and Spices

Always store herbs and spices in airtight containers (glass jars recommended) away from heat and light. In general, whole spices and herbs will retain their flavor for about one year. Ground spices and herbs will keep for six months to one year. When the aroma becomes faint, replace the spices and herbs or use more of them to compensate for flavor loss.

slow-cooker tuscan chicken

SERVES 8

Effortless meals like this one are perfect for serving either guests or family members.

2 pounds boneless, skinless chicken breasts

1 teaspoon dried basil, crumbled

1 teaspoon dried oregano, crumbled

1 14.5-ounce can no-salt-added diced tomatoes, undrained

1 9-ounce package frozen artichoke hearts, thawed

1 cup fat-free, low-sodium chicken broth

1 2.25-ounce can sliced black olives, drained

½ teaspoon salt

¼ teaspoon pepper

¼ teaspoon crushed red pepper flakes (optional)

Discard all visible fat from the chicken. Sprinkle both sides with the basil and oregano. Put the chicken in a 3½- to 4-quart slow cooker.

Stir in the remaining ingredients. Cook, covered, on high for 3 to 4 hours or on low for 7 to 8 hours.

PER SERVING

Calories 162	Carbohydrates 6 g
Total Fat 2.5 g	Fiber 4 g
Saturated Fat 0.5 g	Sugar 2 g
Trans Fat 0.0 g	Protein 28 g
Polyunsaturated Fat 0.5 g	DIETARY EXCHANGES:
Monounsaturated Fat 1.0 g	1 Vegetable
Cholesterol 66 mg	3 Very Lean Meat
Sodium 334 mg	

chicken
with mustard and herbs

SERVES 4

Just because you don't have a lot of time to fix dinner doesn't mean you have to sacrifice flavor—or eat high-fat, high-sodium takeout food. With only a few ingredients, you can whip up an elegant entrée in minutes. Make extra to use for special sandwiches.

Cooking spray

¼ cup spicy brown mustard

1 tablespoon salt-free herb seasoning blend

1 tablespoon light mayonnaise

1 teaspoon salt-free lemon pepper

4 boneless, skinless chicken breast halves (about 4 ounces each)

Preheat the oven to 350° F. Lightly spray a baking dish with cooking spray.

In a small bowl, stir together the mustard, seasoning blend, mayonnaise, and lemon pepper to make a paste.

Discard all visible fat from the chicken. Put the chicken in the dish. Spread the mustard mixture thickly over the top of each breast.

Bake for 20 minutes, or until the chicken is no longer pink in the center.

PER SERVING

Calories 152

Total Fat 2.5 g

  Saturated Fat 0.5 g

  Trans Fat 0.0 g

  Polyunsaturated Fat 0.5 g

  Monounsaturated Fat 0.5 g

Cholesterol 67 mg

Sodium 253 mg

Carbohydrates 0 g

  Fiber 0 g

  Sugar 0 g

Protein 26 g

DIETARY EXCHANGES:

3 Very Lean Meat

chicken ragout

SERVES 6

This easy French stew is delicately flavored with thyme and tarragon. Using fresh instead of dried herbs will make it exceptionally tasty. Serve it with crusty whole-grain bread to absorb the savory liquid.

Cooking spray

⅓ cup all-purpose flour

½ teaspoon pepper, or to taste

6 boneless, skinless chicken breast halves (about 4 ounces each)

1 tablespoon olive oil, divided use

1 medium onion, sliced

1 pound button mushrooms, sliced

1 cup dry white wine (regular or nonalcoholic)

1 cup fat-free, low-sodium chicken broth

¼ cup finely snipped fresh parsley

¼ cup fresh thyme leaves or 1 tablespoon plus 1 teaspoon dried, crumbled

¼ cup fresh tarragon leaves or 1 tablespoon plus 1 teaspoon dried, crumbled

2 medium garlic cloves, minced

¼ teaspoon salt

2 tablespoons all-purpose flour

¼ cup cold water

2 cups frozen green peas

Preheat the oven to 400° F. Lightly spray a large ovenproof casserole dish or Dutch oven with cooking spray.

PER SERVING	
Calories 279	Carbohydrates 20 g
Total Fat 4.5 g	Fiber 4 g
Saturated Fat 1.0 g	Sugar 5 g
Trans Fat 0.0 g	Protein 33 g
Polyunsaturated Fat 1.0 g	DIETARY EXCHANGES:
Monounsaturated Fat 2.0 g	1 Starch
Cholesterol 66 mg	1 Vegetable
Sodium 244 mg	3 Very Lean Meat

Combine ⅓ cup flour and the pepper in a paper or resealable plastic bag.

Discard all visible fat from the chicken. Add several pieces of chicken at a time to the bag and shake well to coat. Shake off any excess.

In a large skillet, heat 1 teaspoon oil over medium-high heat, swirling to coat the bottom. Add half the chicken and brown on both sides. Transfer to the casserole dish. Repeat with 1 teaspoon oil and the remaining chicken.

Pour the remaining 1 teaspoon oil into the skillet and swirl to coat the bottom. Cook the onion for 2 to 3 minutes, or until soft, stirring occasionally.

Stir in the mushrooms, wine, broth, parsley, thyme, tarragon, garlic, and salt. Pour over the chicken.

Bake, covered, for 45 minutes.

Put the 2 tablespoons flour in a cup. Add the water, stirring to dissolve. Gradually pour into the liquid in the casserole, stirring gently. Stir in the peas.

Bake, covered, for 15 to 20 minutes, or until the chicken is no longer pink in the center, the peas are tender, and the sauce has thickened.

quick curry-roasted chicken
with cucumber raita

SERVES 4

In a hurry but tired of the typical? This simple curry-flavored chicken goes nicely with the cool and refreshing cucumber raita (RI-tah), *an Indian yogurt sauce. Try this dish over quick-and-easy couscous.*

Cooking spray

Curry-Roasted Chicken

1 teaspoon curry powder

½ teaspoon ground cumin

¼ teaspoon onion powder or garlic powder

⅛ teaspoon cayenne

4 boneless, skinless chicken breast halves (about 4 ounces each)

Cucumber Raita

1 small cucumber

⅛ teaspoon salt

8 ounces fat-free plain yogurt

¼ cup finely diced red bell pepper

2 tablespoons finely snipped fresh parsley or cilantro

½ teaspoon grated peeled gingerroot

¼ teaspoon cumin seeds or ground cumin

Pepper to taste

Preheat the oven to 350° F. Lightly spray a baking sheet with cooking spray.

In a small bowl, stir together the curry powder, cumin, onion powder, and cayenne.

PER SERVING	
Calories 168	Carbohydrates 7 g
Total Fat 2.0 g	Fiber 1 g
Saturated Fat 0.5 g	Sugar 5 g
Trans Fat 0.0 g	Protein 30 g
Polyunsaturated Fat 0.5 g	DIETARY EXCHANGES:
Monounsaturated Fat 0.5 g	½ Other Carbohydrate
Cholesterol 67 mg	3 Very Lean Meat
Sodium 193 mg	

Discard all visible fat from the chicken. Sprinkle the curry powder mixture over both sides. Place the chicken with the smooth side up on the baking sheet. Lightly spray the chicken with cooking spray.

Bake for 20 minutes, or until the chicken is no longer pink in the center.

Meanwhile, peel the cucumber. Slice in half lengthwise and discard the seeds. Grate the cucumber. Put in a colander and sprinkle with the salt. Let drain for at least 5 minutes. Squeeze the cucumber to remove excess liquid. Pat dry with paper towels.

In a medium serving bowl, thoroughly whisk the yogurt. Stir in the cucumber and remaining raita ingredients except the pepper. Cover and refrigerate until the chicken is done. Just before serving, sprinkle the pepper over the raita. Serve with the chicken.

moroccan chicken

SERVES 4

The power of spice is beautifully demonstrated in this classic dish with Moroccan influences. Fluffy couscous absorbs and distributes the flavors. Serve with steamed spinach and fresh orange slices.

1 pound boneless, skinless chicken breasts

2 teaspoons olive oil

1 medium onion, cut into eighths

4 medium garlic cloves, minced

¾ cup fat-free, low-sodium chicken broth

½ cup dry white wine (regular or nonalcoholic) or water

½ cup kalamata olives, coarsely chopped

1 medium lemon, quartered

1 teaspoon grated peeled gingerroot

½ teaspoon paprika

¼ teaspoon ground turmeric

⅛ teaspoon pepper

¾ cup uncooked couscous

¼ teaspoon salt

Discard all visible fat from the chicken. Cut each breast into quarters.

In a large nonstick skillet, heat the oil over medium-high heat, swirling to coat the bottom. Cook the chicken for 2 minutes on each side.

Stir in the onion and garlic. Cook for 4 to 5 minutes, or until the onion is tender-crisp, stirring occasionally.

PER SERVING

Calories 360	Carbohydrates 32 g
Total Fat 8.5 g	Fiber 2 g
Saturated Fat 1.5 g	Sugar 3 g
Trans Fat 0.0 g	Protein 32 g
Polyunsaturated Fat 1.0 g	DIETARY EXCHANGES:
Monounsaturated Fat 5.5 g	2 Starch
Cholesterol 66 mg	3 Lean Meat
Sodium 526 mg	

Stir in the broth, wine, olives, lemon, gingerroot, paprika, turmeric, and pepper. Bring to a boil, stirring occasionally. Reduce the heat and simmer, covered, for 15 to 20 minutes, or until the chicken is no longer pink in the center.

Stir in the couscous and salt. Remove from the heat and let stand, covered, for 5 minutes, or until the liquid is absorbed and the couscous is tender. (Do not stir while the mixture is standing.) Using a fork, fluff the mixture. Discard the lemon before serving the dish.

garlic chicken fillets
in balsamic vinegar

SERVES 8

This easy, elegant entrée is perfect when you have unexpected company.

8 boneless, skinless chicken breast halves (about 4 ounces each)

½ cup all-purpose flour

2 teaspoons olive oil

Cooking spray

6 to 8 medium garlic cloves, minced

1 cup fat-free, low-sodium chicken broth

⅓ cup balsamic vinegar

Pepper to taste

1 tablespoon cornstarch

2 tablespoons water

Discard all visible fat from the chicken. Put the chicken on a plate. Dust both sides with the flour, shaking off the excess.

In a large nonstick skillet, heat the oil over medium-high heat, swirling to coat the bottom. Cook the chicken on one side for 2 to 3 minutes, or until golden. Spray the tops with cooking spray. Turn over. Sprinkle with the garlic. Cook for 2 to 3 minutes, or until golden.

Add the broth, vinegar, and pepper. Reduce the heat to medium low. Cook, covered, for 5 to 10 minutes, or until the chicken is tender and no longer pink in the center. Leaving the liquid in the skillet, transfer the chicken to a platter. Cover to keep warm.

Put the cornstarch in a cup. Add the water, stirring to dissolve. Pour into the skillet. Increase the heat to high and boil for 1 to 2 minutes, or until thick and smooth, stirring occasionally. Pour over the chicken.

PER SERVING

Calories 181	Carbohydrates 10 g
Total Fat 2.5 g	Fiber 0 g
Saturated Fat 0.5 g	Sugar 2 g
Trans Fat 0.0 g	Protein 28 g
Polyunsaturated Fat 0.5 g	DIETARY EXCHANGES:
Monounsaturated Fat 1.0 g	½ Starch
Cholesterol 66 mg	3 Very Lean Meat
Sodium 85 mg	

greek-style stewed chicken

Stock your kitchen with the flavors of Greece—tomatoes, olives, lemons, oregano—and you'll be ready to prepare this robust dish at any time. Serve with steamed green beans and whole-wheat pita bread.

1 pound chicken breast tenders

1 teaspoon olive oil

1 medium green bell pepper, cut into 1-inch strips

2 medium shallots, quartered

1 14.5-ounce can no-salt-added diced tomatoes, undrained

½ cup fat-free, low-sodium chicken broth

¼ cup kalamata olives, coarsely chopped

1 teaspoon dried oregano, crumbled

1 teaspoon grated lemon zest

2 tablespoons fresh lemon juice

¼ teaspoon salt

¼ teaspoon pepper

⅛ teaspoon ground cinnamon

Discard all visible fat from the chicken.

In a large nonstick skillet, heat the oil over medium-high heat, swirling to coat the bottom. Cook the chicken for 2 minutes on each side.

Stir in the bell pepper and shallots. Cook for 2 to 3 minutes, or until the vegetables are tender-crisp, stirring occasionally.

Stir in the remaining ingredients. Bring to a simmer. Reduce the heat and simmer, covered, for 25 to 30 minutes, or until the chicken is no longer pink in the center.

PER SERVING

Calories 197	Carbohydrates 10 g
Total Fat 5.0 g	Fiber 3 g
Saturated Fat 1.0 g	Sugar 4 g
Trans Fat 0.0 g	Protein 28 g
Polyunsaturated Fat 0.5 g	DIETARY EXCHANGES:
Monounsaturated Fat 3.0 g	2 Vegetable
Cholesterol 66 mg	3 Lean Meat
Sodium 414 mg	

cajun chicken pasta

SERVES 4

Tender twists of gemelli pasta, browned chicken, and a creamy, moderately spicy sauce make this combination hard to resist.

8 ounces dried pasta, such as gemelli, rotini, or penne

1 pound chicken breast tenders

1 teaspoon canola or corn oil

1½ teaspoons salt-free Cajun or Creole seasoning blend

1 medium green bell pepper, chopped

1 medium onion, chopped

2 medium ribs of celery, chopped

2 medium garlic cloves, minced

1½ cups fat-free, low-sodium chicken broth

½ cup fat-free half-and-half

2 tablespoons all-purpose flour

¼ teaspoon salt

Prepare the pasta using the package directions, omitting the salt and oil. Drain well in a colander. Set aside.

Meanwhile, discard all visible fat from the chicken.

In a large nonstick skillet, heat the oil over medium-high heat, swirling to coat the bottom. Put the chicken in the skillet. Sprinkle with the seasoning blend. Brown the chicken for 2 minutes on each side.

Stir in the bell pepper, onion, celery, and garlic. Cook for 2 to 3 minutes, or until the vegetables are tender-crisp, stirring occasionally.

PER SERVING

Calories 410	Carbohydrates 55 g
Total Fat 3.5 g	Fiber 3 g
Saturated Fat 0.5 g	Sugar 7 g
Trans Fat 0.0 g	Protein 38 g
Polyunsaturated Fat 1.0 g	DIETARY EXCHANGES:
Monounsaturated Fat 1.0 g	3 Starch
Cholesterol 66 mg	1 Vegetable
Sodium 294 mg	3 Very Lean Meat

Pour in the broth. Bring to a simmer. Reduce the heat and simmer, covered, for 8 to 10 minutes, or until the vegetables are tender and the chicken is no longer pink in the center.

In a small bowl, whisk together the half-and-half and flour until smooth. Pour into the chicken mixture. Increase the heat to medium high and cook for 3 to 4 minutes, or until thickened, stirring occasionally.

Stir in the pasta and salt and heat through.

skillet chicken
with bell pepper sauce

SERVES 4

Salt-free steak seasoning blend works as well in this quick-enough-for-a-weeknight entrée as it does in your favorite beef dishes.

2 teaspoons salt-free steak seasoning blend

½ teaspoon paprika

1 pound chicken breast tenders

2 tablespoons olive oil, divided use

1 large green bell pepper, thinly sliced lengthwise

1 medium onion, thinly sliced lengthwise

½ cup water

2 tablespoons no-salt-added ketchup

1½ tablespoons Worcestershire sauce (lowest sodium available)

¼ teaspoon salt

In a small bowl, stir together the seasoning blend and paprika.

Discard all visible fat from the chicken. Sprinkle the seasoning blend mixture on both sides of the chicken.

In a large nonstick skillet, heat 2 teaspoons oil over medium heat, swirling to coat the bottom. Cook the chicken with the smooth side down for 2 minutes. Transfer with the browned side up to a plate.

Heat the remaining 1 tablespoon plus 1 teaspoon oil in the skillet, swirling to coat the bottom. Cook the bell pepper and onion for 5 minutes, or until the bell pepper is tender-crisp, stirring frequently.

PER SERVING

Calories 215	Carbohydrates 7 g
Total Fat 8.5 g	Fiber 2 g
Saturated Fat 1.5 g	Sugar 5 g
Trans Fat 0.0 g	Protein 27 g
Polyunsaturated Fat 1.0 g	DIETARY EXCHANGES:
Monounsaturated Fat 5.5 g	1 Vegetable
Cholesterol 66 mg	3 Lean Meat
Sodium 233 mg	

Stir in the water, ketchup, and Worcestershire sauce. Place the chicken with the browned side up on the bell-pepper mixture. Cook, covered, for 3 minutes, or until the chicken is no longer pink in the center. Transfer the chicken to a platter.

Stir the salt into the bell-pepper mixture. Spoon over the chicken.

asparagus-chicken à la king
with roasted peppers

SERVES 4

Although this creamy chicken mixture is typically served over toast points, try it with cooked whole-grain pasta, brown rice, couscous, or spaghetti squash strands for a change.

1 10.5-ounce can fat-free, low-sodium chicken broth

8 ounces fresh asparagus, trimmed and sliced on the diagonal into bite-size pieces, or 1 10-ounce package frozen cut asparagus

¼ teaspoon dried tarragon or thyme, crumbled

⅛ teaspoon salt

⅛ teaspoon pepper

⅓ cup all-purpose flour

1½ cups fat-free evaporated milk, divided use

2 medium red or green bell peppers, or a combination, roasted, peeled, rinsed, and chopped

2 cups chopped cooked chicken or turkey breast, cooked without salt, skin and all visible fat discarded

In a large saucepan, stir together the broth, asparagus, tarragon, salt, and pepper. Bring to a boil over high heat. Reduce the heat and simmer, covered, for 5 minutes.

In a small bowl, whisk together the flour and about half the milk. Stir into the asparagus mixture. Stir in the remaining milk. Cook for 10 minutes, or until thickened and bubbly, stirring occasionally. Cook for 2 minutes, stirring constantly.

Stir in the roasted peppers and chicken. Heat through.

PER SERVING

Calories 258	Carbohydrates 24 g
Total Fat 3.0 g	Sugar 13 g
Saturated Fat 1.0 g	Fiber 3 g
Trans Fat 0.0 g	Protein 32 g
Polyunsaturated Fat 0.5 g	DIETARY EXCHANGES:
Monounsaturated Fat 1.0 g	½ Starch
Cholesterol 63 mg	1 Fat-Free Milk
Sodium 256 mg	3 Very Lean Meat

COOK'S TIP on Roasting Bell Peppers

Roasted bell peppers add color, flavor, and texture to food. You can buy them in jars (look for them in the condiment section of the grocery) or make them at home. Prepare several at one time so you'll have some to use in salads, casseroles, sandwiches—you name it! Halve the bell peppers lengthwise, discarding the stems, ribs, and seeds. Preheat the broiler. Lightly spray a broiler pan with cooking spray. Put the peppers with the cut side down in the broiler pan. Broil about 4 inches from the heat for 3 to 5 minutes, or until the skin is black and bubbly all over. Transfer the peppers to a plastic or paper bag, seal, and let stand until cool enough to handle. Discard the skin. Rinse the peppers and pat dry with paper towels. Roasted bell peppers will keep in an airtight container in the freezer for up to four months.

cumin-roasted turkey breast
with raspberry sauce

SERVES 6 (With half the turkey [about 18 ounces] reserved for another use)

Frozen raspberries, available year-round, are the base for the terrific sauce that complements this nicely spiced entrée.

    1 teaspoon canola or corn oil

    2 teaspoons ground cumin

    ½ teaspoon garlic powder

    ¼ teaspoon salt

    ½ teaspoon pepper

    1 4½-pound bone-in turkey breast with skin, thawed and patted dry with paper towels if frozen

Sauce

    12 ounces frozen unsweetened raspberries, thawed

    2 teaspoons grated orange zest

    ½ cup fresh orange juice

    ¼ cup sugar

    2 tablespoons balsamic vinegar

    1½ tablespoons cornstarch

    ¼ teaspoon crushed red pepper flakes (optional)

    ⅛ teaspoon ground allspice

PER SERVING

Calories 232	Carbohydrates 23 g
Total Fat 2.0 g	Fiber 3 g
Saturated Fat 0.5 g	Sugar 16 g
Trans Fat 0.0 g	Protein 29 g
Polyunsaturated Fat 0.5 g	DIETARY EXCHANGES:
Monounsaturated Fat 0.5 g	1 Fruit
Cholesterol 80 mg	½ Other Carbohydrate
Sodium 152 mg	4 Very Lean Meat

Preheat the oven to 325°F. Spread the oil over a glass baking dish large enough to hold the turkey.

In a small bowl, stir together the cumin, garlic powder, salt, and pepper.

Using your fingers, gently loosen but don't remove the turkey skin. Being careful to avoid tearing the skin, spread the cumin mixture over as much of the meat as possible. Gently pull the skin over any exposed meat. Put the turkey with the breast side up in the baking dish.

Roast for 1 hour 25 minutes, or until the internal temperature registers 175°F on an instant-read thermometer and the juices run clear. For easier carving, let stand on a cooling rack for 15 minutes. Discard the skin. Cut the breast in half, thinly slicing one of the pieces and reserving the remaining piece for a later use.

Meanwhile, in a medium saucepan, stir together the sauce ingredients until the cornstarch is completely dissolved. Bring to a boil over medium-high heat. Boil for 1 minute, stirring frequently. Remove from the heat. Let cool completely.

Serve the sliced turkey with the sauce.

COOK'S TIP

If the turkey tips over when you put it in the baking dish, crumple a sheet of aluminum foil and wedge it under the turkey to stabilize it. A ball of foil placed in the cavity will work as well.

turkey patties
with fresh basil-mushroom sauce

SERVES 4

A thin layer of Dijon mustard and a sprinkle of fresh basil provide layers of flavor in every bite of these turkey patties.

1 pound lean ground turkey breast, skin removed before grinding

¼ cup chopped fresh basil leaves

¼ teaspoon salt

¼ teaspoon garlic powder

1½ tablespoons olive oil, divided use

8 ounces button mushrooms, sliced

1 large onion, chopped

⅛ teaspoon cayenne

1 tablespoon chopped fresh basil leaves

¼ teaspoon salt

2 teaspoons Dijon mustard

In a medium bowl, stir together the turkey, ¼ cup basil, ¼ teaspoon salt, and garlic powder. Form into 4 patties.

In a large nonstick skillet, heat 1 tablespoon oil over medium-high heat, swirling to coat the bottom. Cook the patties for 5 minutes. Turn over and cook for 4 minutes, or until no longer pink in the center. Transfer to a plate. Cover to keep warm.

Still on medium high, heat the remaining 1½ teaspoons oil in the skillet, swirling to coat the bottom. Cook the mushrooms, onion, and cayenne for 4 minutes, or until the onion is soft, stirring frequently. Remove from the heat.

Stir in the remaining 1 tablespoon basil and ¼ teaspoon salt.

To serve, spread the mustard over the patties. Top with the mushroom mixture.

PER SERVING

Calories 208	Carbohydrates 7 g
Total Fat 6.5 g	Fiber 2 g
Saturated Fat 1.0 g	Sugar 4 g
Trans Fat 0.0 g	Protein 30 g
Polyunsaturated Fat 1.0 g	DIETARY EXCHANGES:
Monounsaturated Fat 4.0 g	1 Vegetable
Cholesterol 77 mg	3 Lean Meat
Sodium 397 mg	

turkey tetrazzini

A great way to use turkey leftovers, this is a tasty twist on an old favorite.

12 ounces dried rotini or other pasta (whole-wheat preferred)

Cooking spray

1 medium onion, diced

½ medium green bell pepper, diced

2 medium garlic cloves, minced

8 ounces button mushrooms, sliced

12 ounces cooked turkey breast, cooked without salt, skin and all visible fat discarded, cubed (about 2 cups)

1 10.75-ounce can low-fat condensed cream of chicken soup (lowest sodium available)

½ cup fat-free evaporated milk

2 ounces diced pimientos, drained

2 tablespoons shredded or grated Parmesan cheese

2 tablespoons dry sherry or dry white wine (regular or nonalcoholic) (optional)

⅛ teaspoon pepper

¼ cup plain dry bread crumbs

Prepare the pasta using the package directions, omitting the salt and oil. Drain well in a colander.

Meanwhile, preheat the oven to 350° F. Spray a 3-quart casserole dish and a deep skillet with cooking spray.

Heat the skillet over medium heat. Cook the onion, bell pepper, and garlic for 2 to 3 minutes, or until soft, stirring occasionally.

Stir in the mushrooms. Cook for 2 minutes, or until tender.

Stir the pasta and the remaining ingredients except the bread crumbs into the skillet. Pour into the casserole dish. Sprinkle with the bread crumbs.

Bake, covered, for 35 to 40 minutes, or until heated through.

PER SERVING

Calories 279	Carbohydrates 44 g
Total Fat 2.5 g	Fiber 5 g
Saturated Fat 1.0 g	Sugar 5 g
Trans Fat 0.0 g	Protein 23 g
Polyunsaturated Fat 0.5 g	DIETARY EXCHANGES:
Monounsaturated Fat 0.5 g	3 Starch
Cholesterol 40 mg	2 Very Lean Meat
Sodium 231 mg	

meats

elegant beef tenderloin

Perfect for a grand entrance, this roast is flavored with a variety of aromatic ingredients. Serve it on your most decorative platter, and enjoy the applause.

Cooking spray

1 2-pound beef tenderloin

Rub

¼ cup chopped fresh rosemary

¼ cup Dijon mustard

¼ cup bottled white horseradish

2 tablespoons pink peppercorns, crushed, or 2 teaspoons black pepper (coarsely ground preferred)

1 tablespoon onion powder

4 medium garlic cloves, minced

2 teaspoons olive oil

Preheat the oven to 400° F. Lightly spray a heavy roasting pan with cooking spray (no rack needed). Discard the silver skin and all visible fat from the beef.

In a small bowl, stir together the rub ingredients. Coat the beef with the rub. Transfer to the roasting pan.

Bake for 40 minutes to 1 hour 5 minutes, or until the internal temperature of the beef registers 5 to 10 degrees below the desired doneness when tested with a meat thermometer. Transfer the beef to a carving board. Cover with aluminum foil. Let stand for 10 to 15 minutes to continue cooking and allow the beef to firm up a bit before thinly slicing.

PER SERVING

Calories 194	Carbohydrates 4 g
Total Fat 8.5 g	Fiber 1 g
Saturated Fat 2.5 g	Sugar 2 g
Trans Fat 0.0 g	Protein 25 g
Polyunsaturated Fat 0.5 g	DIETARY EXCHANGES:
Monounsaturated Fat 3.5 g	3 Lean Meat
Cholesterol 67 mg	
Sodium 228 mg	

COOK'S TIP on Meat Thermometers

The best way to know when meat and poultry are properly cooked is to use a meat thermometer to gauge the internal temperature. Insert the thermometer into the thickest part of the meat, making sure it doesn't touch bone or gristle. The regular type of meat thermometer stays in the meat during the cooking process. The popular instant-read thermometer cannot withstand the constant heat of the oven, however, so insert it when you think the food is done.

COOK'S TIP on Peppercorns

Peppercorns are berries produced on the vines of pepper plants. Depending on when they are picked, the berries vary quite a bit in flavor. The green peppercorn is mild and fresh tasting. The common black peppercorn is pungent, yet slightly sweet. For a mild-flavored pepper, try the white peppercorn. Pink peppercorns add a flavorful touch (similar to that of black pepper) to sauces and other dishes. They aren't true peppercorns; they are the dried berries of a rose-family plant traditionally cultivated in Madagascar.

grilled teriyaki sirloin

SERVES 4

Fire up the grill for this teriyaki-inspired steak, which is topped with toasted sesame seeds and accompanied by plump sugar snap peas tossed with sesame oil.

Marinade

2 tablespoons soy sauce (lowest sodium available)

1 tablespoon dry sherry or white wine vinegar

2 medium garlic cloves, minced

1 teaspoon peeled grated gingerroot or ¼ teaspoon ground ginger

1 teaspoon light brown sugar

1 teaspoon toasted sesame oil

❉ ❉ ❉

1 1-pound boneless sirloin steak

Cooking spray

1 tablespoon sesame seeds

6 ounces fresh sugar snap peas, trimmed

¼ cup water

½ teaspoon toasted sesame oil

In a large resealable plastic bag, combine the marinade ingredients.

Discard all visible fat from the steak. Cut into 4 pieces. Add to the marinade. Seal the bag and turn to coat. Refrigerate for 15 minutes to 8 hours, turning occasionally.

Lightly spray the grill rack with cooking spray. Preheat the grill on medium high.

Meanwhile, put the sesame seeds in a single layer in a small skillet. Dry-roast over medium heat for 2 to 3 minutes, or until golden brown, stirring frequently. Transfer to a small bowl. Set aside.

PER SERVING	
Calories 190	Carbohydrates 4 g
Total Fat 6.5 g	Fiber 1 g
Saturated Fat 2.0 g	Sugar 2 g
Trans Fat 0.0 g	Protein 26 g
Polyunsaturated Fat 1.0 g	DIETARY EXCHANGES:
Monounsaturated Fat 2.5 g	3 Lean Meat
Cholesterol 46 mg	
Sodium 252 mg	

Remove the steak pieces from the bag, discarding the marinade. Grill for 4 to 7 minutes on each side, or until the desired doneness. Transfer to a plate. Slice if desired. Cover with aluminum foil to keep warm.

Put the peas and water in a medium microwaveable bowl. Cover and microwave on 100 percent power (high) for 1 minute, or until the peas are tender-crisp. Drain well in a colander. Return to the bowl.

Stir in the sesame oil to coat.

To serve, spoon the peas onto four plates. Place the steak on the peas. Sprinkle with the sesame seeds.

COOK'S TIP on Gingerroot

If the produce section of your grocery store has only large pieces of gingerroot, it is appropriate to break off what you need. Use a spoon, knife, or vegetable peeler to remove the skin before grating, slicing, or finely chopping the flesh.

grilled sirloin steak
with chimichurri sauce

SERVES 4

A modified version of chimichurri (chihm-ee-CHOOR-ee), *a savory fresh parsley sauce that's very popular in Argentina, tops sizzling sirloin steak.*

Chimichurri Sauce

1 cup fresh parsley, loosely packed

2 tablespoons red wine vinegar

2 tablespoons fresh orange juice

1 teaspoon light brown sugar

1 teaspoon olive oil

1 medium garlic clove

❋ ❋ ❋

Cooking spray

1 teaspoon dried thyme, crumbled

1 teaspoon dried oregano, crumbled

½ teaspoon black pepper

¼ teaspoon salt

1 1-pound sirloin steak

In a food processor or blender, process the sauce ingredients for 20 to 30 seconds, or until the parsley is finely chopped. Pour the mixture into an airtight container and refrigerate until ready to use.

Lightly spray the grill rack with cooking spray. Preheat the grill on medium high.

PER SERVING	
Calories 172	Carbohydrates 4 g
Total Fat 6.0 g	Fiber 1 g
Saturated Fat 2.0 g	Sugar 2 g
Trans Fat 0.0 g	Protein 25 g
Polyunsaturated Fat 0.5 g	DIETARY EXCHANGES:
Monounsaturated Fat 2.5 g	3 Lean Meat
Cholesterol 46 mg	
Sodium 205 mg	

In a small bowl, stir together the thyme, oregano, pepper, and salt.

Discard all visible fat from the steak. Cut into 4 pieces. Sprinkle the thyme mixture over both sides of the steak. Using your fingers or a spoon, gently press the mixture into the steak so it will adhere.

Grill for 3 to 5 minutes on each side, or until the desired doneness.

To serve, spoon 2 tablespoons sauce over each serving.

COOK'S TIP on Healthy Steak Cuts

Steak on a cholesterol-lowering diet? Sure. Just select the cut of meat carefully and trim away all visible fat. Besides sirloin steak, wise beef choices include tenderloin, flank, eye of round, and round steak.

spiced shish kebabs
with horseradish cream

SERVES 4

These attractive kebabs combine the earthiness of chili powder with the bite of a creamy horseradish sauce.

   1 pound boneless top sirloin steak

   2 teaspoons chili powder

   2 teaspoons dried oregano, crumbled

   1 teaspoon ground cumin

   ¾ teaspoon garlic powder

   1 large red onion

   1 medium yellow bell pepper

   Cooking spray

Horseradish Cream

   ⅓ cup fat-free sour cream

   2 tablespoons light mayonnaise

   1 tablespoon bottled white horseradish

   ½ teaspoon garlic powder

   Chili powder to taste

   ❄ ❄ ❄

   16 cherry tomatoes

Discard all visible fat from the steak. Cut into 16 cubes. Put the cubes in a shallow casserole dish. Sprinkle with the 2 teaspoons chili powder, oregano, cumin, and ¾ teaspoon garlic powder. Toss gently to coat. Cover and refrigerate for 15 minutes.

PER SERVING	
Calories 241	Carbohydrates 15 g
Total Fat 8.0 g	Fiber 3 g
Saturated Fat 2.5 g	Sugar 6 g
Trans Fat 0.0 g	Protein 27 g
Polyunsaturated Fat 0.5 g	DIETARY EXCHANGES:
Monounsaturated Fat 2.0 g	1 Other Carbohydrate
Cholesterol 52 mg	3 Lean Meat
Sodium 159 mg	

Meanwhile, quarter the onion and separate the layers so there are at least 16 pieces. Cut the bell pepper into 16 pieces.

Preheat the broiler. Lightly spray a broiler pan and rack with cooking spray.

In a small serving bowl, stir together all the horseradish cream ingredients except the chili powder. Sprinkle the chili powder on top. Set aside.

Thread the vegetables and steak onto four long metal skewers as follows, repeating until all are used: onion, bell pepper, tomato, and steak. Put the kebabs on the broiler rack.

Broil about 4 inches from the heat for 4 minutes. Turn over and broil for 3 minutes, or until the desired doneness. Serve with the horseradish cream.

sirloin steak
with portobello mushrooms

SERVES 4

This combination of peppery sirloin and meaty portobellos is made to match up with robust mashed potatoes, perhaps flavored with garlic and horseradish.

1 1-pound boneless sirloin steak

1 teaspoon dried thyme, crumbled

½ teaspoon pepper (coarsely ground preferred)

8 ounces portobello mushrooms, cut into 1-inch squares

1 large red onion, sliced

½ cup fat-free, no-salt-added beef broth

1 tablespoon Dijon mustard

1 tablespoon Worcestershire sauce (lowest sodium available)

2 tablespoons brandy (optional)

Discard all visible fat from the steak. Cut into 4 pieces. Sprinkle both sides with the thyme and pepper.

Heat a large nonstick skillet over medium-high heat. Cook the steak for 4 to 6 minutes on each side, or to the desired doneness. Transfer to a platter and cover with aluminum foil to keep warm.

In the same skillet, cook the mushrooms and onion over medium-high heat for 1 to 2 minutes, or until the onion is tender-crisp, stirring occasionally.

Stir in the remaining ingredients. Cook for 5 to 6 minutes, or until the mushrooms are tender and the liquid is reduced by half, stirring occasionally. Spoon over the steak.

PER SERVING	
Calories 184	Carbohydrates 8 g
Total Fat 5.0 g	Fiber 2 g
Saturated Fat 2.0 g	Sugar 3 g
Trans Fat 0.0 g	Protein 27 g
Polyunsaturated Fat 0.0 g	DIETARY EXCHANGES:
Monounsaturated Fat 2.0 g	1 Vegetable
Cholesterol 46 mg	3 Lean Meat
Sodium 153 mg	

marinated steak

This simple marinade is a favorite among steak lovers.

Marinade

½ cup dry red wine (regular or nonalcoholic) or fat-free, no-salt-added beef broth

3 tablespoons tarragon vinegar or wine vinegar

3 tablespoons finely snipped fresh parsley

1 tablespoon chopped fresh oregano or 1 teaspoon dried, crumbled

1 tablespoon chopped fresh tarragon or 1 teaspoon dried, crumbled

3 medium garlic cloves, crushed

1 teaspoon olive oil

1 bay leaf

½ teaspoon pepper

⁂

1 1- to 1½-pound flank steak

Cooking spray

Pepper to taste

In a large resealable plastic bag, combine the marinade ingredients.

Discard the silver skin and all visible fat from the steak. Put the steak in the bag. Seal and turn to coat. Refrigerate for at least 8 hours, turning occasionally.

Preheat the broiler. Lightly spray a broiler pan and rack with cooking spray.

Remove the steak from the bag, discarding the marinade. Sprinkle the steak with pepper. Transfer to the broiler rack.

Broil the meat 4 to 6 inches from the heat for 3 to 7 minutes on each side, or to the desired doneness (3 to 5 minutes for medium rare, 4 to 7 for medium). Cut diagonally across the grain into very thin slices.

PER SERVING

Calories 131
Total Fat 5.5 g
   Saturated Fat 2.5 g
   Trans Fat 0.0 g
   Polyunsaturated Fat 0.0 g
   Monounsaturated Fat 2.0 g
Cholesterol 37 mg
Sodium 38 mg

Carbohydrates 0 g
   Fiber 0 g
   Sugar 0 g
Protein 19 g

DIETARY EXCHANGES:
2½ Lean Meat

peppery beef
with blue cheese sauce

SERVES 4

A little blue cheese has a big impact on the rich-tasting sauce in this recipe.

Cooking spray

12 ounces flank steak

2 teaspoons pepper (coarsely ground preferred)

Sauce

1 tablespoon light tub margarine

1 medium garlic clove, minced

1 tablespoon all-purpose flour

⅔ cup fat-free milk

2 tablespoons crumbled blue cheese

2 tablespoons finely chopped green onions

1 tablespoon dry white wine (regular or nonalcoholic) (optional)

Preheat the broiler. Lightly spray a broiler pan and rack with cooking spray.

Discard the silver skin and all visible fat from the steak. Make three widely spaced, shallow *X*s on one side of the steak. Rub that side with half the pepper. Make three *X*s on the other side. Rub that side with the remaining pepper. Transfer to the broiler rack.

Broil the steak about 4 inches from the heat for 5 minutes. Turn over and broil for 3 to 5 minutes, or until the desired doneness. Transfer to a cutting board and let stand for 5 minutes. Cut diagonally across the grain into very thin slices.

Meanwhile, in a small saucepan, heat the margarine over medium heat. Cook the garlic for 1 minute.

PER SERVING

Calories 169	Carbohydrates 5 g
Total Fat 7.5 g	Fiber 1 g
Saturated Fat 3.0 g	Sugar 2 g
Trans Fat 0.0 g	Protein 20 g
Polyunsaturated Fat 0.5 g	DIETARY EXCHANGES:
Monounsaturated Fat 3.0 g	2½ Lean Meat
Cholesterol 37 mg	
Sodium 134 mg	

Whisk in the flour. Whisk in the milk all at once. Cook for 5 minutes, or until thickened and bubbly, whisking constantly. Cook for 1 minute more, whisking constantly. Remove from the heat.

Stir in the blue cheese, green onions, and wine. Serve over the steak.

COOK'S TIP on Silver Skin

A thin, tough membrane found on flank steak and tenderloin, silver skin should be discarded before you cook the meat. If left on, silver skin tends to make the meat curl.

steak and vegetable roll-ups

SERVES 4

If you like tender pot roast with vegetables, you will love these roll-ups. They are seasoned with fresh rosemary and braised in a pan gravy enhanced with Dijon mustard. Serve over mashed potatoes or with a baked sweet potato.

8 thin boneless eye-of-round steaks (about 2 ounces each)

2 medium ribs of celery, halved crosswise

2 medium carrots, halved crosswise

4 medium green onions, halved crosswise

1 tablespoon chopped fresh rosemary or 1 teaspoon dried, crushed

¼ teaspoon pepper

1 teaspoon olive oil

1 cup fat-free, no-salt-added beef broth

⅓ cup water

1½ tablespoons all-purpose flour

1 tablespoon Dijon mustard

Discard all visible fat from the steaks. Put on a sturdy flat surface. Cover the steaks with plastic wrap. Using the smooth side of a meat mallet, lightly flatten the steaks to a thickness of about ¼ inch, being careful not to tear the meat.

Put 2 steaks lengthwise on a cutting board, slightly overlapping the steaks. Place 1 piece of celery, 1 of carrot, and 2 of green onion lengthwise in the center of the overlapping steaks. Starting from a short side, roll up jelly-roll style to enclose the filling. Secure with a wooden toothpick. Repeat with the remaining steaks and vegetables.

PER SERVING	
Calories 194	Carbohydrates 9 g
Total Fat 5.0 g	Fiber 3 g
Saturated Fat 1.5 g	Sugar 3 g
Trans Fat 0.0 g	Protein 26 g
Polyunsaturated Fat 0.5 g	DIETARY EXCHANGES:
Monounsaturated Fat 2.5 g	½ Other Carbohydrate
Cholesterol 47 mg	3 Lean Meat
Sodium 186 mg	

Sprinkle with the rosemary and pepper.

In a deep skillet, heat the oil over medium-high heat, swirling to coat the bottom. Cook the roll-ups for 1 minute on each side (4 minutes total), or until browned.

Pour in the broth. Bring to a simmer. Reduce the heat and simmer, covered, for 45 to 50 minutes, or until the beef and vegetables are tender. Transfer to a plate, leaving the liquid in the skillet. Cover the plate with aluminum foil to keep warm.

In a small bowl, whisk together the water and flour. Whisk into the pan juices.

Whisk in the mustard. Increase the heat to medium-high and cook for 2 to 3 minutes, or until thickened, whisking constantly.

To serve, transfer the roll-ups to four plates. Discard the toothpicks from the roll-ups. Top with the sauce.

COOK'S TIP

If you don't see thinly sliced eye-of-round steaks in the meat section of your grocery, ask the butcher to cut some for you. You can purchase an eye-of-round roast and cut it yourself if you prefer.

balsamic-braised beef
with exotic mushrooms

SERVES 4

Slow braising not only makes the lean meat in this recipe fork-tender but also helps provide savory gravy.

1 1-pound boneless eye-of-round or sirloin steak

1 pound mixed mushrooms, such as shiitake, chanterelle, and morel, cut into ¼-inch slices if large

1 cup fat-free, no-salt-added beef broth

2 tablespoons balsamic vinegar

1 tablespoon chopped fresh rosemary or 1 teaspoon dried, crushed

1 teaspoon onion powder

1 teaspoon garlic powder

1 bay leaf

2 tablespoons all-purpose flour

¼ cup water

Discard all visible fat from the steak. In a large nonstick skillet over medium-high heat, cook the steak for 2 minutes on each side.

Stir in the mushrooms. Cook for 2 to 3 minutes, or until they are slightly tender, stirring occasionally. Stir in the broth, vinegar, rosemary, onion powder, garlic powder, and bay leaf. Bring to a simmer, stirring occasionally. Reduce the heat and simmer, covered, for 45 to 50 minutes, or until the meat is tender.

Put the flour in a small bowl. Add the water, stirring until well combined. Pour into the beef mixture. Increase the heat to medium high and cook for 2 to 3 minutes, or until thickened, stirring occasionally. Remove the bay leaf before serving the dish.

PER SERVING	
Calories 191	Carbohydrates 9 g
Total Fat 4.0 g	Fiber 1 g
Saturated Fat 1.5 g	Sugar 4 g
Trans Fat 0.0 g	Protein 30 g
Polyunsaturated Fat 0.5 g	DIETARY EXCHANGES:
Monounsaturated Fat 1.5 g	½ Other Carbohydrate
Cholesterol 47 mg	3 Lean Meat
Sodium 71 mg	

slow-cooker pepper steak

Cherry tomatoes stirred in just before serving add a burst of freshness to this Asian-style one-dish meal.

1 pound boneless top round steak

2 cups fat-free, no-salt-added beef broth

1 medium red bell pepper, cut into 1-inch strips

1 medium green bell pepper, cut into 1-inch strips

½ medium onion, cut into 1-inch strips

2 tablespoons soy sauce (lowest sodium available)

1 teaspoon toasted sesame oil

¼ teaspoon crushed red pepper flakes (optional)

1 cup uncooked quick-cooking brown rice

1 cup cherry tomatoes, whole or halved

Discard all visible fat from the steak. Cut into thin strips.

Put the strips along with the broth, bell peppers, onion, soy sauce, sesame oil, and red pepper flakes in a 3½- to 4-quart slow cooker. Stir. Cover and cook on high for 2 to 3 hours or on low for 6 to 8 hours. Five minutes before the end of the cooking time if cooking on high or 15 minutes before if cooking on low, stir in the rice.

Just before serving, stir in the cherry tomatoes.

COOK'S TIP

To halve or not to halve—that is the question when cooking with cherry tomatoes. If left whole, they provide more intense flavor when you bite into them. If halved, they tend to soak up the flavors from the sauces, dressings, and marinades they are in.

PER SERVING	
Calories 279	Carbohydrates 25 g
Total Fat 6.0 g	Fiber 3 g
Saturated Fat 1.5 g	Sugar 5 g
Trans Fat 0.0 g	Protein 30 g
Polyunsaturated Fat 1.0 g	DIETARY EXCHANGES:
Monounsaturated Fat 2.0 g	1 Starch
Cholesterol 64 mg	2 Vegetable
Sodium 300 mg	3 Lean Meat

chili

SERVES 6

Every cook has a favorite chili recipe—we think this one will be yours. Like many other soups and stews, it tastes best when made in advance, allowing the flavors to blend.

Cooking spray

1 pound extra-lean ground beef

2 large onions, chopped

2 8-ounce cans no-salt-added tomato sauce

1½ cups water

2 to 4 medium garlic cloves, minced

2 15-ounce cans no-salt-added pinto beans, rinsed and drained

3 tablespoons chili powder

1 or 2 fresh jalapeño peppers, seeds and ribs discarded, chopped (optional)

1 tablespoon chopped fresh oregano or 1 teaspoon dried, crumbled

1 teaspoon ground cumin

½ teaspoon salt

⅛ teaspoon cayenne, or to taste

Pepper to taste

2 tablespoons cornstarch

¼ cup water

Lightly spray a large, heavy saucepan or Dutch oven with cooking spray. Cook the beef over medium-high heat for 4 to 5 minutes, or until no longer pink, stirring occasionally to turn and break up the beef. Drain well in a colander. Wipe the pan with paper towels. Lightly spray the pan with cooking spray. Return it to the heat.

PER SERVING	
Calories 301	Carbohydrates 39 g
Total Fat 4.5 g	Fiber 9 g
Saturated Fat 1.5 g	Sugar 12 g
Trans Fat 0.0 g	Protein 26 g
Polyunsaturated Fat 0.5 g	DIETARY EXCHANGES:
Monounsaturated Fat 0.5 g	1½ Starch
Cholesterol 42 mg	3 Vegetable
Sodium 304 mg	3 Very Lean Meat

Cook the onions over medium-high heat for 3 to 4 minutes, or until soft, stirring frequently.

Stir in the beef, tomato sauce, 1½ cups water, and garlic. Reduce the heat and simmer, partially covered, for 20 minutes.

Stir in the beans, chili powder, jalapeños, oregano, cumin, salt, cayenne, and pepper. Simmer, partially covered, for 30 minutes.

Put the cornstarch in a cup. Add the water, stirring to dissolve. Stir into the chili mixture. Cook for 3 to 4 minutes, or until the desired consistency.

ground beef ragout

SERVES 6

The ingredients in this recipe may seem like those for chili, but true to its name, this ragout is a rich-tasting, well-seasoned stew. For economy in cost but not in taste, prepare whole-wheat spaghetti or yolk-free noodles to make a bed for the ragout, thus stretching the dish to serve more people.

1½ pounds extra-lean ground beef

1 large onion, chopped

2 large tomatoes, chopped

1 8-ounce can no-salt-added tomato sauce

¾ cup dry red wine (regular or nonalcoholic) and ½ cup water, or 1¼ cups water

1 tablespoon fresh oregano or 1 teaspoon dried, crumbled

3 medium garlic cloves, minced

1 teaspoon chili powder, or to taste

1 teaspoon ground cumin

½ teaspoon salt

Pepper to taste

1 red chile pepper, ribs and seeds discarded, chopped (optional)

1 15-ounce can no-salt-added kidney beans, rinsed and drained

1 15-ounce can reduced-sodium great northern beans, rinsed and drained

¼ cup snipped fresh parsley

Heat a Dutch oven over medium-high heat. Cook the beef for 4 to 5 minutes, or until no longer pink, stirring occasionally to turn and break up the beef. Drain well in a colander. Wipe the skillet with paper towels. Return the beef to the skillet.

PER SERVING

Calories 328	Carbohydrates 30 g
Total Fat 6.0 g	Fiber 7 g
Saturated Fat 2.5 g	Sugar 8 g
Trans Fat 0.0 g	Protein 34 g
Polyunsaturated Fat 0.5 g	DIETARY EXCHANGES:
Monounsaturated Fat 2.5 g	1½ Starch
Cholesterol 62 mg	2 Vegetable
Sodium 369 mg	3½ Lean Meat

Stir the onion into the beef. Cook over medium-high heat for about 4 minutes, or until the onion is soft, stirring occasionally.

Stir in the tomatoes, tomato sauce, wine, water, oregano, garlic, chili powder, cumin, salt, pepper, and chile pepper. Bring to a boil. Reduce the heat and simmer, partially covered, for 45 minutes, stirring occasionally.

Stir in the beans. Simmer for 10 to 15 minutes, or until thoroughly heated.

To serve, ladle into six soup bowls. Sprinkle with the parsley.

COOK'S TIP

Sometimes a small change makes a big difference. To see what we mean, substitute 1 cup of fresh pearl onions (about 4 ounces) for the chopped onion in this recipe. Add the raw pearl onions with the wine, water, and other ingredients just after draining the cooked beef.

meat loaf
with apricot glaze

SERVES 6

A grated apple is the surprise ingredient that helps make this meat loaf extra moist. The apricot glaze provides the finishing touch.

Cooking spray

Meat Loaf

1 small onion, grated (about ½ cup)

1 small apple, peeled and grated (about ½ cup)

Whites of 2 large eggs

2 tablespoons snipped fresh parsley

2 tablespoons Worcestershire sauce (lowest sodium available)

2 tablespoons no-salt-added ketchup

2 medium garlic cloves, minced

1 teaspoon dried oregano, crumbled

¼ teaspoon salt

1 pound extra-lean ground beef

½ cup uncooked quick-cooking rolled oats

Glaze

½ cup all-fruit apricot spread

3 tablespoons no-salt-added ketchup

2 tablespoons fresh orange juice

1 tablespoon honey

2 teaspoons cornstarch

½ teaspoon ground ginger

¼ teaspoon red hot-pepper sauce

PER SERVING	
Calories 231	Carbohydrates 30 g
Total Fat 4.5 g	Fiber 2 g
Saturated Fat 1.5 g	Sugar 19 g
Trans Fat 0.0 g	Protein 19 g
Polyunsaturated Fat 0.5 g	DIETARY EXCHANGES:
Monounsaturated Fat 1.5 g	2 Other Carbohydrate
Cholesterol 42 mg	2½ Lean Meat
Sodium 187 mg	

Preheat the oven to 350° F. Lightly spray a 9 × 5 × 3-inch loaf pan with cooking spray.

In a large bowl, stir together the onion, apple, egg whites, parsley, Worcestershire sauce, ketchup, garlic, oregano, and salt.

Using your hands, work the beef and oats into the onion mixture just until blended. Transfer to the pan and lightly pat into a rectangle slightly smaller than the pan.

Bake for 45 minutes. Remove the meat loaf from the oven and pour off and discard any fat.

Meanwhile, in a small saucepan, whisk together the glaze ingredients. Cook over medium-high heat for 8 to 10 minutes, or until thickened and bubbling, whisking constantly.

Spoon the glaze over the cooked meat loaf.

Bake for 15 minutes, or until the meat loaf reaches an internal temperature of 160° F and is no longer pink in the center. Let stand for 5 to 10 minutes before slicing.

COOK'S TIP

You can easily double this recipe and make two meat loaves. Cook both at the same time, then freeze the extra one to have on hand for a busy day. An interesting side note: Ranking after oatmeal cereal and oatmeal cookies, meat loaf is the third most popular use for oats.

saucy stroganoff

SERVES 6

Transform time-consuming classic beef stroganoff into a quick and healthy dinner by using lean ground beef, whole-wheat noodles, and tangy fat-free yogurt.

6 ounces dried whole-wheat or whole-grain noodles

1 pound extra-lean ground beef

8 ounces button mushrooms, sliced

1 medium onion, chopped

1 cup hot water

2 teaspoons sodium-free instant powdered beef bouillon

2 tablespoons Worcestershire sauce (lowest sodium available)

1 tablespoon snipped fresh parsley

2 medium garlic cloves, minced

1 teaspoon dried basil, crumbled

1 teaspoon salt-free all-purpose seasoning blend

¼ teaspoon salt

¼ teaspoon pepper

2 tablespoons cornstarch

¼ cup dry white wine (regular or nonalcoholic)

¾ cup fat-free plain yogurt

Fresh parsley sprigs (optional)

Prepare the noodles using the package directions, omitting the salt and oil. Drain well in a colander. Transfer to a large bowl. Cover and set aside.

Meanwhile, in a Dutch oven or a large nonstick skillet, cook the beef, mushrooms, and onion over medium-high heat for 10 to 12 minutes, or until the beef

PER SERVING	
Calories 258	Carbohydrates 31 g
Total Fat 4.5 g	Fiber 5 g
Saturated Fat 1.5 g	Sugar 6 g
Trans Fat 0.0 g	Protein 24 g
Polyunsaturated Fat 0.5 g	DIETARY EXCHANGES:
Monounsaturated Fat 1.5 g	2 Starch
Cholesterol 42 mg	2½ Very Lean Meat
Sodium 194 mg	

is browned and the mushrooms and onion are soft, stirring occasionally to turn and break up the beef. Drain well in a colander. Wipe the Dutch oven or skillet with a paper towel. Return the beef mixture to the Dutch oven or skillet.

Pour the hot water into a small bowl. Add the bouillon, stirring until dissolved.

Stir in the Worcestershire sauce, snipped parsley, garlic, basil, seasoning blend, salt, and pepper. Stir into the beef mixture.

Put the cornstarch in the same small bowl. Pour in the wine, whisking until dissolved. Stir into the beef mixture. Bring to a boil over medium-high heat, stirring occasionally. Reduce the heat and simmer for 2 to 3 minutes, or until thickened, stirring frequently.

Gently stir in the yogurt. Heat through, but do not let the mixture come to a boil.

To serve, spoon the beef mixture over the noodles. Garnish with the parsley sprigs.

mexican beef and corn bread pie

SERVES 6

A blend of the Old South and south of the border, this family favorite is a winner.

Meat Mixture

1 pound extra-lean ground beef

1 large onion, chopped

2 large tomatoes, chopped

1 large green bell pepper, chopped

1 10-ounce package frozen whole-kernel corn

1 cup fat-free, low-sodium chicken broth or fat-free, no-salt-added beef broth

1 tablespoon Worcestershire sauce (lowest sodium available)

1 teaspoon ground cumin

1 teaspoon chili powder, or to taste

¼ teaspoon salt

Corn Bread Mixture

1½ cups yellow cornmeal

¼ cup all-purpose flour

2 teaspoons baking powder

1 teaspoon sugar (optional)

¼ teaspoon salt

Whites of 3 large eggs

½ cup fat-free milk

1 tablespoon canola or corn oil

PER SERVING

Calories 353	Carbohydrates 51 g
Total Fat 7.5 g	Fiber 5 g
Saturated Fat 2.0 g	Sugar 8 g
Trans Fat 0.0 g	Protein 25 g
Polyunsaturated Fat 1.5 g	DIETARY EXCHANGES:
Monounsaturated Fat 3.0 g	3 Starch
Cholesterol 42 mg	1 Vegetable
Sodium 446 mg	2½ Lean Meat

Preheat the oven to 400° F.

Heat a large nonstick skillet over medium-high heat. Cook the beef for 4 to 5 minutes, or until no longer pink, stirring occasionally to turn and break up the beef. Drain well in a colander. Wipe the skillet with paper towels. Return the beef to the skillet.

Stir the onion into the beef. Cook for 3 minutes, or until the onion is soft, stirring occasionally.

Stir in the remaining meat mixture ingredients. Reduce the heat and simmer for about 20 minutes. Spoon into a 10-inch square baking pan.

In a medium bowl, stir together the cornmeal, flour, baking powder, sugar, and salt.

In a small bowl, whisk together the egg whites, milk, and oil. Pour into the cornmeal mixture. Stir gently, just enough to combine the ingredients thoroughly. Spoon over the meat mixture, spreading gently to cover the surface.

Bake for 30 to 40 minutes, or until the corn bread is golden brown.

bulgur and ground beef casserole

SERVES 4

The bulgur adds a crunchy chewiness to this hearty casserole.

Cooking spray

1 pound extra-lean ground beef

2 medium onions, chopped

1 cup uncooked bulgur

4 medium tomatoes, chopped

½ cup finely snipped fresh cilantro or parsley

½ cup canned low-sodium mixed-vegetable juice

2 tablespoons fresh lemon juice

1 tablespoon chopped fresh dillweed or 1 heaping teaspoon dried, crumbled

½ teaspoon salt

¼ plus ⅛ teaspoon garlic powder

¼ teaspoon pepper

Preheat the oven to 350° F.

Lightly spray a Dutch oven with cooking spray. Cook the beef over medium-high heat for 4 to 5 minutes, or until no longer pink, stirring occasionally to turn and break up the beef. Drain well in a colander. Wipe the skillet with paper towels. Return the beef to the skillet.

Stir the onions into the beef. Cook for 3 to 4 minutes, or until the onions are soft, stirring occasionally. Spoon into a 10-inch square or 11 × 9 × 2-inch baking pan or casserole dish.

Stir the remaining ingredients into the beef mixture.

Bake for 15 to 20 minutes, or until thoroughly heated.

PER SERVING	
Calories 334	Carbohydrates 42 g
Total Fat 6.5 g	Fiber 10 g
Saturated Fat 2.5 g	Sugar 10 g
Trans Fat 0.0 g	Protein 31 g
Polyunsaturated Fat 1.0 g	DIETARY EXCHANGES:
Monounsaturated Fat 2.5 g	2 Starch
Cholesterol 62 mg	2 Vegetable
Sodium 411 mg	3 Lean Meat

spicy baked pork chops

SERVES 4

Fixing dinner is as easy as 1-2-3! Simplify preparation with an assembly line: Place the bowl with the egg substitute mixture at the left, the plate of crumb mixture in the center, and the baking pan at the right.

Cooking spray

¼ cup egg substitute

2 tablespoons fat-free milk

⅓ cup cornflake crumbs

2 tablespoons cornmeal

½ teaspoon dried marjoram, crumbled

⅛ teaspoon pepper

⅛ teaspoon dry mustard

⅛ teaspoon ground ginger

⅛ teaspoon cayenne

4 boneless pork loin chops (about 4 ounces each), all visible fat discarded

Preheat the oven to 375° F. Using cooking spray, lightly spray a shallow baking pan large enough to hold the pork chops in a single layer.

In a shallow bowl, stir together the egg substitute and milk.

In a shallow dish, such as a pie pan, combine the crumbs, cornmeal, marjoram, pepper, mustard, ginger, and cayenne.

Using tongs, dip the pork in the egg substitute mixture, letting any excess liquid drip off. Coat both sides of the pork with the crumb mixture. Put the pork in the baking pan.

Bake for 15 minutes. Turn over. Bake for 10 minutes, or until tender and no longer pink in the center.

PER SERVING

Calories 213	Carbohydrates 11 g
Total Fat 6.5 g	Fiber 0 g
Saturated Fat 2.5 g	Sugar 1 g
Trans Fat 0.0 g	Protein 27 g
Polyunsaturated Fat 0.5 g	DIETARY EXCHANGES:
Monounsaturated Fat 3.0 g	½ Starch
Cholesterol 65 mg	3 Lean Meat
Sodium 136 mg	

skillet pork chops
with cinnamon-apple salsa

This easy-to-prepare dish will appeal to "kids" of all ages. What a delicious way to incorporate more fruit into your diet!

4 lean pork chops with bone (about 5 ounces each)

½ teaspoon dried thyme, crumbled

¼ teaspoon garlic powder

Cinnamon-Apple Salsa

8 ounces Granny Smith apples, finely chopped

4 dried plums with orange essence, finely chopped

1 tablespoon firmly packed dark brown sugar

½ teaspoon grated orange zest

2 tablespoons fresh orange juice

¼ teaspoon ground cinnamon

Discard all visible fat from the pork. Sprinkle both sides of the pork with the thyme and garlic powder.

In a large nonstick skillet over medium heat, cook the pork for 5 minutes on each side, or until no longer pink in the center.

Meanwhile, in a medium serving bowl, gently stir the salsa ingredients to combine thoroughly. Serve with the pork.

COOK'S TIP on Cutting Dried Fruit

To prevent your scissors or knife from becoming sticky when you snip or chop dried fruit, lightly spray the utensil with cooking spray or dip it in hot water or sugar before using.

PER SERVING	
Calories 213	Carbohydrates 18 g
Total Fat 6.0 g	Fiber 2 g
Saturated Fat 2.0 g	Sugar 13 g
Trans Fat 0.0 g	Protein 22 g
Polyunsaturated Fat 0.5 g	DIETARY EXCHANGES:
Monounsaturated Fat 2.5 g	1 Fruit
Cholesterol 58 mg	3 Lean Meat
Sodium 45 mg	

pork with savory sauce

SERVES 4

Flavored vinegar and port wine give this dish a dash of elegance.

¾ cup fat-free, low-sodium chicken broth

¼ cup raspberry or balsamic vinegar

2 tablespoons port wine

1 teaspoon olive oil

½ teaspoon pepper (coarsely ground preferred)

½ teaspoon dried oregano, crumbled

1 medium garlic clove, minced

1 pound pork tenderloin

1 teaspoon cornstarch

2 tablespoons water

In a small saucepan, stir together the broth, vinegar, port, oil, pepper, oregano, and garlic. Cook over medium-high heat for 20 minutes, or until reduced to ½ cup.

Meanwhile, discard all visible fat from the pork. Cut the pork into ¼-inch medallions.

Put the cornstarch in a cup. Add the water, stirring to dissolve. Stir into the reduced sauce. Reduce the heat to medium. Cook for 1 minute, or until thickened, stirring constantly. Remove from the heat and cover to keep warm.

Heat a large nonstick skillet over medium-high heat. Cook the pork for 3 to 4 minutes on each side, or until no longer pink in the center. Serve with the sauce.

PER SERVING

Calories 173
Total Fat 5.0 g
  Saturated Fat 1.5 g
  Trans Fat 0.0 g
  Polyunsaturated Fat 0.5 g
  Monounsaturated Fat 2.5 g
Cholesterol 63 mg
Sodium 61 mg

Carbohydrates 6 g
  Fiber 0 g
  Sugar 4 g
Protein 23 g

DIETARY EXCHANGES:
½ Other Carbohydrate
3 Lean Meat

pork
with corn-cilantro pesto

SERVES 4 (Plus about ½ cup pesto remaining)

The delicious pesto inside these pork pinwheels is a southwestern rendition of an Italian favorite. The recipe makes more pesto than you need for the pork, so try some of the extra with pasta or stir a dollop into vegetable soup for a fresh flavor boost.

Cooking spray

Corn-Cilantro Pesto

1 cup firmly packed fresh cilantro

⅓ cup no-salt-added whole-kernel corn, drained if canned or thawed if frozen

¼ cup firmly packed fresh parsley

¼ cup shredded or grated Parmesan or Romano cheese

2 tablespoons chopped pecans

1 tablespoon chopped shallot

1 tablespoon fresh lime juice

2 medium garlic cloves, quartered

¼ teaspoon salt

1 tablespoon plus 1 teaspoon olive oil

Fresh lime juice or water (if needed)

❋ ❋ ❋

1 1-pound pork tenderloin

Tomato Sauce

½ cup chopped onion

1 medium garlic clove, minced

1 8-ounce can no-salt-added tomato sauce

¼ teaspoon sugar

¼ teaspoon salt

⅛ teaspoon pepper

PER SERVING

Calories 198
Total Fat 7.0 g
  Saturated Fat 2.0 g
  Trans Fat 0.0 g
  Polyunsaturated Fat 1.0 g
  Monounsaturated Fat 3.5 g
Cholesterol 64 mg
Sodium 276 mg

Carbohydrates 9 g
  Fiber 2 g
  Sugar 4 g
Protein 25 g

DIETARY EXCHANGES:
½ Other Carbohydrate
3 Lean Meat

Lightly spray a shallow roasting pan and a wire rack or a broiler pan and broiler rack with cooking spray.

In a food processor or blender, process the cilantro, corn, parsley, Parmesan, pecans, shallot, 1 tablespoon lime juice, quartered garlic, and salt until well combined, stopping and scraping the sides occasionally.

With the machine running, gradually pour in the oil. Process until well combined. If the pesto is thicker than you like, gradually add lime juice or water as needed.

Preheat the oven to 425° F.

Discard all visible fat from the pork. Cut the pork lengthwise almost in half. Lay it flat between two pieces of plastic wrap. Using the smooth side of a meat mallet, lightly pound the pork to a thickness of ¼ inch, being careful not to tear it.

Spread ¼ cup pesto over the cut surface of the pork. (Reserve the remaining pesto for later uses.) Roll up the pork from a short end. Tie in several places with kitchen twine to keep the filling in place. Put the pork on the rack.

Bake for 20 minutes. Turn over. Bake for 10 to 20 minutes, or until a meat thermometer registers an internal temperature of 160° F. Remove from the oven. Let stand for 5 minutes. Slice into medallions.

Meanwhile, lightly spray a medium saucepan with cooking spray. Cook the onion and minced garlic over medium heat for 3 to 4 minutes, or until the onion is soft, stirring occasionally.

Stir in the remaining sauce ingredients. Increase the heat to high and bring to a boil. Reduce the heat and simmer for 5 minutes, or until the desired consistency. Serve with the pork.

vegetarian entrées

pumpkin gnocchi

SERVES 4

You'll get a sense of satisfaction from making your own gnocchi, and the pumpkin flavor and silky sauce you add will please your family.

8 ounces frozen Italian-cut green beans

1 cup canned solid-pack pumpkin (not pie filling)

½ cup egg substitute

¼ teaspoon salt

¼ teaspoon pepper

2 cups all-purpose flour

Flour for rolling out dough

1 cup fat-free half-and-half

1½ tablespoons all-purpose flour

¼ cup shredded or grated Parmesan cheese

1 teaspoon grated lemon zest

⅛ teaspoon salt

¼ teaspoon pepper

Prepare the green beans using the package directions, omitting the salt and margarine. Drain well in a colander. Cover to keep warm.

Meanwhile, fill a stockpot with water. Bring to a simmer over high heat.

While the water heats, in a medium bowl, stir together the pumpkin, egg substitute, ¼ teaspoon salt, and ¼ teaspoon pepper.

Add 2 cups flour to the pumpkin mixture, stirring just until the dough forms a ball. Do not overmix or the dough may become gummy. Divide the dough into 4 equal pieces.

PER SERVING	
Calories 352	Carbohydrates 67 g
Total Fat 2.5 g	Fiber 6 g
Saturated Fat 1.0 g	Sugar 8 g
Trans Fat 0.0 g	Protein 17 g
Polyunsaturated Fat 0.5 g	DIETARY EXCHANGES:
Monounsaturated Fat 0.5 g	4 Starch
Cholesterol 4 mg	1 Vegetable
Sodium 494 mg	

Lightly flour a flat surface. Using your hands, lightly roll each piece of the dough into a 12-inch-long cylinder. Cut each crosswise into twenty-four ½-inch pieces. If desired, use a fork to slightly flatten each piece and create grooves, which help hold the sauce.

Put half the gnocchi in the simmering water. After the pieces float to the surface (about 1 minute), cook for 3 to 4 minutes, or until tender and cooked through (when cut in half, they shouldn't look chalky, which indicates uncooked flour), stirring occasionally. Using a slotted spoon, transfer the gnocchi to a medium bowl. Cover with aluminum foil to keep warm. Repeat with the remaining gnocchi.

Meanwhile, in a small saucepan, whisk together the half-and-half and 1½ tablespoons flour. The mixture will be slightly lumpy. Bring to a simmer over medium-high heat, whisking occasionally. Simmer for 1 to 2 minutes, or until thickened, whisking occasionally. Remove from the heat and stir in the remaining ingredients except the green beans.

To serve, spoon the gnocchi into each bowl. Spoon the green beans over the gnocchi. Ladle the sauce on top.

polenta
with sautéed vegetables

SERVES 4

Make your own polenta—it's easy—and add a mixture of colorful vegetables and Parmesan cheese for an Italian-style comfort dish.

1 tablespoon olive oil

2 medium garlic cloves, minced

1 medium eggplant (about 1 pound), diced

1 small yellow summer squash (about 4 ounces), thinly sliced

1 small zucchini (about 4 ounces), thinly sliced

1 medium red bell pepper, cut into strips about ½ inch wide

1 8-ounce can no-salt-added tomato sauce

½ cup low-sodium vegetable broth

1 teaspoon dried oregano, crumbled

¼ teaspoon salt

¼ teaspoon pepper

1 cup low-sodium vegetable broth

1 cup fat-free milk

½ cup yellow cornmeal (coarse-grained for more robust texture, fine-grained for creamier texture)

¼ cup shredded or grated Parmesan cheese

In a large nonstick skillet, heat the oil over medium-high heat, swirling to coat the bottom. Cook the garlic for 10 seconds, stirring constantly. Watch carefully so it doesn't burn.

PER SERVING	
Calories 217	Carbohydrates 34 g
Total Fat 6.0 g	Fiber 7 g
Saturated Fat 2.0 g	Sugar 11 g
Trans Fat 0.0 g	Protein 10 g
Polyunsaturated Fat 1.0 g	DIETARY EXCHANGES:
Monounsaturated Fat 3.0 g	1 Starch
Cholesterol 6 mg	3 Vegetable
Sodium 323 mg	1 Fat

Stir in the eggplant, summer squash, zucchini, and bell pepper. Cook for 5 to 6 minutes, or until tender, stirring occasionally. Add water, 1 tablespoon at a time, if the mixture begins to stick to the skillet.

Stir in the tomato sauce, ½ cup broth, oregano, salt, and pepper. Bring to a simmer. Reduce the heat and simmer, partially covered, for 15 minutes.

Meanwhile, in a medium saucepan, bring 1 cup broth and the milk to a simmer over medium-high heat. Gradually add the cornmeal, whisking constantly. Reduce the heat to medium and cook for 10 to 12 minutes, or until thickened (soft and creamy, not gritty), whisking constantly.

To serve, spoon the polenta into bowls. Spoon the vegetables on top. Sprinkle with the Parmesan.

COOK'S TIP

For this and other recipes calling for Parmesan cheese, you may want to buy a wedge of the cheese and shave the specified amount as you need it. A potato peeler works well for this. For a real taste treat, try Parmigiano-Reggiano, a pricey Italian import that practically melts in your mouth.

whole-wheat pasta
with vegetable sauce

SERVES 6

Whole-wheat pasta gives this dish a nutty quality. You can make the sauce in advance and reheat it at serving time for extra flavor.

    Cooking spray

Sauce

    1 teaspoon olive oil

    6 medium green onions, chopped

    1 large red or white onion, chopped

    4 medium garlic cloves, minced

    1 16-ounce can no-salt-added kidney beans, rinsed and drained

    1 16-ounce can no-salt-added tomatoes, undrained

    8 ounces button mushrooms, sliced

    2 medium red, green, or yellow bell peppers, or any combination, chopped

    2 medium ribs of celery with leaves, chopped

    1 cup water

    ½ cup dry red wine (regular or nonalcoholic) (optional)

    ¼ cup finely snipped fresh parsley

    1 tablespoon chopped fresh oregano or 1 teaspoon dried, crumbled

    1 tablespoon chopped fresh basil or ½ teaspoon dried, crumbled

    1 bay leaf

    Pepper to taste

    ✻ ✻ ✻

    12 ounces dried whole-wheat pasta, such as spaghetti

    1 cup shredded part-skim mozzarella cheese

PER SERVING	
Calories 393	Carbohydrates 69 g
Total Fat 5.0 g	Fiber 14 g
Saturated Fat 2.0 g	Sugar 11 g
Trans Fat 0.0 g	Protein 20 g
Polyunsaturated Fat 0.5 g	DIETARY EXCHANGES:
Monounsaturated Fat 1.5 g	4 Starch
Cholesterol 12 mg	2 Vegetable
Sodium 178 mg	1 Very Lean Meat

Lightly spray a large saucepan or Dutch oven with cooking spray. Put the oil in and swirl to coat the bottom. Cook the onions and garlic over medium-high heat for 2 to 3 minutes, or until the onions are soft.

Stir in the remaining sauce ingredients. Increase the heat to high and bring to a boil. Reduce the heat and simmer, covered, for 1 hour, stirring frequently. Discard the bay leaf.

Meanwhile, prepare the pasta using the package directions, omitting the salt and oil. Drain well in a colander. Spoon onto six plates.

Sprinkle the mozzarella over the pasta. Spoon the sauce on top.

penne and cannellini bean casserole

with sun-dried tomatoes

SERVES 8

Penne pasta and vegetables team up with cannellini beans (white kidney beans) for a winning casserole combination.

8 ounces dried penne pasta (whole-wheat preferred)

8 dry-packed sun-dried tomato halves (about 1 ounce total)

Cooking spray

2 medium shallots, finely chopped

1 tablespoon low-sodium vegetable broth

4 ounces fresh asparagus, trimmed and cut diagonally into ½-inch pieces

½ medium red bell pepper, diced

1 teaspoon dried oregano, crumbled

⅛ teaspoon pepper

1 15-ounce can cannellini beans, rinsed and drained

½ cup low-sodium vegetable broth

¼ cup fat-free milk

1 cup shredded part-skim mozzarella cheese

1 tablespoon light tub margarine

Prepare the pasta using the package directions, omitting the salt and oil. With a large slotted spoon, transfer the pasta to a colander, leaving the pot of water heating on the stovetop. Set the pasta aside.

PER SERVING	
Calories 205	Carbohydrates 33 g
Total Fat 3.5 g	Fiber 7 g
Saturated Fat 1.5 g	Sugar 3 g
Trans Fat 0.0 g	Protein 11 g
Polyunsaturated Fat 0.5 g	DIETARY EXCHANGES:
Monounsaturated Fat 1.0 g	3 Starch
Cholesterol 9 mg	½ Very Lean Meat
Sodium 211 mg	

Add the tomatoes to the cooking water. Turn off the heat. Let the tomatoes soak for 15 to 20 minutes.

About halfway through the soaking time, preheat the oven to 350°F. Lightly spray a shallow 2½-quart glass casserole dish with cooking spray. Set aside.

In a large nonstick skillet over medium heat, cook the shallots and 1 tablespoon vegetable broth for 1 minute.

Stir in the asparagus, bell pepper, oregano, and pepper. Cook for 1 to 2 minutes, or until the vegetables are tender-crisp, stirring occasionally. Turn off the heat.

Remove the tomatoes from the soaking liquid and squeeze out any excess liquid. Dice the tomatoes and stir into the asparagus mixture.

In the casserole dish, layer half the beans, half the pasta, and half the asparagus mixture. Repeat. Pour ½ cup vegetable broth and the milk over all. Sprinkle with the mozzarella. Dot with the margarine.

Bake, covered, for 20 minutes. Uncover and bake for 5 minutes.

soba lo mein
with bok choy and sugar snap peas

SERVES 4

The secret to success for this dish is not to overcook the soba—thin Japanese noodles made from buckwheat and wheat flour. The noodles have an earthy flavor that distinguishes them from other noodles.

8 cups water

4 ounces dried soba noodles

Sauce

¼ cup low-sodium vegetable broth

2 tablespoons hoisin sauce

1 tablespoon soy sauce (lowest sodium available)

1 teaspoon sugar (optional)

    ❈ ❈ ❈

1 teaspoon canola or corn oil

2 medium garlic cloves, minced

2 medium carrots, thinly sliced

4 ounces sugar snap peas, trimmed

2 stalks bok choy, stems and leaves thinly sliced

½ medium onion, thinly sliced

In a large saucepan or Dutch oven, bring the water to a boil over high heat. Stir in the noodles. Reduce the heat to medium-high. Cook for 2 to 3 minutes, or until tender, stirring occasionally. Drain well in a colander. Set aside.

In a small bowl, stir together the sauce ingredients. Set aside.

PER SERVING

Calories 157	Carbohydrates 32 g
Total Fat 1.5 g	Fiber 4 g
Saturated Fat 0.0 g	Sugar 8 g
Trans Fat 0.0 g	Protein 6 g
Polyunsaturated Fat 0.5 g	DIETARY EXCHANGES:
Monounsaturated Fat 0.5 g	1½ Starch
Cholesterol 0 mg	2 Vegetable
Sodium 207 mg	

Pour the oil into a large nonstick skillet or wok and swirl to coat the bottom. Cook the garlic over medium-high heat for 15 seconds.

Stir in the carrots and peas. Cook for 1 minute, stirring constantly.

Stir in the bok choy and onion. Cook for 1 to 2 minutes, or until the vegetables are tender-crisp, stirring constantly.

Stir in the sauce and noodles. Cook for 1 minute, or until the mixture is heated through, stirring constantly.

COOK'S TIP on Bok Choy

Both the crunchy white stems and the delicate leafy green part of bok choy are edible. Cook the stems or eat them raw like celery. Cook the green parts as you would spinach. Both stems and greens are good stir-fried or added to soups (the greens cook quickly, so add them near the end of cooking time).

pan-fried pasta pancake
with vegetables

SERVES 4

Try this tasty alternative to plain pasta. It's fun to make, it reheats well, and thanks to the egg substitute, it contains no cholesterol.

> 8 ounces dried pasta, such as linguine, vermicelli, or spaghetti (whole-wheat preferred)
>
> 1 medium carrot, shredded
>
> 2 medium green onions, thinly sliced
>
> ½ cup fresh snow peas, trimmed and cut into ½-inch pieces
>
> 1 teaspoon toasted sesame oil
>
> 1 teaspoon canola or corn oil
>
> 1 cup egg substitute
>
> ¼ teaspoon salt
>
> ⅛ teaspoon pepper

Prepare the pasta using the package directions, omitting the salt and oil. Drain well in a colander. Transfer to a large bowl. Refrigerate for at least 10 minutes.

Stir the carrot, green onions, snow peas, and sesame oil into the cooled pasta.

Heat a 10-inch nonstick omelet pan or skillet over medium heat. Pour the canola oil into the pan and swirl to coat the bottom. Heat for 30 seconds. Spread the pasta mixture evenly in the pan. Cook for 1 minute without stirring. Reduce the heat to low.

In a small bowl, whisk together the egg substitute, salt, and pepper. Pour over the pasta, tilting the pan to distribute the egg mixture evenly (do not stir).

Cook, covered, for 10 to 12 minutes, or until thoroughly cooked. To brown the other side, invert the pancake onto a plate, slide it back into the pan, and cook for 1 to 2 minutes.

PER SERVING

Calories 265	Carbohydrates 47 g
Total Fat 3.0 g	Fiber 9 g
Saturated Fat 0.5 g	Sugar 5 g
Trans Fat 0.0 g	Protein 15 g
Polyunsaturated Fat 1.0 g	DIETARY EXCHANGES:
Monounsaturated Fat 1.5 g	3 Starch
Cholesterol 0 mg	1 Very Lean Meat
Sodium 290 mg	

spinach, chickpea, and olive pasta

SERVES 4

This one-dish meal is an eye-pleasing and satisfying combination of ingredients.

   4 ounces dried radiatore or rotini pasta (whole-wheat preferred)

   2 ounces fresh spinach leaves, coarsely chopped

   1 15-ounce can no-salt-added chickpeas, rinsed and drained

   1 cup coarsely chopped roasted red bell peppers, rinsed and drained if bottled

   12 kalamata olives, chopped

   2 tablespoons cider vinegar

   1 tablespoon dried basil, crumbled

   ½ cup crumbled fat-free feta cheese

Prepare the pasta using the package directions, omitting the salt and oil. Pour into a colander and run under cold water until completely cooled. Drain well.

Meanwhile, in a medium serving bowl, stir together the remaining ingredients except the feta.

Gently stir in the pasta, then the feta.

PER SERVING

Calories 263	Carbohydrates 44 g
Total Fat 4.5 g	Fiber 7 g
Saturated Fat 0.5 g	Sugar 3 g
Trans Fat 0.0 g	Protein 14 g
Polyunsaturated Fat 0.5 g	DIETARY EXCHANGES:
Monounsaturated Fat 2.5 g	3 Starch
Cholesterol 0 mg	1 Very Lean Meat
Sodium 498 mg	

grilled portobello mushrooms
with couscous and greens

SERVES 4

The grand size and meaty texture of the portobello mushroom make it a perfect base for fluffy couscous and vibrant greens.

4 portobello mushrooms

¼ cup balsamic vinegar

Cooking spray

½ cup low-sodium vegetable broth

½ cup water

¼ teaspoon ground turmeric

⅔ cup uncooked couscous

¼ cup dried cranberries

½ teaspoon grated lemon zest

¼ teaspoon salt

1 teaspoon olive oil

2 medium garlic cloves, minced

6 ounces fresh collard greens or kale or 8 ounces fresh spinach, chopped

2 tablespoons water

1 tablespoon light tub margarine

½ medium red bell pepper, finely chopped

On the smooth side of each mushroom, cut four slits, each 2 to 3 inches long and about ½ inch deep. Discard the stems. Place the mushrooms with the smooth side up in a single layer in a 13 × 9 × 2-inch glass casserole dish.

PER SERVING

Calories 203	Carbohydrates 38 g
Total Fat 3.0 g	Fiber 5 g
Saturated Fat 0.0 g	Sugar 11 g
Trans Fat 0.0 g	Protein 6 g
Polyunsaturated Fat 0.5 g	DIETARY EXCHANGES:
Monounsaturated Fat 1.5 g	1½ Starch
Cholesterol 0 mg	½ Fruit
Sodium 226 mg	1 Vegetable
	½ Fat

Sprinkle the mushrooms with half the balsamic vinegar. Lightly spray with cooking spray. Turn the mushrooms over and sprinkle with the remaining vinegar. Lightly spray with cooking spray. Cover with plastic wrap. Set aside. (Mushrooms will keep in the refrigerator for up to 1 hour.)

In a medium saucepan, bring the broth, ½ cup water, and turmeric to a boil over high heat.

Stir in the couscous, cranberries, lemon zest, and salt. Remove from the heat. Let stand, covered, for at least 5 minutes. Fluff with a fork.

Meanwhile, lightly spray a grill rack with cooking spray. Preheat the grill on medium-high.

Pour the oil into a medium saucepan and swirl to coat the bottom. Cook the garlic over medium heat for 1 minute, stirring occasionally.

Stir in the greens and 2 tablespoons water. Cook, covered, for 2 to 3 minutes, or until the greens are tender.

Add the margarine. Stir for 30 seconds, or until melted. Remove from the heat and cover to keep warm.

Grill the mushrooms for 2 to 3 minutes on each side.

To assemble, place a mushroom with the stem side up on each of four plates. Spoon the couscous over each mushroom. Spoon the greens over the couscous. Sprinkle with the bell pepper.

COOK'S TIP

The couscous mixture and cooked greens can be covered and refrigerated separately for up to five days. Reheat each part in a microwaveable container at 100 percent power (high) for 1 to 2 minutes.

whole-grain pilaf
with pecans

SERVES 4

Whether you prepare this dish as a vegetarian entrée or opt for the version with chicken, you will find it colorful, flavorful, and fiber-full!

1 6.5-ounce packet no-salt-added whole-grain pilaf

½ teaspoon dried thyme, crumbled

1 tablespoon olive oil

2 medium onions, chopped

1 cup matchstick-size carrot strips

1 medium rib of celery, thinly sliced

1 cup frozen whole-kernel corn, thawed

½ medium red bell pepper, finely chopped

½ teaspoon salt

¼ to ½ teaspoon pepper

1½ ounces finely chopped pecans, dry-roasted

Prepare the pilaf using the package directions, adding the thyme with the pilaf packet.

Meanwhile, in a large nonstick skillet, heat the oil over medium-high heat, swirling to coat the bottom. Cook the onions, carrots, and celery for 6 minutes, or until tender-crisp and beginning to richly brown. Remove from the heat.

Stir in the corn, bell pepper, salt, and pepper.

To serve, spoon the pilaf onto a platter. Spoon the vegetable mixture on top. Sprinkle with the pecans.

PER SERVING	
Calories 352	Carbohydrates 54 g
Total Fat 13.5 g	Fiber 10 g
Saturated Fat 1.5 g	Sugar 10 g
Trans Fat 0.0 g	Protein 10 g
Polyunsaturated Fat 4.0 g	DIETARY EXCHANGES:
Monounsaturated Fat 7.0 g	3 Starch
Cholesterol 0 mg	2 Vegetable
Sodium 324 mg	2 Fat

whole-grain pilaf with chicken and pecans
SERVES 4

Replace the corn with 1 cup diced cooked chicken, cooked without salt, skin and all visible fat discarded.

COOK'S TIP
If you can't find the whole-grain pilaf mix, you can substitute 2 cups of cooked brown rice, cooked without salt or margarine.

PER SERVING (with chicken and pecans)

Calories 410	Carbohydrates 54 g
Total Fat 15.0 g	Fiber 10 g
Saturated Fat 2.0 g	Sugar 10 g
Trans Fat 0.0 g	Protein 21 g
Polyunsaturated Fat 4.0 g	DIETARY EXCHANGES:
Monounsaturated Fat 7.5 g	3 Starch 1½ Fat
Cholesterol 30 mg	2 Vegetable
Sodium 350 mg	1½ Lean Meat

spinach and black bean enchiladas

SERVES 6

Dress up these hearty enchiladas with a side of seasoned brown rice or corn on the cob and sliced watermelon or other seasonal fruit.

1 pound fresh spinach leaves or 1 10-ounce package frozen leaf spinach

Cooking spray

1 15-ounce can no-salt-added black beans, rinsed and drained

½ cup salsa

¼ teaspoon ground cumin

¼ teaspoon chili powder

6 6-inch corn tortillas

½ cup fat-free sour cream

1½ to 2 teaspoons fresh lime juice

1 cup shredded reduced-fat Monterey Jack cheese

2 medium Italian plum tomatoes, diced

2 medium green onions, thinly sliced

In a soup pot or Dutch oven, bring several quarts of water to a boil over high heat. Cook the fresh spinach for 1 minute. Or prepare the frozen spinach using the package directions, omitting the salt and margarine. Drain well in a colander. Using the back of a spoon, press out as much liquid as possible.

Preheat the oven to 350°F. Lightly spray a large shallow baking pan or casserole dish with cooking spray.

In a medium bowl, stir together the spinach, black beans, salsa, cumin, and chili powder. Spoon one-sixth of the mixture down the center of one tortilla.

PER SERVING

Calories 197	Carbohydrates 27 g
Total Fat 4.0 g	Fiber 6 g
Saturated Fat 2.0 g	Sugar 6 g
Trans Fat 0.0 g	Protein 14 g
Polyunsaturated Fat 0.5 g	DIETARY EXCHANGES:
Monounsaturated Fat 1.0 g	1½ Starch
Cholesterol 14 mg	1 Vegetable
Sodium 298 mg	1 Lean Meat

Roll the tortilla around the filling, jelly-roll style. Place the tortilla with the seam side down in the baking pan. Repeat the process with the remaining tortillas and filling.

Bake for 15 minutes.

Meanwhile, stir together the sour cream and lime juice.

Remove the cooked enchiladas from the oven. Spread the sour cream mixture over the top. Sprinkle with the cheese, tomatoes, and green onions.

Bake for 5 minutes.

broiled vegetables, white beans, and tomatoes

with feta

SERVES 4

The rich flavor of broiled vegetables combined with the freshness of tomatoes and herbs makes this easy one-dish meal a perfect choice after a stress-filled day.

Cooking spray

2 medium zucchini, coarsely chopped

1 medium red bell pepper, coarsely chopped

1 medium yellow bell pepper, coarsely chopped

1 medium onion, coarsely chopped

12 ounces whole grape tomatoes or cherry tomatoes, quartered

2 tablespoons capers, rinsed and drained

2 teaspoons dried basil, crumbled

1 15-ounce can no-salt-added navy beans

¾ cup crumbled fat-free feta cheese

Preheat the broiler.

Lightly spray a large baking sheet with cooking spray. Put the zucchini, peppers, and onion in a single layer on the baking sheet. Lightly spray the vegetables with cooking spray.

Broil the vegetables about 4 inches from the heat for 10 minutes, or until richly browned, stirring halfway through.

PER SERVING	
Calories 179	Carbohydrates 32 g
Total Fat 0.5 g	Fiber 8 g
Saturated Fat 0.0 g	Sugar 12 g
Trans Fat 0.0 g	Protein 13 g
Polyunsaturated Fat 0.5 g	DIETARY EXCHANGES:
Monounsaturated Fat 0.0 g	1 Starch
Cholesterol 0 mg	3 Vegetable
Sodium 472 mg	1 Very Lean Meat

PER SERVING (with orzo)	
Calories 192	Carbohydrates 37 g
Total Fat 1.0 g	Fiber 5 g
Saturated Fat 0.0 g	Sugar 10 g
Trans Fat 0.0 g	Protein 11 g
Polyunsaturated Fat 0.5 g	DIETARY EXCHANGES:
Monounsaturated Fat 0.0 g	1½ Starch
Cholesterol 0 mg	3 Vegetable
Sodium 470 mg	½ Very Lean Meat

Meanwhile, in a medium bowl, stir together the tomatoes, capers, and basil.

Put the beans in a colander and rinse under very hot water until heated through. Drain well.

To assemble, spoon the beans onto four plates. Top with the broiled vegetables. Spoon the tomato mixture over all. Sprinkle with the feta.

variation

broiled vegetables, orzo, and tomatoes with feta

You can substitute 4 ounces dried orzo for the beans. While the vegetables are broiling, prepare the orzo using the package directions, omitting the salt and oil.

spicy lentil curry

SERVES 6

Serve this curry by itself or try it over brown rice with a dollop of fat-free plain yogurt topping each serving. For a delicious way to use leftovers, spoon the curry into whole-wheat pita pockets.

6 cups water

1½ cups dried lentils, sorted for stones and shriveled lentils and rinsed

1 teaspoon cumin seeds or ground cumin

1 teaspoon canola or corn oil

1 large onion, chopped

1 medium tomato, chopped

1 red chile pepper (optional)

1 tablespoon grated peeled gingerroot or 1 teaspoon ground ginger

½ teaspoon ground turmeric

½ teaspoon salt

1 medium garlic clove, minced

2 tablespoons snipped fresh cilantro or parsley

In a large, heavy saucepan, bring the water and lentils to a boil over medium-high heat. Reduce the heat and simmer, partially covered, for 45 to 50 minutes, or until tender, skimming off the foam and stirring occasionally.

Meanwhile, heat a medium nonstick skillet over medium-high heat. If using the cumin seeds, cook them for 1 minute, being careful not to burn them. Stir in the oil and onion. Add the ground cumin if using. Cook for 4 to 5 minutes, or until the onion is light brown, stirring occasionally.

PER SERVING

Calories 204	Carbohydrates 37 g
Total Fat 1.0 g	Fiber 8 g
Saturated Fat 0.0 g	Sugar 6 g
Trans Fat 0.0 g	Protein 15 g
Polyunsaturated Fat 0.5 g	DIETARY EXCHANGES:
Monounsaturated Fat 0.5 g	2 Starch
Cholesterol 0 mg	1 Vegetable
Sodium 204 mg	1 Very Lean Meat

Stir in the tomato and chile pepper. Cook for 5 minutes, or until the tomato is reduced to pulp, stirring frequently. Discard the chile pepper.

When the lentils are tender, stir in the tomato mixture and remaining ingredients except the cilantro. Simmer for 10 to 15 minutes.

To serve, sprinkle with the cilantro.

COOK'S TIP on Turmeric

Sometimes known as poor man's saffron because it is more affordable than the pricey saffron threads, turmeric adds a beautiful reddish-orange color to foods. It is pungent, so use it sparingly if you want only to enhance the color of your dish.

thai coconut curry
with vegetables

SERVES 4

This light yet filling stir-fry boasts a variety of vegetables and a spicy coconut-flavored sauce. Fresh lime zest and juice add a final burst of freshness. Serve over steaming brown or jasmine rice if you wish.

2 teaspoons canola or corn oil

½ medium onion, chopped

14 ounces light firm tofu, cut into ½-inch cubes

2 cups broccoli florets

2 medium carrots, thinly sliced

1 cup canned baby corn, rinsed and drained

1 cup low-sodium vegetable broth

⅔ cup light coconut milk

⅓ cup fat-free evaporated milk

2 teaspoons red curry paste (Thai-style preferred)

½ teaspoon coconut extract

2 tablespoons cornstarch

3 tablespoons water

2 teaspoons grated lime zest

1 tablespoon fresh lime juice

Pour the oil into a large nonstick skillet over medium-high heat and swirl to coat the bottom. Cook the onion for 1 to 2 minutes, or until tender-crisp.

Stir in the tofu, broccoli, carrots, and corn. Cook for 2 to 3 minutes, or until the broccoli and carrots are tender-crisp, stirring frequently.

PER SERVING	
Calories 179	Carbohydrates 21 g
Total Fat 5.5 g	Fiber 6 g
Saturated Fat 0.5 g	Sugar 7 g
Trans Fat 0.0 g	Protein 12 g
Polyunsaturated Fat 0.5 g	DIETARY EXCHANGES:
Monounsaturated Fat 2.0 g	1 Vegetable
Cholesterol 1 mg	1 Other Carbohydrate
Sodium 375 mg	1 Very Lean Meat
	1 Fat

Stir in the broth, coconut milk, evaporated milk, curry paste, and coconut extract. Reduce the heat and simmer, covered, for 2 to 3 minutes, or until the vegetables are tender.

Put the cornstarch in a cup. Add the water, stirring to dissolve. Pour into the skillet. Increase the heat to medium high and cook for 1 to 2 minutes, or until thickened, stirring occasionally.

Stir in the lime zest and juice.

COOK'S TIP on Curry Paste

A richly flavored blend of clarified butter, spices, and vinegar, curry paste is used instead of curry powder in many Indian dishes. Thai curry pastes feature a blend of ingredients that includes dried chiles, pepper, coriander, cumin, lemongrass, galanga (peppery Thai ginger), lime, garlic, and shrimp paste. You can find both types of curry paste in many supermarkets and in Asian markets.

grilled vegetable
quesadillas

SERVES 4

*Quesadillas are the answer if you need a last-minute appetizer or lunch. Our version
includes grilled vegetables—a great way to add healthy variety to your meals.*

  Cooking spray

1 medium ear of corn, shucked and desilked

1 medium red bell pepper, halved lengthwise

1 medium yellow summer squash, ends trimmed, halved lengthwise

½ small onion

¾ cup plus 2 tablespoons shredded low-fat Monterey Jack cheese

1 medium Italian plum tomato, diced

2 teaspoons fresh lime juice

¼ teaspoon chili powder

⅛ teaspoon pepper

4 6-inch corn tortillas

½ cup salsa

½ cup fat-free sour cream

Lightly spray the grill rack with cooking spray. Preheat the grill on medium high.

Lightly spray all sides of the corn, bell pepper, squash, and onion with cooking spray.

Grill the corn for 2 minutes on each side. Grill the bell pepper, squash, and onion for 1 to 2 minutes on each side. Transfer to a cutting board. Let cool for 10 minutes. Dice the bell pepper, squash, and onion. Transfer to a medium bowl. Hold the corn with the stem end down in a medium bowl. Using a sharp knife,

---

PER SERVING

Calories 193	Carbohydrates 24 g
Total Fat 6.0 g	Fiber 3 g
Saturated Fat 3.5 g	Sugar 8 g
Trans Fat 0.0 g	Protein 12 g
Polyunsaturated Fat 0.5 g	DIETARY EXCHANGES:
Monounsaturated Fat 1.5 g	1 Starch
Cholesterol 21 mg	1 Vegetable
Sodium 311 mg	1 Medium-Fat Meat

cut several rows at a time from the top down to remove the kernels. Add to the bell pepper mixture.

Stir in the Monterey Jack, tomato, lime juice, chili powder, and pepper.

Heat a nonstick griddle or large cast-iron skillet over medium heat. Lightly spray one side of a tortilla with cooking spray. Put the tortilla on the griddle with the sprayed side down. Spread a heaping ⅓ cup vegetable mixture on half the tortilla. Fold the other half over the filling. Cook for 1 to 2 minutes on each side, or until the tortilla is golden brown and the cheese has melted. Transfer to a cutting board and keep warm. Repeat with the remaining tortillas and filling.

To serve, cut the quesadillas in half and place on a platter. Top each piece with salsa and sour cream.

mediterranean strata

SERVES 6

As this savory strata bakes, your kitchen will fill with an appealing aroma similar to that of a pizzeria. The strata is an excellent choice for brunch, lunch, or dinner.

> Cooking spray
>
> 1 tablespoon olive oil
>
> 2 medium garlic cloves, minced
>
> 3 small zucchini (about 12 ounces total), diced
>
> 2 medium red bell peppers, thinly sliced
>
> 6 slices light whole-grain bread, cubed
>
> ½ cup loosely packed fresh basil leaves, coarsely chopped
>
> ½ cup cherry tomatoes, halved
>
> 1½ cups low-sodium vegetable broth
>
> 1½ cups egg substitute
>
> ¼ cup plus 2 tablespoons shredded or grated Asiago or Parmesan cheese

Preheat the oven to 350° F. Lightly spray a 13 × 9 × 2-inch baking pan with cooking spray.

In a large skillet, heat the oil over medium-high heat, swirling to coat the bottom. Heat the garlic for about 10 seconds, stirring occasionally. Watch carefully so it doesn't burn.

Stir in the zucchini and bell peppers. Cook for 5 to 6 minutes, or until tender-crisp. Transfer to the baking pan.

Gently stir in the bread, basil, and cherry tomatoes, spreading evenly.

In a medium bowl, whisk together the broth, egg substitute, and Asiago. Pour over the zucchini mixture. (Can be covered and refrigerated for up to 8 hours before baking if desired.)

PER SERVING	
Calories 139	Carbohydrates 16 g
Total Fat 4.0 g	Fiber 5 g
Saturated Fat 1.0 g	Sugar 6 g
Trans Fat 0.0 g	Protein 12 g
Polyunsaturated Fat 0.5 g	DIETARY EXCHANGES:
Monounsaturated Fat 2.0 g	½ Starch
Cholesterol 3 mg	1 Vegetable
Sodium 337 mg	1 Lean Meat

Bake for 50 to 55 minutes, or until the center is set (doesn't jiggle when gently shaken). (If refrigerated, uncover the strata before placing in a cold oven and baking at 350°F for 1 hour to 1 hour 5 minutes.) Let cool slightly before slicing.

COOK'S TIP

Because of its rich, nutty flavor, a small amount of Asiago cheese goes a long way. That can be helpful if you are watching the amount of saturated fat, cholesterol, and sodium in your diet. Experiment by substituting the same amount of Asiago (or slightly less) for the Parmesan in your favorite recipes.

rosemary-artichoke frittata

SERVES 4

This Italian omelet boasts layers of flavor and an enticing aroma.

4 ounces button mushrooms, sliced

1 14-ounce can artichoke hearts, rinsed, drained, and coarsely chopped

1 cup egg substitute

¼ cup fat-free milk

¼ cup finely chopped green onions

¼ cup finely snipped fresh parsley

½ teaspoon dried oregano, crumbled

¼ teaspoon dried rosemary, crushed

3 medium Italian plum tomatoes, thinly sliced

⅛ teaspoon salt

¼ teaspoon dried oregano, crumbled

⅛ teaspoon dried rosemary, crushed

⅔ cup shredded part-skim mozzarella cheese

In a 12-inch nonstick skillet, cook the mushrooms over medium heat for 3 to 4 minutes, or until slightly limp, stirring occasionally.

In a medium bowl, stir together the artichoke hearts, egg substitute, milk, green onions, parsley, ½ teaspoon oregano, and ¼ teaspoon rosemary. Pour over the mushrooms. Reduce the heat to medium low and cook, covered, without stirring, for 10 minutes, or until almost set (the frittata doesn't jiggle when gently shaken and appears to be very moist). Remove from the heat.

Meanwhile, preheat the broiler.

Arrange the tomato slices over the frittata. Sprinkle with the salt, ¼ teaspoon oregano, and ⅛ teaspoon rosemary. Top with the mozzarella.

PER SERVING

Calories 125	Carbohydrates 10 g
Total Fat 3.5 g	Fiber 2 g
Saturated Fat 2.0 g	Sugar 5 g
Trans Fat 0.0 g	Protein 14 g
Polyunsaturated Fat 0.0 g	DIETARY EXCHANGES:
Monounsaturated Fat 1.0 g	2 Vegetable
Cholesterol 12 mg	1½ Lean Meat
Sodium 492 mg	

Broil 3 or 4 inches from the heat for 2 minutes, or until the cheese is just beginning to turn golden. Let stand for about 5 minutes so the flavors blend and the frittata is easier to cut. Cut into 4 wedges.

COOK'S TIP

Because of the generous amount of moisture in the artichokes, it may appear that the frittata is not cooked at the recommended time. After the frittata stands for a few minutes and the cheese has melted, however, the liquid will absorb properly.

eggplant parmigiana

SERVES 6

Broiling the eggplant instead of frying it is the key to reducing the fat in this recipe. To complete the meal, add a garden salad and chunks of ciabatta.

Sauce

2 8-ounce cans no-salt-added tomato sauce

1 14-ounce can artichoke hearts, rinsed and drained

1 6-ounce can no-salt-added tomato paste

1 tablespoon Italian seasoning

2 medium garlic cloves, minced

1 teaspoon olive oil

⅛ teaspoon pepper

Dash of red hot-pepper sauce

¼ teaspoon fennel seeds, crushed (optional)

❖ ❖ ❖

Olive oil spray

1 medium eggplant (about 1 pound), cut into ⅜-inch rounds

10 ounces light firm tofu, patted dry with paper towels

White of 1 large egg

1 cup shredded part-skim mozzarella cheese

1 tablespoon all-purpose flour

⅓ cup grated or shredded Parmesan cheese

⅓ cup plain dry bread crumbs

In a food processor or blender, process the sauce ingredients for 30 seconds, or until no lumps remain. Set aside.

Preheat the broiler.

PER SERVING	
Calories 208	Carbohydrates 25 g
Total Fat 6.0 g	Fiber 6 g
Saturated Fat 3.0 g	Sugar 10 g
Trans Fat 0.0 g	Protein 15 g
Polyunsaturated Fat 0.5 g	DIETARY EXCHANGES:
Monounsaturated Fat 2.0 g	½ Starch
Cholesterol 16 mg	4 Vegetable
Sodium 425 mg	1½ Lean Meat

Lightly spray a large baking sheet with olive oil spray. Place the eggplant slices in a single layer on the baking sheet.

Broil about 4 inches from the heat for 3 to 4 minutes on each side, being careful not to burn the eggplant. Set aside to let cool.

Preheat the oven to 350°F.

In a food processor or blender, process the tofu and egg white until smooth.

In a small bowl, toss the mozzarella with the flour to keep the cheese from clumping.

In an 11 × 7 × 2-inch glass baking dish, layer the ingredients as follows: one-third sauce, one-half eggplant slices, one-third sauce, all the mozzarella, all the tofu mixture, remaining eggplant slices, remaining sauce, Parmesan, and bread crumbs.

Bake for 35 minutes. Let stand for 5 minutes before serving.

edamame stir-fry

Serve this very colorful dish warm or chilled.

> 4 cups low-sodium vegetable broth or water
>
> 2 cups frozen edamame (shelled green soybeans)
>
> Cooking spray
>
> 4 medium garlic cloves, minced
>
> 2 medium yellow summer squash, diced
>
> 1 large onion, diced
>
> 1 medium red bell pepper, diced
>
> 1 cup frozen whole-kernel corn
>
> 1 4-ounce can diced green chiles, rinsed and drained
>
> 3 tablespoons fresh lemon juice
>
> 1½ teaspoons ground coriander
>
> ½ teaspoon ground ginger
>
> ½ teaspoon salt
>
> ⅛ teaspoon pepper
>
> ¼ medium head red cabbage, thinly sliced

In a large saucepan, combine the broth and edamame. Bring to a boil over high heat. Reduce the heat and simmer, partially covered, for 6 to 7 minutes, or until tender. Drain well in a colander.

Lightly spray a medium skillet with cooking spray. Cook the garlic over medium-low heat for 30 seconds. Stir in the squash, onion, bell pepper, and corn. Cook for 5 to 7 minutes, or until tender-crisp, stirring occasionally.

Stir in the edamame and remaining ingredients except the cabbage. Cook for 1 to 2 minutes, or until warmed through.

Garnish with the cabbage.

PER SERVING	
Calories 115	Carbohydrates 17 g
Total Fat 3.0 g	Fiber 6 g
Saturated Fat 0.5 g	Sugar 6 g
Trans Fat 0.0 g	Protein 7 g
Polyunsaturated Fat 1.5 g	DIETARY EXCHANGES:
Monounsaturated Fat 0.5 g	½ Starch
Cholesterol 0 mg	1½ Vegetable
Sodium 209 mg	1 Lean Meat

bulgur and butternut squash

SERVES 4

Convenient frozen butternut squash takes center stage in this comforting main dish.

1 cup low-sodium vegetable broth

½ cup uncooked bulgur

2 teaspoons olive oil

1 medium red bell pepper, chopped

1 medium onion, chopped

2 10-ounce bags frozen diced butternut squash

¼ teaspoon salt

¼ teaspoon pepper

2 tablespoons balsamic vinegar

1 tablespoon light brown sugar

1 tablespoon Dijon mustard

¼ cup chopped pecans, dry-roasted

In a medium saucepan, bring the broth to a simmer over medium-high heat. Stir in the bulgur. Reduce the heat and simmer, covered, for 15 minutes, or until the broth is absorbed. Remove from the heat. Let stand for 5 minutes. Fluff with a fork.

Meanwhile, in a large nonstick skillet, heat the oil over medium-high heat, swirling to coat the bottom. Cook the bell pepper and onion for 3 to 4 minutes, or until tender, stirring occasionally.

Stir in the squash, salt, and pepper. Cook for 4 to 5 minutes, or until warmed through, stirring gently if you want the squash to stay chunky (no need to be careful if you want the squash more mashed).

In a small microwaveable bowl, stir together the vinegar, sugar, and mustard. Microwave on 100 percent power (high) for 15 to 20 seconds, or until warmed through. Transfer to a small serving bowl.

To serve, spoon the cooked bulgur into four soup bowls. Spoon the vegetable mixture over each serving. Sprinkle with the pecans. Serve the sauce on the side.

PER SERVING

Calories 264	Carbohydrates 46 g
Total Fat 8.5 g	Fiber 7 g
Saturated Fat 1.0 g	Sugar 13 g
Trans Fat 0.0 g	Protein 7 g
Polyunsaturated Fat 2.0 g	DIETARY EXCHANGES:
Monounsaturated Fat 4.5 g	3 Starch
Cholesterol 0 mg	1 Fat
Sodium 245 mg	

quinoa
in vegetable nests

SERVES 4

Orange carrots, yellow bell pepper, and red and green cabbage make very distinctive nests for delicately flavored quinoa.

    ¾ cup uncooked quinoa

    1½ cups water

    2 medium carrots, cut into very thin strips

    1½ cups shredded napa cabbage

    1 cup thinly sliced red cabbage

    ½ medium yellow bell pepper, cut into very thin strips

    2 teaspoons fresh lime juice

    2 teaspoons plain rice vinegar

    2 teaspoons soy sauce (lowest sodium available)

    1 medium garlic clove, minced

    ⅛ teaspoon pepper

    2 medium green onions, halved crosswise and cut into very thin strips

Rinse the quinoa in a fine strainer under cold running water for 1 to 2 minutes to remove the coating. Shake off excess water. In a medium saucepan, cook the quinoa over medium heat for about 5 minutes, stirring occasionally.

Stir in the water. Bring to a boil over high heat. Reduce the heat and simmer, covered, for 15 minutes. Remove from the heat. Let stand, covered, for 5 minutes. Transfer to a large bowl. Cover and refrigerate for at least 30 minutes.

Meanwhile, in a medium bowl, combine the carrots, cabbages, and bell pepper.

PER SERVING	
Calories 158	Carbohydrates 30 g
Total Fat 2.0 g	Fiber 4 g
Saturated Fat 0.0 g	Sugar 5 g
Trans Fat 0.0 g	Protein 6 g
Polyunsaturated Fat 1.0 g	DIETARY EXCHANGES:
Monounsaturated Fat 0.5 g	1½ Starch
Cholesterol 0 mg	1½ Vegetable
Sodium 111 mg	

Stir the remaining ingredients except the green onions into the cooled quinoa.

To assemble, spoon the carrot mixture into four shallow bowls. Make a "nest" in the center of the vegetables. Spoon the quinoa mixture into the nests. Garnish with the green onions.

COOK'S TIP

You can prepare this recipe up to four days in advance, keeping the vegetable and quinoa mixtures separate. Warm both mixtures, combine as directed above, and garnish with the green onions.

COOK'S TIP on Quinoa

Often called a supergrain because of the amount of protein and other nutrients it contains, quinoa actually is not a grain at all. It is the fruit of a plant related to spinach, Swiss chard, and beets. It looks like a grain and can be substituted for other grains, however. Look for this very nutritious ingredient in the grain section of supermarkets and health food stores.

vegetables and side dishes

asparagus
with dill and pine nuts

SERVES 4

Take advantage of fresh asparagus during its peak season, February through June, by preparing this tasty side dish. Try it with Rosemary-Dijon Fish Fillets (page 125).

   1 teaspoon olive oil

   2 medium shallots, finely chopped

   1 pound fresh asparagus spears, trimmed

   2 tablespoons shredded or grated Parmesan cheese

   1 tablespoon snipped fresh dillweed or 1 teaspoon dried, crumbled

   1 teaspoon grated lemon zest

   ⅛ teaspoon pepper

   2 tablespoons pine nuts, dry-roasted

In a large nonstick skillet, heat the oil over medium heat, swirling to coat the bottom. Cook the shallots for 1 to 2 minutes, or until tender-crisp, stirring occasionally.

   Add the asparagus. Cook for 3 to 4 minutes, or until tender-crisp, stirring occasionally.

   Stir in the remaining ingredients except the pine nuts. Cook for 1 minute, or until the Parmesan is melted, stirring occasionally.

   Sprinkle with the pine nuts.

PER SERVING

Calories 74	Carbohydrates 6 g
Total Fat 4.0 g	Fiber 3 g
Saturated Fat 1.0 g	Sugar 3 g
Trans Fat 0.0 g	Protein 5 g
Polyunsaturated Fat 1.0 g	DIETARY EXCHANGES:
Monounsaturated Fat 2.0 g	1 Vegetable
Cholesterol 2 mg	1 Fat
Sodium 46 mg	

baked beans
with chipotle peppers

SERVES 10

High-flavor chipotle peppers—dried smoked jalapeño peppers—are a great substitute for high-fat bacon or salt pork in this classic recipe.

3 15-ounce cans no-salt-added navy beans, rinsed and drained
1 large onion, chopped
½ cup water
¼ cup molasses (dark preferred)
¼ cup maple syrup
¼ cup firmly packed dark brown sugar
2 to 3 canned chipotle peppers in adobo sauce, finely chopped
2 tablespoons Worcestershire sauce (lowest sodium available)
1 teaspoon dry mustard
½ teaspoon salt
¼ teaspoon pepper

Preheat the oven to 300°F.

In a 2-quart casserole dish or a Dutch oven, stir together all the ingredients.

Bake for 1 hour. Stir. Bake for 30 minutes to 1 hour, or until the desired consistency, stirring occasionally and checking to be sure the mixture doesn't burn on the bottom. If the mixture starts to become dry, stir in small amounts of water as needed.

PER SERVING	
Calories 188	Carbohydrates 39 g
Total Fat 0.5 g	Fiber 5 g
Saturated Fat 0.0 g	Sugar 20 g
Trans Fat 0.0 g	Protein 7 g
Polyunsaturated Fat 0.0 g	DIETARY EXCHANGES:
Monounsaturated Fat 0.0 g	2 Starch
Cholesterol 0 mg	½ Other Carbohydrate
Sodium 180 mg	½ Very Lean Meat

beets in orange sauce

SERVES 6

Fresh orange sauce adds zest and flair to brightly colored beets. For an even prettier dish, garnish with orange sections.

2 quarts water

2 pounds fresh beets

Sauce

1 tablespoon sugar

1 tablespoon cornstarch

⅛ teaspoon salt

2 teaspoons grated orange zest, or to taste

⅔ cup fresh orange juice

1 teaspoon light tub margarine

❊ ❊ ❊

1 orange, peeled and divided into sections (optional)

In a large saucepan, bring the water to a boil over high heat.

Meanwhile, cut off all but 1 to 2 inches of stems from the beets. Add the beets to the boiling water. Reduce the heat and simmer, covered, for 40 to 50 minutes, or until tender. Drain well in a colander. Let cool for about 5 minutes, or until cool enough to handle. Slip the skins off. Slice the beets into wedges. Transfer to a serving bowl and cover to keep warm.

While the beets cool, in a small saucepan, stir together the sugar, cornstarch, salt, and orange zest.

Slowly add the orange juice, stirring until smooth. Cook over medium heat for 5 to 8 minutes, or until thickened, stirring constantly.

PER SERVING

Calories 93	Carbohydrates 21 g
Total Fat 0.5 g	Fiber 4 g
Saturated Fat 0.0 g	Sugar 15 g
Trans Fat 0.0 g	Protein 3 g
Polyunsaturated Fat 0.0 g	DIETARY EXCHANGES:
Monounsaturated Fat 0.0 g	3 Vegetable
Cholesterol 0 mg	½ Other Carbohydrate
Sodium 172 mg	

Add the margarine, stirring until melted. Pour over the beets. Garnish with orange sections, if using.

COOK'S TIP on Fresh Beets

Fresh beets stain what they touch, so you may want to wear disposable plastic gloves to protect your hands.

TIME-SAVER

You can substitute two 16- or 17-ounce cans of no-salt-added beets for the fresh beets. Warm them over medium heat, then drain well. Prepare the sauce as described on page 250.

sweet-and-sour broccoli and red bell pepper

SERVES 6

Take this innovative, Asian-inspired side dish along on your next picnic. It doesn't need space in the cooler, and thanks to the tangy dressing, it will perk up simple grilled chicken and meats.

1 pound fresh broccoli florets

1 medium red bell pepper, cut into thin strips

½ cup plain rice vinegar

3 tablespoons light brown sugar

1 medium green onion (green part only), thinly sliced

1 tablespoon plus 1 teaspoon soy sauce (lowest sodium available)

1 tablespoon toasted sesame oil

1 tablespoon grated peeled gingerroot

2 medium garlic cloves, minced

2 tablespoons sliced almonds, dry-roasted

In a medium saucepan, steam the broccoli and bell pepper for 5 to 7 minutes, or until tender-crisp. Plunge into cold water to stop the cooking. Drain well in a colander. Dry on paper towels. Transfer to a medium serving bowl.

In a small bowl, whisk together the remaining ingredients except the almonds. Pour over the vegetables. Toss gently to coat. Cover and refrigerate for at least 1 hour so the flavors blend.

Shortly before serving, bring to room temperature. Sprinkle with the almonds.

PER SERVING	
Calories 94	Carbohydrates 14 g
Total Fat 3.5 g	Fiber 3 g
Saturated Fat 0.5 g	Sugar 9 g
Trans Fat 0.0 g	Protein 3 g
Polyunsaturated Fat 1.5 g	DIETARY EXCHANGES:
Monounsaturated Fat 1.5 g	1½ Vegetable
Cholesterol 0 mg	½ Other Carbohydrate
Sodium 117 mg	½ Fat

roasted brussels sprouts

SERVES 4

Once you try roasted brussels sprouts with this zesty balsamic dressing, you will be hooked.

Cooking spray

8 ounces fresh brussels sprouts

Dressing

1 tablespoon balsamic vinegar

1 tablespoon Dijon mustard

2 teaspoons olive oil (extra-virgin preferred)

1 medium garlic clove, minced

½ teaspoon light brown sugar

¼ teaspoon pepper

Preheat the oven to 400°F. Lightly spray a 13 × 9 × 2-inch glass baking dish with cooking spray.

Trim the stem ends of the brussels sprouts. Discard any loose or yellow outer leaves. Cut the sprouts in half lengthwise. Transfer to the baking dish, spreading in a single layer. Lightly spray with cooking spray.

Bake for 20 to 25 minutes, or until tender when pierced with the tip of a sharp knife, stirring once or twice.

Meanwhile, in a large serving bowl, whisk together the dressing ingredients.

Stir the sprouts into the dressing to coat. Serve warm or cover and refrigerate for up to three days to serve cold.

PER SERVING

Calories 56	Carbohydrates 7 g
Total Fat 2.5 g	Fiber 2 g
Saturated Fat 0.5 g	Sugar 3 g
Trans Fat 0.0 g	Protein 2 g
Polyunsaturated Fat 0.5 g	DIETARY EXCHANGES:
Monounsaturated Fat 1.5 g	1 Vegetable
Cholesterol 0 mg	½ Fat
Sodium 92 mg	

carrot and barley pilaf

The convenience, flavor, and texture of quick-cooking barley, coupled with its health benefits, will make you want to prepare this side dish often. It pairs nicely with roasted pork tenderloin or grilled salmon.

1⅓ cups fat-free, low-sodium chicken broth

⅔ cup uncooked quick-cooking barley

1 teaspoon olive oil

2 medium carrots, shredded

2 medium green onions, thinly sliced

2 tablespoons chopped pecans, dry-roasted

½ teaspoon ground cumin

¼ teaspoon salt

⅛ teaspoon pepper

In a medium saucepan, bring the broth to a boil over medium-high heat. Stir in the barley. Reduce the heat and simmer, covered, for 10 to 12 minutes, or until the barley is tender and almost all the liquid is absorbed. Remove from the heat. Let stand, covered, for 5 minutes. Fluff with a fork.

Meanwhile, pour the oil into a medium skillet, swirling to coat the bottom. Stir in the remaining ingredients. Cook for 1 to 2 minutes, or until the carrots are tender-crisp. Stir into the cooked barley.

PER SERVING

Calories 177	Carbohydrates 31 g
Total Fat 4.5 g	Fiber 7 g
Saturated Fat 0.5 g	Sugar 3 g
Trans Fat 0.0 g	Protein 5 g
Polyunsaturated Fat 1.0 g	DIETARY EXCHANGES:
Monounsaturated Fat 2.5 g	1½ Starch
Cholesterol 0 mg	1 Vegetable
Sodium 196 mg	½ Fat

apple-lemon carrots

Tired of plain carrots? Try this distinctive dish for a change. The apple and lemon juices add a tangy sweetness.

1 pound carrots, grated

2 tablespoons frozen unsweetened apple juice concentrate, thawed

1 tablespoon fresh lemon juice

1 teaspoon light tub margarine

1 teaspoon poppy seeds

In a medium nonstick skillet, stir together the carrots, apple juice concentrate, and lemon juice. Cook over medium-high heat for 3 minutes, or until the carrots are tender, stirring constantly.

Add the margarine, stirring to coat. Transfer to a medium serving bowl. Sprinkle with the poppy seeds.

PER SERVING

Calories 46	Carbohydrates 10 g
Total Fat 0.5 g	Fiber 2 g
Saturated Fat 0.0 g	Sugar 6 g
Trans Fat 0.0 g	Protein 1 g
Polyunsaturated Fat 0.5 g	DIETARY EXCHANGES:
Monounsaturated Fat 0.0 g	½ Other Carbohydrate
Cholesterol 0 mg	
Sodium 59 mg	

cauliflower au gratin

SERVES 8

Just as satisfying as classic cauliflower with cheese sauce but updated to be heart-healthy, this soothing side dish has everything you expect: creamy texture, crisp topping, and the goodness of cauliflower.

1 medium head cauliflower (about 1½ pounds), cut into florets, or 2 10-ounce packages frozen cauliflower florets

½ teaspoon salt-free all-purpose seasoning

½ cup fat-free milk

½ cup fat-free, low-sodium chicken broth

1½ tablespoons all-purpose flour

⅛ teaspoon ground nutmeg

½ cup shredded low-fat sharp Cheddar cheese or 3 slices (about ¾ ounce each) low-fat sharp Cheddar cheese, torn into pieces

2 tablespoons panko or plain dry bread crumbs

2 tablespoons shredded or grated Parmesan cheese

If using fresh cauliflower, put it in a steamer basket. Sprinkle with the seasoning. Steam for 8 to 10 minutes, or until tender. If using frozen cauliflower, sprinkle with the seasoning and cook using the package directions. Drain well in a colander if needed. Transfer to an 8-inch square nonstick baking pan.

Preheat the oven to 350°F.

In a small saucepan, whisk together the milk, broth, flour, and nutmeg. Bring to a simmer over medium-high heat, whisking constantly to prevent scorching. Adjusting the heat if needed, simmer for 2 to 3 minutes, or until thickened, whisking constantly. Reduce the heat to medium low.

Stir in the Cheddar. Cook for 1 minute, or until melted, whisking occasionally. Pour over the cauliflower, stirring to coat.

PER SERVING	
Calories 51	Carbohydrates 7 g
Total Fat 1.0 g	Fiber 2 g
Saturated Fat 0.5 g	Sugar 3 g
Trans Fat 0.0 g	Protein 5 g
Polyunsaturated Fat 0.0 g	DIETARY EXCHANGES:
Monounsaturated Fat 0.5 g	1 Vegetable
Cholesterol 3 mg	½ Very Lean Meat
Sodium 103 mg	

In a small bowl, stir together the panko and Parmesan. Sprinkle over the cauliflower mixture.

Bake for 20 minutes, or until golden brown on top.

COOK'S TIP on Panko

Panko, or Japanese bread crumbs, are coarser, lighter, and usually lower in sodium than regular bread crumbs. Though the products are interchangeable in almost any recipe, panko gives a crisper crust. Look in the Asian section of your supermarket for panko.

individual corn puddings

SERVES 4

Looking for something different to cook when fresh corn is in abundance? Try this succulent side dish made with corn cut from the cob.

Cooking spray

1 large or 2 small ears of corn, or 1 cup frozen whole-kernel corn, thawed

1 cup fat-free milk

¼ cup egg substitute

1 tablespoon imitation bacon bits

1 tablespoon olive oil

¼ teaspoon pepper

⅓ cup all-purpose flour

Preheat the oven to 350°F. Lightly spray four 8-ounce custard cups with cooking spray. Put on a baking sheet.

If using fresh corn, in a medium bowl, hold an ear of corn with the stem end down. Using a sharp knife, cut several rows at a time from the top down to remove the kernels. Repeat if using 2 ears. Measure and reserve 1 cup kernels, using any remaining for other purposes.

In the same bowl, whisk together the remaining ingredients except the flour. Add the flour, whisking just until combined. The flour mixture will be lumpy. Stir in the reserved corn. Spoon into the custard cups.

Bake for 35 to 40 minutes, or until the center is set (doesn't jiggle when the pudding is gently shaken) or a cake tester or wooden toothpick inserted in the center comes out clean. The corn pudding will rise like a soufflé, then fall quickly when removed from the oven.

PER SERVING

Calories 132	Carbohydrates 19 g
Total Fat 4.0 g	Fiber 1 g
Saturated Fat 0.5 g	Sugar 5 g
Trans Fat 0.0 g	Protein 6 g
Polyunsaturated Fat 0.5 g	DIETARY EXCHANGES:
Monounsaturated Fat 2.5 g	1 Starch
Cholesterol 1 mg	1 Fat
Sodium 83 mg	

green beans amandine

Cook fresh green beans quickly to preserve their color and texture, then add oregano for flavor and almonds for crunch. This is an ideal side dish for roast turkey or grilled chicken or fish.

1 teaspoon light tub margarine

1 pound fresh green beans, trimmed and cut into 2-inch pieces

¼ cup low-sodium vegetable broth or fat-free, low-sodium chicken broth

1 tablespoon chopped fresh oregano or 1 teaspoon dried, crumbled

Pepper to taste

1 cup frozen pearl onions

¼ cup plain dry bread crumbs

2 tablespoons sliced almonds, dry-roasted

In a large nonstick skillet, heat the margarine over medium-high heat, swirling to coat the bottom. Cook the beans for 1 to 2 minutes, stirring constantly.

Stir in the broth, oregano, and pepper. Cook for 20 to 30 seconds.

Stir in the onions. Reduce the heat to medium low and cook, covered, for 6 to 8 minutes, or until the beans are tender-crisp. Transfer to a medium serving bowl.

Sprinkle with the bread crumbs and almonds.

COOK'S TIP on Fresh Green Beans

When green beans are in season, buy extra to freeze. Trim and slice the beans. Blanch them in boiling water to cover by 1 inch for 1 minute. Remove them from the hot water and run them under cold water. Let the beans cool, then freeze them for up to six months. For this recipe, thaw them before cooking.

PER SERVING	
Calories 78	Carbohydrates 14 g
Total Fat 1.5 g	Fiber 3 g
Saturated Fat 0.0 g	Sugar 3 g
Trans Fat 0.0 g	Protein 3 g
Polyunsaturated Fat 0.5 g	DIETARY EXCHANGES:
Monounsaturated Fat 1.0 g	2 Vegetable
Cholesterol 0 mg	½ Fat
Sodium 48 mg	

sautéed greens and cabbage

SERVES 6

Cabbage and rice vinegar enhance the flavor of the greens used in this simple dish.

3 quarts water

1 bunch collard greens, kale, turnip greens, or spinach (12 to 16 ounces), stems discarded, leaves finely chopped

⅓ medium head cabbage, coarsely shredded (2½ to 3 cups)

Olive oil spray

1 teaspoon olive oil

1 medium onion, quartered and sliced

1 medium garlic clove, minced

2 teaspoons plain rice vinegar or white wine vinegar

¼ teaspoon salt

Red hot-pepper sauce to taste

In a large saucepan or Dutch oven, bring the water to a boil over high heat. Stir in the greens. Return to a boil. Cook for 3 to 4 minutes, or until tender-crisp. Using a large slotted spoon, transfer the greens to a colander, leaving the water in the pan. Drain the greens and leave them in the colander.

Return the water to a boil. Stir in the cabbage. Cook for 1 minute. Drain in the colander with the greens.

Lightly spray a large skillet with olive oil spray. Pour in the oil, swirling to coat the bottom. Cook the onion and garlic over medium-low heat for 2 to 3 minutes, or until tender-crisp, stirring occasionally.

Stir in the greens and cabbage. Cook for 2 to 3 minutes, or until heated through, stirring occasionally.

Stir in the vinegar, salt, and hot-pepper sauce.

PER SERVING

Calories 47	Carbohydrates 9 g
Total Fat 1.0 g	Fiber 4 g
Saturated Fat 0.0 g	Sugar 4 g
Trans Fat 0.0 g	Protein 2 g
Polyunsaturated Fat 0.0 g	DIETARY EXCHANGES:
Monounsaturated Fat 0.5 g	2 Vegetable
Cholesterol 0 mg	
Sodium 172 mg	

home-fried potatoes

SERVES 6

When it's too hot to use the oven but you want meat and potatoes, serve this zippy side dish with Marinated Steak (page 185).

1 tablespoon canola or corn oil

1½ pounds small unpeeled red potatoes, cooked and quartered

2 medium shallots, chopped

1 teaspoon paprika

½ teaspoon dried rosemary, crushed

½ teaspoon dry mustard

¼ teaspoon salt

Pepper to taste

In a large, heavy nonstick skillet, heat the oil over medium-high heat, swirling to coat the bottom. Heat the potatoes on one side for 3 to 4 minutes. Turn the potatoes over.

Stir in the shallots. Cook for 3 to 4 minutes.

Stir in the remaining ingredients. Cook for 1 to 2 minutes so the flavors blend.

PER SERVING

Calories 106	Carbohydrates 19 g
Total Fat 2.5 g	Fiber 2 g
Saturated Fat 0.0 g	Sugar 1 g
Trans Fat 0.0 g	Protein 2 g
Polyunsaturated Fat 1.0 g	DIETARY EXCHANGES:
Monounsaturated Fat 0.5 g	1½ Starch
Cholesterol 0 mg	
Sodium 105 mg	

twice-baked potatoes and herbs

SERVES 4

Varying the fresh herbs gives you lots of options for these potatoes.

4 medium baking potatoes (russets preferred)

⅓ cup fat-free sour cream or fat-free plain yogurt

2 tablespoons chopped fresh herbs, such as basil, chives, thyme, marjoram, oregano, parsley, or any combination

2 tablespoons shredded or grated Parmesan cheese

1 to 2 tablespoons fat-free milk (as needed)

¼ cup shredded part-skim mozzarella cheese

Preheat the oven to 425°F.

Prick the potatoes in several places. Put on a baking sheet.

Bake for 40 minutes to 1 hour, or until tender. Transfer the potatoes to a cooling rack and let cool.

Cut a thin lengthwise slice from the top of each potato. Using a spoon, carefully scoop out all the pulp from those slices and discard the skins. Scoop out most of the pulp from each potato, leaving a thin shell (about ¼ inch thick) of pulp and skin. Put all the scooped-out pulp in a large mixing bowl.

Using an electric mixer on low speed or a potato masher, beat or mash the potato pulp. Stir in the sour cream, herbs, and Parmesan. Beat or mash until smooth. Stir in enough milk to reach the desired consistency. Spoon into the shells. Place in a medium shallow baking dish.

Sprinkle each potato with mozzarella.

Bake for 15 to 20 minutes, or until lightly browned.

PER SERVING

Calories 163	Carbohydrates 30 g
Total Fat 2.0 g	Fiber 2 g
Saturated Fat 1.0 g	Sugar 3 g
Trans Fat 0.0 g	Protein 7 g
Polyunsaturated Fat 0.0 g	DIETARY EXCHANGES:
Monounsaturated Fat 0.5 g	2 Starch
Cholesterol 10 mg	
Sodium 112 mg	

COOK'S TIP on Leftover Fresh Herbs

Small amounts of fresh herbs, such as basil, oregano, cilantro, or a mixture, are the basis for an easy herb cream cheese spread. Combine 2 tablespoons chopped fresh herbs with 1 minced garlic clove and 8 ounces low-fat cream cheese. Try a little on a whole-grain bagel or steamed red potatoes.

red and green pilaf

SERVES 4

This pretty rice dish is speckled with sliced okra or green peas and bits of red and green bell pepper and tomato, then seasoned with a touch of cayenne.

   Cooking spray
   ½ large onion, chopped
   ⅓ medium green bell pepper, chopped
   ⅓ medium red bell pepper, chopped
   ½ cup uncooked brown rice
   2 medium garlic cloves, minced
   1½ cups fat-free, low-sodium chicken broth
   ¼ teaspoon salt
   ⅛ teaspoon cayenne
   1 cup sliced fresh or frozen okra or ⅔ cup fresh or frozen green peas, thawed if frozen
   1 medium Italian plum tomato, seeds discarded, chopped

Lightly spray a medium saucepan with cooking spray. Cook the onion and bell peppers over medium-high heat for 5 minutes, stirring occasionally.

Stir in the rice and garlic. Cook for 1 minute.

Stir in the broth, salt, and cayenne. Increase the heat to high and bring to a boil. Reduce the heat and simmer, covered, for 30 minutes.

Stir in the okra. Cook, covered, for 5 to 10 minutes, or until the rice is tender and the liquid is absorbed.

Stir in the tomato. Let stand for 5 minutes before serving.

PER SERVING

Calories 117	Carbohydrates 24 g
Total Fat 1.0 g	Fiber 3 g
Saturated Fat 0.0 g	Sugar 3 g
Trans Fat 0.0 g	Protein 4 g
Polyunsaturated Fat 0.5 g	DIETARY EXCHANGES:
Monounsaturated Fat 0.5 g	1 Starch
Cholesterol 0 mg	1 Vegetable
Sodium 176 mg	

golden rice

Known as "pilau" in Indian cuisine and "pilaf" in the Middle East and Greece, this dish is intriguing regardless of what you call it.

1 cup uncooked basmati or other long-grain rice

1 cup fat-free, low-sodium chicken broth

1 cup water

1 cinnamon stick (about 3 inches long)

1 bay leaf

¼ teaspoon salt

¼ teaspoon ground turmeric or saffron

2 tablespoons slivered almonds, dry-roasted

Rinse the rice in several changes of water before cooking. Drain well in a colander.

In a medium saucepan, bring the broth and water to a boil over medium-high heat. Stir in the rice, cinnamon stick, bay leaf, and salt. Reduce the heat and simmer, covered, for 20 minutes.

Using a fork, lightly stir in the turmeric. Cook, covered, over low heat for 10 minutes, or until the rice is tender and the liquid is absorbed. Discard the cinnamon stick and bay leaf.

Sprinkle the rice mixture with the almonds just before serving.

COOK'S TIP on Basmati Rice

In Hindi, *basmati* means "fragrant," which aptly describes the aroma of this long-grain rice. Basmati rice is aged after harvest, which lessens its moisture content and intensifies its distinctive nutlike flavor. Several varieties, such as Texmati and Kasmati, are now grown in the United States. Store the rice in a cool, dry area in a sealed container away from the open air and moisture.

PER SERVING	
Calories 116	Carbohydrates 24 g
Total Fat 1.0 g	Fiber 0 g
Saturated Fat 0.0 g	Sugar 0 g
Trans Fat 0.0 g	Protein 3 g
Polyunsaturated Fat 0.5 g	DIETARY EXCHANGES:
Monounsaturated Fat 0.5 g	1½ Starch
Cholesterol 0 mg	
Sodium 108 mg	

spinach parmesan

If you have company coming, you can easily double or triple this side dish. You can even make it the night before, then quickly reheat it in the microwave.

Cooking spray

2 10-ounce packages frozen chopped spinach, thawed and squeezed dry

¾ cup finely chopped onion

½ cup fat-free sour cream

3 tablespoons shredded or grated Parmesan cheese

⅓ cup fat-free milk

¼ teaspoon garlic powder

1 tablespoon shredded or grated Parmesan cheese

Preheat the oven to 350°F.

Lightly spray a pie pan with cooking spray. In the pan, stir together all the ingredients except 1 tablespoon Parmesan. Cover with aluminum foil.

Bake for 25 minutes, or just until the onion is soft.

Sprinkle with the remaining Parmesan.

PER SERVING	
Calories 114	Carbohydrates 15 g
Total Fat 2.5 g	Fiber 5 g
Saturated Fat 1.0 g	Sugar 6 g
Trans Fat 0.0 g	Protein 11 g
Polyunsaturated Fat 0.0 g	DIETARY EXCHANGES:
Monounsaturated Fat 0.5 g	2 Vegetable
Cholesterol 9 mg	½ Other Carbohydrate
Sodium 225 mg	½ Lean Meat

wilted spinach

SERVES 4

If you like wilted spinach salad, you'll love this cooked version. The warm sweet-and-sour dressing is accented with capers and lemon zest. You can leave out the chopped egg whites to save time, but they add a nice color contrast to the dish.

1 pound fresh spinach leaves

1 teaspoon olive oil

2 medium green onions, thinly sliced

2 medium garlic cloves, minced

2 tablespoons imitation bacon bits

1 tablespoon white wine vinegar

2 teaspoons capers, rinsed and drained

1 teaspoon grated lemon zest

1 teaspoon light brown sugar

⅛ teaspoon pepper

Whites of 2 large hard-cooked eggs, chopped (yolks discarded)

Put the spinach in a colander. Rinse, leaving any water still clinging to the spinach.

In a large nonstick skillet, heat the oil over medium heat, swirling to coat the bottom. Cook the green onions and garlic for 1 to 2 minutes, or until the green onions are tender-crisp, stirring occasionally.

Stir in the spinach. Reduce the heat to medium low and cook, covered, for 3 to 4 minutes, or until the spinach is wilted and soft.

Stir in the remaining ingredients except the egg whites. Cook, covered, for 1 to 2 minutes, or until the mixture is warmed through. Transfer to a small serving bowl.

Sprinkle with the chopped egg whites.

PER SERVING

Calories 68	Carbohydrates 8 g
Total Fat 2.0 g	Fiber 3 g
Saturated Fat 0.0 g	Sugar 2 g
Trans Fat 0.0 g	Protein 6 g
Polyunsaturated Fat 0.5 g	DIETARY EXCHANGES:
Monounsaturated Fat 1.0 g	1½ Vegetable
Cholesterol 0 mg	½ Fat
Sodium 200 mg	

praline butternut squash

SERVES 8

Pureed butternut squash topped with maple-flavored fruit—this is a perfect dish for fall entertaining, especially during the holidays.

1 2- to 2½-pound butternut squash

1 cup water

1 15.25-ounce can pineapple chunks, packed in their own juice, drained

½ cup dried fruit, such as apricots, peaches, apples, or any combination, diced

2 tablespoons chopped pecans, dry-roasted

2 tablespoons maple syrup

1 tablespoon dark brown sugar

1 teaspoon grated lemon zest

Preheat the oven to 350°F.

Cut the squash in half. Using a spoon, scoop out and discard the seeds and strings. Put the squash with the cut side down in a shallow baking pan. Pour the water around the squash.

Bake for 45 to 50 minutes, or until the squash is tender. Transfer to a cooling rack and let cool for at least 15 minutes.

Using a spoon, remove the squash pulp from the skin. In a food processor, process the pulp for 1 minute, or until smooth. (You can use a potato masher if you prefer.) Spoon into a 1-quart glass casserole dish.

In a medium bowl, stir together the remaining ingredients. Spoon over the squash.

Bake for 30 minutes, or until warmed through.

PER SERVING

Calories 133	Carbohydrates 31 g
Total Fat 1.5 g	Fiber 3 g
Saturated Fat 0.0 g	Sugar 17 g
Trans Fat 0.0 g	Protein 2 g
Polyunsaturated Fat 0.5 g	DIETARY EXCHANGES:
Monounsaturated Fat 1.0 g	1 Starch
Cholesterol 0 mg	1 Fruit
Sodium 6 mg	

COOK'S TIP on Butternut Squash

Cutting butternut squash is easier if you have the right tools and a little know-how. Here's one method you might want to try: Use a sharp, sturdy knife, such as an 8- or 10-inch chef's knife. Pierce the middle of the squash with the tip of the knife and very carefully rock the knife downward to slice through the squash all the way to the round bottom end. Pull out the knife. Turn the squash so that you can cut from the same midpoint to the stem end, cutting the entire squash in half. Using a vegetable peeler or a paring knife, peel off the thick skin. Using a spoon, remove and discard the stringy fibers and seeds. Place each squash half with the cut side down so it won't rock. Cut into strips or cubes, as needed.

yellow squash sauté

The light dusting of bread crumbs adds a touch of substance to this satisfying side dish.

2 teaspoons olive oil

1 medium garlic clove, minced

2 cups thinly sliced yellow summer squash

3 tablespoons finely snipped fresh parsley

¼ cup plain dry bread crumbs

⅛ teaspoon pepper, or to taste

In a medium skillet, heat the oil over medium-high heat, swirling to coat the bottom. Cook the garlic for 30 seconds.

Stir in the squash and parsley. Cook for 5 to 7 minutes, or until the squash is tender-crisp, stirring occasionally.

Stir in the bread crumbs and pepper. Increase the heat to high and cook for 1 minute, stirring to coat.

PER SERVING

Calories 58	Carbohydrates 7 g
Total Fat 2.5 g	Fiber 1 g
Saturated Fat 0.5 g	Sugar 2 g
Trans Fat 0.0 g	Protein 2 g
Polyunsaturated Fat 0.5 g	DIETARY EXCHANGES:
Monounsaturated Fat 1.5 g	½ Starch
Cholesterol 0 mg	½ Fat
Sodium 52 mg	

sweet potatoes
in creamy cinnamon sauce

SERVES 6

The aroma of spices fills the air as this dish bakes. It's perfect for the holiday season or anytime you want a boost from vitamin-rich sweet potatoes. Serve with Pork with Savory Sauce (page 205) and steamed green beans.

1 pound sweet potatoes (about 2 large), peeled and cut crosswise into ¼-inch slices

½ cup fat-free half-and-half

2 tablespoons light brown sugar

1 teaspoon grated orange zest

½ teaspoon ground cinnamon

¼ teaspoon ground nutmeg

1 tablespoon light tub margarine

Preheat the oven to 400°F.

Arrange the sweet potato slices in even layers in an 8-inch round or square nonstick baking pan.

In a small bowl, whisk together the remaining ingredients except the margarine. Pour over the sweet potatoes.

Dot with the margarine.

Bake for 35 to 40 minutes, or until the sweet potatoes are tender, stirring once halfway through the baking time.

PER SERVING

Calories 120
Total Fat 1.0 g
  Saturated Fat 0.0 g
  Trans Fat 0.0 g
  Polyunsaturated Fat 0.0 g
  Monounsaturated Fat 0.5 g
Cholesterol 0 mg
Sodium 63 mg

Carbohydrates 26 g
  Fiber 3 g
  Sugar 10 g
Protein 3 g

DIETARY EXCHANGES:
1½ Starch

swiss chard
with hot-pepper sauce

SERVES 4

This recipe for Swiss chard takes just a matter of minutes to prepare—with delicious results.

8 ounces Swiss chard leaves with stems
½ cup fat-free, low-sodium chicken broth
½ medium onion, finely chopped
1 medium garlic clove, minced
½ cup fat-free, low-sodium chicken broth
2 teaspoons olive oil (extra-virgin preferred)
Red hot-pepper sauce to taste

Remove the stems from the Swiss chard leaves. Thinly slice the stems. Coarsely chop the leaves.

In a large skillet, bring ½ cup broth to a boil over high heat. Stir in the chard stems, onion, and garlic. Cook for 3 to 4 minutes, or until the liquid has evaporated and the vegetables are beginning to lightly brown, stirring frequently.

Stir in the remaining ½ cup broth. Bring to a boil.

Stir in the chard leaves. Return to a boil and cook for 3 minutes, or until the liquid has evaporated. Remove from the heat.

To serve, drizzle with the oil. Sprinkle with the hot-pepper sauce.

PER SERVING

Calories 42	Carbohydrates 4 g
Total Fat 2.5 g	Fiber 1 g
Saturated Fat 0.5 g	Sugar 2 g
Trans Fat 0.0 g	Protein 2 g
Polyunsaturated Fat 0.5 g	DIETARY EXCHANGES:
Monounsaturated Fat 1.5 g	½ Fat
Cholesterol 0 mg	
Sodium 137 mg	

oven-fried green tomatoes
with poppy seeds

SERVES 6

A typical end-of-summer tradition in the South is to pick the last of the garden tomatoes while they are still green, slice them, coat them with cornmeal, and fry them. This dish captures the same tradition and flavor, but without the fat.

　　Cooking spray

¼ cup egg substitute

　2 tablespoons fat-free milk

½ cup cornmeal

¼ cup all-purpose flour

　1 teaspoon poppy seeds

¼ teaspoon salt

⅛ teaspoon pepper

　1 pound green tomatoes or firm red tomatoes (about 3 medium), cut crosswise into ¼-inch slices.

Preheat the oven to 450°F. Lightly spray a baking sheet with cooking spray.

In a small bowl, whisk together the egg substitute and milk.

In a pie pan or shallow baking pan, stir together the remaining ingredients except the tomatoes.

Set the tomato slices, the bowl with the egg substitute mixture, the pan with the cornmeal mixture, and the baking sheet in a row, assembly-line fashion. Using tongs, dip the tomato slices in the egg substitute mixture, letting any excess drip off. Lightly coat both sides of the tomatoes with the cornmeal mixture. Place the tomatoes in a single layer on the baking sheet.

Bake for 10 minutes. Turn over. Bake for 5 minutes, or until golden-brown.

PER SERVING	
Calories 86	Carbohydrates 18 g
Total Fat 0.5 g	Fiber 2 g
Saturated Fat 0.0 g	Sugar 4 g
Trans Fat 0.0 g	Protein 4 g
Polyunsaturated Fat 0.5 g	DIETARY EXCHANGES:
Monounsaturated Fat 0.0 g	1 Starch
Cholesterol 0 mg	
Sodium 130 mg	

italian-style zucchini slices

SERVES 6

Bring some Italian flair to your meal. Herbs and spices blend with Parmesan cheese and crunchy almonds to make this side dish special.

> 1 teaspoon canola or corn oil
>
> 8 small zucchini (about 4 ounces each), cut crosswise into ½-inch slices
>
> ½ cup whole-wheat bread crumbs, toasted
>
> ¼ cup finely snipped fresh parsley
>
> 2 tablespoons minced almonds, dry-roasted
>
> 1 tablespoon shredded or grated Parmesan cheese
>
> 1 tablespoon chopped fresh oregano or 1 teaspoon dried, crumbled
>
> 1 medium garlic clove, minced
>
> Pepper to taste

In a large nonstick skillet, heat the oil over medium-high heat, swirling to coat the bottom. Cook the zucchini for 8 to 10 minutes, or just until tender and lightly browned, stirring frequently.

Meanwhile, in a medium bowl, stir together the remaining ingredients. Gently stir into the cooked zucchini to coat thoroughly.

PER SERVING

Calories 60	Carbohydrates 8 g
Total Fat 2.5 g	Fiber 2 g
Saturated Fat 0.5 g	Sugar 3 g
Trans Fat 0.0 g	Protein 3 g
Polyunsaturated Fat 0.5 g	DIETARY EXCHANGES:
Monounsaturated Fat 1.0 g	1 Vegetable
Cholesterol 1 mg	½ Fat
Sodium 58 mg	

ratatouille

SERVES 6

Excellent with chicken or fish, this French stew of vegetables is also wonderful served hot on a baked potato or cold with crusty whole-grain bread. Ratatouille is best made a day ahead so the flavors blend.

1 teaspoon olive oil

2 medium onions, sliced

1 large eggplant, peeled (unless very young), cut into 1-inch cubes

4 medium zucchini, cut into ½-inch slices

2 medium red, green, or yellow bell peppers, or any combination, chopped

2 large tomatoes, chopped

1 tablespoon chopped fresh thyme or 1 teaspoon dried, crumbled

1 tablespoon chopped fresh oregano or 1 teaspoon dried, crumbled

1 tablespoon chopped fresh basil or 1 teaspoon dried, crumbled

2 medium garlic cloves, minced

¼ teaspoon salt

Pepper to taste

In a large, heavy nonstick skillet, heat the oil over medium-high heat, swirling to coat the bottom. Cook the onions for 2 to 3 minutes, or until soft, stirring occasionally.

Stir in the remaining ingredients. Reduce the heat and simmer, covered, for 30 to 45 minutes, or until the vegetables are thoroughly cooked, stirring occasionally to prevent sticking. Cook, uncovered, for 5 minutes to reduce the liquid.

Serve warm or transfer to a covered container and refrigerate to serve chilled.

PER SERVING

Calories 88	Carbohydrates 18 g
Total Fat 1.5 g	Fiber 7 g
Saturated Fat 0.0 g	Sugar 10 g
Trans Fat 0.0 g	Protein 4 g
Polyunsaturated Fat 0.5 g	DIETARY EXCHANGES:
Monounsaturated Fat 0.5 g	3 Vegetable
Cholesterol 0 mg	½ Fat
Sodium 166 mg	

breads
and
breakfast
dishes

speckled spoon bread

SERVES 6

This soufflélike bread requires a spoon for serving, hence its name. The bread may deflate slightly when it comes out of the oven, but it will still be light.

Cooking spray
1 cup water
½ cup cornmeal
½ cup canned no-salt-added or frozen whole-kernel corn
¼ cup finely chopped green onions (green part only)
2 tablespoons chopped pimiento, patted dry with paper towels
1 tablespoon light tub margarine
2 medium garlic cloves, minced
½ teaspoon salt-free all-purpose seasoning blend
⅛ teaspoon pepper
¾ cup fat-free milk
¼ cup egg substitute
1 teaspoon baking powder
Whites of 3 large eggs

Preheat the oven to 325° F. Lightly spray a 1½-quart glass casserole dish with cooking spray. Set aside.

In a medium saucepan, stir together the water and cornmeal. Bring to a boil over high heat. Reduce the heat to medium low. Cook for about 1 minute, or until very thick, stirring constantly. Remove from the heat.

Stir in the corn, green onions, pimiento, margarine, garlic, seasoning blend, and pepper.

Stir in the milk.

PER SERVING

Calories 90	Carbohydrates 16 g
Total Fat 1.0 g	Fiber 1 g
Saturated Fat 0.0 g	Sugar 3 g
Trans Fat 0.0 g	Protein 5 g
Polyunsaturated Fat 0.5 g	DIETARY EXCHANGES:
Monounsaturated Fat 0.5 g	1 Starch
Cholesterol 1 mg	
Sodium 148 mg	

In a small bowl, stir together the egg substitute and baking powder. Stir into the cornmeal mixture.

Using an electric mixer, in a small stainless steel or glass mixing bowl, beat the egg whites until stiff peaks form (the peaks don't fall when the beaters are lifted). Fold into the cornmeal mixture, just until no whites show. Gently spoon into the baking dish.

Bake for 50 minutes to 1 hour, or until a knife inserted in the center comes out clean.

zucchini bread

SERVES 16

This loaf bread combines good nutrition and great taste in one almost-foolproof recipe.

Cooking spray
1½ cups all-purpose flour
½ cup firmly packed light brown sugar
1½ teaspoons baking powder
½ teaspoon ground cinnamon
¼ teaspoon baking soda
⅛ teaspoon salt
1 cup shredded zucchini

¼ cup raisins
1 tablespoon finely chopped walnuts, dry-roasted
½ cup pineapple juice
¼ cup egg substitute
1 tablespoon canola or corn oil
1 tablespoon light corn syrup
½ teaspoon vanilla extract

Preheat the oven to 350°F. Lightly spray a 9 × 5 × 3-inch loaf pan with cooking spray.

In a large bowl, combine the flour, brown sugar, baking powder, cinnamon, baking soda, and salt.

Stir in the zucchini, raisins, and walnuts.

In a small bowl, whisk together the remaining ingredients. Pour into the flour mixture, stirring just until moistened. Pour the batter into the pan.

Bake for 50 minutes to 1 hour, or until a cake tester or wooden toothpick inserted in the center of the loaf comes out clean. Remove from the oven and let cool in the pan for 10 minutes. Invert onto a cooling rack and let cool completely. Cut into 16 slices.

Wrap any extra bread in plastic wrap and refrigerate for up to seven days.

PER SERVING

Calories 98	Carbohydrates 20 g
Total Fat 1.5 g	Fiber 1 g
Saturated Fat 0.0 g	Sugar 10 g
Trans Fat 0.0 g	Protein 2 g
Polyunsaturated Fat 0.5 g	DIETARY EXCHANGES:
Monounsaturated Fat 0.5 g	1½ Other Carbohydrate
Cholesterol 0 mg	
Sodium 88 mg	

oat bran muffins

You've heard about the healthfulness of oat bran—now taste how good it can be. The almond extract "stretches" the nutty flavor of the pecans. Make an extra batch to freeze so you can enjoy these moist muffins at breakfast, lunch, or snack time.

Cooking spray (optional)

2½ cups uncooked oat bran

¼ cup firmly packed light brown sugar

¼ cup dried currants

2 tablespoons chopped pecans, dry-roasted

1 tablespoon baking powder

¼ teaspoon salt

¾ cup fat-free milk

Whites of 4 large eggs, lightly beaten

¼ cup honey

2 tablespoons canola or corn oil

1 teaspoon almond extract

1 teaspoon vanilla extract

Preheat the oven to 350°F. Lightly spray a 12-cup muffin pan and a 6-cup muffin pan with cooking spray or use paper bake cups.

In a large bowl, stir together the oat bran, brown sugar, currants, pecans, baking powder, and salt.

In a small bowl, whisk together the remaining ingredients. Stir into the oat bran mixture just until moistened. Spoon into the muffin cups.

Bake for 20 to 25 minutes, or until light brown. Serve warm or at room temperature.

PER SERVING

Calories 92	Carbohydrates 18 g
Total Fat 3.0 g	Fiber 2 g
Saturated Fat 0.5 g	Sugar 9 g
Trans Fat 0.0 g	Protein 4 g
Polyunsaturated Fat 1.0 g	DIETARY EXCHANGES:
Monounsaturated Fat 1.5 g	1 Starch
Cholesterol 0 mg	½ Fat
Sodium 118 mg	

oatmeal-fruit muffins

SERVES 12

What a find: so many healthy ingredients in such tasty muffins!

Cooking spray (optional)
1 cup all-purpose flour
¾ cup uncooked old-fashioned or quick-cooking rolled oats
⅓ cup toasted wheat germ
2 teaspoons baking powder
1 teaspoon ground cinnamon
½ teaspoon baking soda
⅛ teaspoon salt
¾ cup fat-free milk
½ cup firmly packed light brown sugar
¼ cup egg substitute
¼ cup unsweetened applesauce
½ teaspoon vanilla extract
½ cup snipped dried figs or dried apricots

Preheat the oven to 400°F. Lightly spray a 12-cup muffin pan with cooking spray or use paper bake cups.

In a medium bowl, stir together the flour, oats, wheat germ, baking powder, cinnamon, baking soda, and salt. Make a well in the center.

In another medium bowl, stir together the remaining ingredients except the figs. Stir into the well just until moistened. The batter should be lumpy.

Fold in the figs. Spoon into the muffin cups.

Bake for 10 to 12 minutes, or until a wooden toothpick or cake tester inserted in the center comes out clean. Transfer to a cooling rack and let cool for 5 minutes.

PER SERVING

Calories 126	Carbohydrates 27 g
Total Fat 1.0 g	Fiber 2 g
Saturated Fat 0.0 g	Sugar 13 g
Trans Fat 0.0 g	Protein 4 g
Polyunsaturated Fat 0.5 g	DIETARY EXCHANGES:
Monounsaturated Fat 0.0 g	1 Starch
Cholesterol 0 mg	1 Other Carbohydrate
Sodium 165 mg	

cardamom-lemon muffins

SERVES 24

Cardamom adds a distinctive flavor to and enhances the sweetness of these muffins. Instead of using a lot of fat for moistness, this recipe calls for applesauce.

Cooking spray (optional)

2 cups unsweetened applesauce

Whites of 4 large eggs

½ cup pineapple juice

½ cup honey

2 tablespoons canola or corn oil

¼ teaspoon almond extract

Grated zest of 1 medium lemon

2½ cups uncooked oat bran

2 cups all-purpose flour

2 teaspoons baking powder

1½ teaspoons baking soda

1 teaspoon ground cardamom

Preheat the oven to 400°F. Lightly spray two 12-cup muffin pans with cooking spray or use paper bake cups.

In a large bowl, stir together the applesauce, egg whites, pineapple juice, honey, oil, almond extract, and lemon zest.

In another large bowl, whisk together the remaining ingredients. Stir into the applesauce mixture just until moistened. The batter should be lumpy. Spoon into the muffin cups.

Put the muffins in the oven and reduce the heat to 375°F. Bake for 18 to 20 minutes, or until golden brown. Serve warm or at room temperature.

PER SERVING

Calories 109	Carbohydrates 23 g
Total Fat 2.0 g	Fiber 2 g
Saturated Fat 0.0 g	Sugar 9 g
Trans Fat 0.0 g	Protein 3 g
Polyunsaturated Fat 0.5 g	DIETARY EXCHANGES:
Monounsaturated Fat 1.0 g	1 Starch
Cholesterol 0 mg	½ Other Carbohydrate
Sodium 123 mg	

pumpkin-pie coffeecake

SERVES 12

Yes, this is a coffeecake, but it tastes like pumpkin pie. The bonus is that you can enjoy this rich-tasting treat any time from breakfast through dinner.

Coffeecake

2 tablespoons canola or corn oil, divided use

1¼ cups low-fat buttermilk

1 cup wheat-bran cereal buds

1 cup canned solid-pack pumpkin (not pie filling)

1½ teaspoons vanilla extract or vanilla, butter, and nut flavoring

Whites of 2 large eggs or ¼ cup egg substitute

1 cup all-purpose flour

½ cup sugar

½ cup finely chopped pecans

2 teaspoons baking powder

2 teaspoons ground cinnamon

½ teaspoon ground nutmeg

¼ teaspoon salt

¼ teaspoon ground allspice (optional)

Topping

¼ cup confectioners' sugar

1 tablespoon low-fat buttermilk

Preheat the oven to 400°F. Coat a 9-inch round cake pan with 1 teaspoon oil.

In a large bowl, stir together the remaining 1 tablespoon plus 2 teaspoons oil, 1¼ cups buttermilk, cereal, pumpkin, and vanilla. Let stand for 15 minutes so the cereal softens. Stir in the egg whites.

PER SERVING	
Calories 177	Carbohydrates 29 g
Total Fat 6.5 g	Fiber 5 g
Saturated Fat 0.5 g	Sugar 15 g
Trans Fat 0.0 g	Protein 4 g
Polyunsaturated Fat 2.0 g	DIETARY EXCHANGES:
Monounsaturated Fat 3.5 g	1 Starch
Cholesterol 1 mg	1 Other Carbohydrate
Sodium 205 mg	1 Fat

Meanwhile, in a medium bowl, stir together the remaining cake ingredients. Add to the bran mixture, stirring just to moisten and blend in the dry ingredients. Spoon into the cake pan, smoothing the top.

Bake for 30 minutes, or until a cake tester or wooden toothpick inserted in the center comes out clean. Transfer to a cooling rack and let cool completely, about 1 hour. Turn out onto a plate.

In a small bowl, whisk together the topping ingredients. Drizzle over the cooled cake. Cut into 12 wedges.

gingerbread pancakes
with apple-berry topping

SERVES 4

You don't need cold weather to enjoy these pancakes. In fact, they're so good, you'll look for excuses to eat them for dinner!

1 cup all-purpose flour

2 tablespoons sugar

2 teaspoons baking powder

½ teaspoon ground cinnamon

¼ teaspoon ground ginger

¼ teaspoon ground allspice

¾ cup fat-free milk

¼ cup egg substitute

2 tablespoons molasses

1 tablespoon canola or corn oil

8 ounces canned light apple pie filling

½ cup blueberry, boysenberry, or strawberry syrup

¼ cup dried cranberries

In a medium bowl, stir together the flour, sugar, baking powder, cinnamon, ginger, and allspice.

In a small bowl, whisk together the milk, egg substitute, molasses, and oil. Stir into the flour mixture just until combined. (Do not overmix or the pancakes will be tough.)

Heat a nonstick griddle over medium heat. Test the griddle by sprinkling a few drops of water on it. If the water evaporates quickly, the griddle is ready.

PER SERVING

Calories 370	Carbohydrates 78 g
Total Fat 4.0 g	Fiber 2 g
Saturated Fat 0.5 g	Sugar 50 g
Trans Fat 0.0 g	Protein 6 g
Polyunsaturated Fat 1.0 g	DIETARY EXCHANGES:
Monounsaturated Fat 2.0 g	2 Starch
Cholesterol 1 mg	3 Other Carbohydrate
Sodium 262 mg	½ Fat

Pour about ¼ cup batter onto the griddle. Cook for 2 to 3 minutes, or until bubbles appear all over the surface. Flip pancake over. Cook for 2 minutes, or until the bottom is golden brown. Repeat with the remaining batter. (You should have 8 pancakes.)

Meanwhile, in a small saucepan, heat the pie filling over low heat for 2 to 3 minutes, or until warmed through.

To serve, place 2 pancakes on each of four plates. Spoon about 2 tablespoons syrup on each serving. Top each with pie filling. Sprinkle with cranberries.

COOK'S TIP

Look for fruit-flavored syrup near the pancake syrup at the supermarket.

dutch baby

Part of the fun of making this pancake is watching it puff up as it bakes. Then it deflates, becoming a bowl that is just right for holding a lemony confectioners' sugar drizzle and vibrantly colored fresh fruit.

    Cooking spray

Batter

½ cup fat-free milk

½ cup egg substitute

2 tablespoons light brown sugar

2 teaspoons canola or corn oil

1 teaspoon lemon zest

1 teaspoon vanilla extract

¼ teaspoon ground cinnamon

½ cup all-purpose flour

    ✳ ✳ ✳

¼ cup confectioners' sugar

2 tablespoons fresh lemon juice

1½ cups sliced fresh hulled strawberries

2 kiwifruit, peeled and thinly sliced

Preheat the oven to 425°F. Heat a 10-inch cast-iron skillet in the oven while preparing the batter. Or lightly spray a 9-inch round cake pan with cooking spray. The pan does not need to be preheated.

In a medium bowl, whisk together all the batter ingredients except the flour. Sift the flour over the batter. Whisk just until combined.

PER SERVING	
Calories 138	Carbohydrates 26 g
Total Fat 2.0 g	Fiber 2 g
Saturated Fat 0.0 g	Sugar 15 g
Trans Fat 0.0 g	Protein 4 g
Polyunsaturated Fat 0.5 g	DIETARY EXCHANGES:
Monounsaturated Fat 1.0 g	½ Starch
Cholesterol 0 mg	½ Fruit
Sodium 54 mg	1 Other Carbohydrate
	½ Fat

Remove the skillet from the oven and lightly spray with cooking spray. Immediately pour the batter into the skillet or cake pan.

Bake for 15 to 20 minutes, or until the pancake is puffy and set in the center (doesn't jiggle when gently shaken). Transfer the pan to a heatproof surface, such as a cooling rack.

To assemble, transfer the pancake to a platter. Mound the confectioners' sugar in the middle of the pancake. Pour the lemon juice over the sugar, stirring gently and distributing over the pancake. (Don't worry if you have a few small lumps.) Arrange the strawberries and kiwifruit over the pancake. Cut into 6 wedges.

breakfast tortilla wrap

SERVES 4

This hearty breakfast sandwich makes an easy meal for busy people on the go.

½ cup egg substitute

⅛ teaspoon pepper

1 cup frozen fat-free shredded potatoes

½ medium red bell pepper, diced

1 ounce Canadian bacon, chopped

⅛ teaspoon pepper

1 teaspoon canola or corn oil

4 6-inch corn tortillas

¼ cup shredded low-fat Cheddar cheese

If using an oven rather than a microwave to warm the tortillas, preheat to 350°F.

In a small nonstick skillet, cook the egg substitute and ⅛ teaspoon pepper over medium-low heat for 3 to 4 minutes, or until cooked through, stirring occasionally. Set aside.

Meanwhile, in a medium bowl, stir together the potatoes, bell pepper, Canadian bacon, and ⅛ teaspoon pepper.

In a medium nonstick skillet, heat the oil over medium-high heat, swirling to coat the bottom. Spread the potato mixture evenly in the skillet. Cook for 6 to 7 minutes on one side, or until the potatoes are a light golden brown. Using a spatula, turn the potato mixture over. Cook for 5 to 6 minutes, or until light golden brown.

Meanwhile, wrap the tortillas in aluminum foil and warm in the oven for 5 minutes. Or wrap the tortillas in damp paper towels and microwave using the package directions.

PER SERVING	
Calories 121	Carbohydrates 17 g
Total Fat 2.5 g	Fiber 2 g
Saturated Fat 0.5 g	Sugar 1 g
Trans Fat 0.0 g	Protein 8 g
Polyunsaturated Fat 0.5 g	DIETARY EXCHANGES:
Monounsaturated Fat 1.0 g	1 Starch
Cholesterol 5 mg	1 Very Lean Meat
Sodium 236 mg	

To assemble, layer the ingredients across the tortilla as follows: one-fourth of the scrambled egg substitute, one-fourth of the potato mixture, and one-fourth of the cheese. Roll up jelly-roll style, starting at the bottom. Secure with a toothpick, if desired. Repeat with the remaining ingredients.

Serve immediately or refrigerate in an airtight container or individually wrapped in plastic wrap. To reheat, place 1 or 2 wraps on a microwaveable plate. Microwave on 100 percent power (high) for 1 to 1½ minutes, or until heated through.

french toast
with peach and praline topping

SERVES 8

For a special breakfast on the weekend—or any other time—try this scrumptious French toast made with whole-grain bread and a fruit topping.

1 cup fat-free milk

½ cup egg substitute

½ teaspoon ground cinnamon

2 teaspoons canola or corn oil, divided use

8 slices reduced-calorie whole-grain bread

1 15-ounce can sliced peaches in juice, undrained

⅓ cup chopped pecans, dry-roasted

2 tablespoons light brown sugar

1 tablespoon fresh lemon juice

1 teaspoon vanilla extract

¼ teaspoon ground cinnamon

¼ teaspoon ground nutmeg

Preheat the oven to 200°F.

In a medium shallow bowl, whisk together the milk, egg substitute, and ½ teaspoon cinnamon.

Heat a nonstick griddle over medium heat. Heat 1 teaspoon oil on the griddle, swirling to coat the surface.

Dip 4 bread slices, one at a time, in the milk mixture to coat both sides. Let any excess drip off. Cook for 2 to 3 minutes on each side, or until golden brown. Transfer to a nonstick metal baking pan (it is okay if the slices overlap). Keep warm in the oven. Repeat.

In a medium saucepan, stir together the peaches with juice, pecans, brown sugar, lemon juice, vanilla, ¼ teaspoon cinnamon, and nutmeg. Bring to a simmer over medium-high heat. Reduce the heat and simmer for 3 to 4 minutes so the flavors blend, stirring occasionally.

Put the French toast on plates. Spoon the topping over each serving.

PER SERVING

Calories 152
Total Fat 5.0 g
  Saturated Fat 0.5 g
  Trans Fat 0.0 g
  Polyunsaturated Fat 1.5 g
  Monounsaturated Fat 2.5 g
Cholesterol 1 mg
Sodium 169 mg

Carbohydrates 23 g
  Fiber 5 g
  Sugar 12 g
Protein 5 g

DIETARY EXCHANGES:
1 Starch
½ Fruit
1 Fat

---

pecan-topped cinnamon oatmeal

SERVES 4

Start the day off right with this sweetly tangy oatmeal.

1 tablespoon plus 1 teaspoon sugar

¾ teaspoon ground cinnamon

2¾ cups fat-free milk

1½ cups uncooked old-fashioned rolled oats

⅓ cup sweetened dried cranberries

⅛ teaspoon salt

1 teaspoon grated orange zest

1 teaspoon light tub margarine

½ teaspoon vanilla extract or vanilla, butter, and nut flavoring

2 ounces finely chopped pecans

In a small bowl, stir together the sugar and cinnamon.

In a large saucepan, bring the milk to a boil over medium-high heat. Stir in the oats, cranberries, salt, and all but 2 teaspoons cinnamon sugar. Reduce the heat and simmer for 5 minutes, stirring occasionally.

Stir in the orange zest, margarine, and vanilla. Let stand for 3 minutes so the flavors blend.

Spoon the oatmeal into four bowls. Sprinkle with the pecans and the reserved 2 teaspoons cinnamon sugar.

PER SERVING	
Calories 327	Carbohydrates 44 g
Total Fat 12.5 g	Fiber 5 g
Saturated Fat 1.5 g	Sugar 22 g
Trans Fat 0.0 g	Protein 12 g
Polyunsaturated Fat 4.0 g	DIETARY EXCHANGES:
Monounsaturated Fat 6.5 g	1½ Starch
Cholesterol 3 mg	½ Fat-Free Milk
Sodium 152 mg	1 Other Carbohydrate
	2 Fat

beverages

sangria-style pomegranate coolers

SERVES 6

Jewel-toned pomegranate juice combines delightfully with tangy citrus juices to make this refreshing drink.

> 2 cups pomegranate juice combination, such as blueberry-pomegranate, or plain pomegranate juice
>
> 2 medium limes, quartered
>
> 1 medium orange, cut into 8 wedges
>
> 2 cups diet ginger ale or champagne, chilled

Pour the pomegranate juice into a medium pitcher. Squeeze the juice of the limes and orange into the pitcher. Stir in the squeezed rinds. Cover with plastic wrap and refrigerate until chilled. (For a more pronounced citrus flavor, refrigerate for up to 24 hours.)

Just before serving, stir in the ginger ale. Serve with or without ice.

COOK'S TIP

Look in the produce section of your supermarket for pomegranate juice bottled alone or combined with other fruit juices.

PER SERVING (with ginger ale)

Calories 57	Carbohydrates 14 g
Total Fat 0.0 g	Fiber 0 g
Saturated Fat 0.0 g	Sugar 13 g
Trans Fat 0.0 g	Protein 1 g
Polyunsaturated Fat 0.0 g	DIETARY EXCHANGES:
Monounsaturated Fat 0.0 g	1 Fruit
Cholesterol 0 mg	
Sodium 30 mg	

PER SERVING (with champagne)

Calories 110	Carbohydrates 15 g
Total Fat 0.0 g	Fiber 0 g
Saturated Fat 0.0 g	Sugar 13 g
Trans Fat 0.0 g	Protein 1 g
Polyunsaturated Fat 0.0 g	DIETARY EXCHANGES:
Monounsaturated Fat 0.0 g	1 Fruit
Cholesterol 0 mg	1 Other Carbohydrate
Sodium 14 mg	

orange-strawberry froth

When you crave something sweet, try this thick, fruity blend.

2 cups fresh orange juice

1½ cups canned apricot nectar

1 cup frozen unsweetened strawberries

In a food processor or blender, process all the ingredients for 20 seconds, or until smooth and frothy. Pour into six glasses and serve immediately.

COOK'S TIP on Canned Nectar

Look for various fruit nectars in the canned juice section of your supermarket. Experiment with different ones in this recipe for a refreshing change.

PER SERVING

Calories 81	Carbohydrates 20 g
Total Fat 0.0 g	Fiber 1 g
Saturated Fat 0.0 g	Sugar 16 g
Trans Fat 0.0 g	Protein 1 g
Polyunsaturated Fat 0.0 g	DIETARY EXCHANGES:
Monounsaturated Fat 0.0 g	1½ Fruit
Cholesterol 0 mg	
Sodium 3 mg	

spiced apple cider

SERVES 16

A warm fire. A cozy room. A comfy chair. This cold-weather favorite completes the scene.

2 quarts unsweetened apple
  juice or apple cider

1 quart water

3 plain tea bags

½ medium orange, thinly
  sliced

½ medium lemon, thinly sliced

2 cinnamon sticks, each about
  3 inches long

12 whole allspice

6 whole cloves

  Ground allspice to taste

1 medium orange, thinly
  sliced (optional)

1 medium lemon, thinly sliced
  (optional)

In a large nonreactive saucepan, bring the apple juice, water, tea bags, slices of ½ orange and ½ lemon, cinnamon sticks, whole allspice, and cloves to a boil over high heat. Reduce the heat and simmer for 3 minutes. Discard the tea bags, orange and lemon slices, cinnamon sticks, allspice, and cloves. Simmer the liquid for 5 minutes.

Stir in the ground allspice.

Serve hot or cover and refrigerate to serve chilled. Garnish with the remaining orange and lemon slices.

COOK'S TIP on Bouquet Garni

For easy removal of the whole allspice and cloves from the cider mixture, make a bouquet garni. Tie the spices in cheesecloth or put them in a tea ball. When the cider is ready, you won't have to round up the spices, piece by piece. Most often made of parsley, thyme, and bay leaf, bouquets garnis are time-savers in soups and stews also.

PER SERVING	
Calories 59	Carbohydrates 15 g
Total Fat 0.0 g	Fiber 0 g
Saturated Fat 0.0 g	Sugar 14 g
Trans Fat 0.0 g	Protein 0 g
Polyunsaturated Fat 0.0 g	DIETARY EXCHANGES:
Monounsaturated Fat 0.0 g	1 Fruit
Cholesterol 0 mg	
Sodium 6 mg	

chocolate cappuccino

SERVES 4

Besides tasting terrific, this cappuccino is convenient—you don't need an espresso/cappuccino machine to prepare it. A blender works well for frothing the milk. (See the Cook's Tip below if you do own an espresso/cappuccino machine.)

2 cups fat-free milk

1⅓ cups strong hot coffee (dark roast preferred)

¼ cup fat-free chocolate syrup

1 tablespoon plus 1 teaspoon sugar

¼ cup fat-free frozen whipped topping, thawed in refrigerator

¼ teaspoon unsweetened cocoa powder

In a medium saucepan, heat the milk over medium heat for 2 to 3 minutes, or until warm (do not boil). Pour into a blender. Blend on high speed for 1 minute.

To assemble, pour ⅓ cup coffee into each of four coffee or cappuccino mugs. Stir 1 tablespoon syrup and 1 teaspoon sugar into each. Pour ½ cup milk into each (do not stir). Top each serving with a dollop of whipped topping and a sprinkle of cocoa powder.

COOK'S TIP

If you have an espresso/cappuccino machine, brew the coffee and steam and froth the milk according to the manufacturer's directions. Add the chocolate syrup, sugar, and whipped topping as directed above.

PER SERVING	
Calories 122	Carbohydrates 25 g
Total Fat 0.0 g	Fiber 0 g
Saturated Fat 0.0 g	Sugar 19 g
Trans Fat 0.0 g	Protein 4 g
Polyunsaturated Fat 0.0 g	DIETARY EXCHANGES:
Monounsaturated Fat 0.0 g	½ Fat-Free Milk
Cholesterol 3 mg	1 Other Carbohydrate
Sodium 68 mg	

desserts

chocolate custard cake
with raspberries

SERVES 10

You'll love the richness and creamy texture of this flanlike cake, but it doesn't contain any flour or leavening agent so it won't be a high riser. Serve it warm or chilled with a double dose of raspberries.

  Cooking spray

Cake

  1 14-ounce can fat-free sweetened condensed milk

  1¼ cups egg substitute

  ½ cup fat-free milk

  ½ cup sugar

  ¼ cup unsweetened cocoa powder

  ¼ cup fat-free chocolate syrup

  ❋ ❋ ❋

  1¼ cups all-fruit seedless raspberry spread

  10 ounces fresh or frozen unsweetened raspberries, thawed if frozen

  1 tablespoon confectioners' sugar

Preheat the oven to 350° F. Line the bottom of an 8-inch nonstick round cake pan with parchment paper or wax paper. If using wax paper, spray the top with cooking spray.

In a large bowl, whisk together the cake ingredients. Pour into the cake pan. Place the cake pan in the middle of a large baking pan (the bottom of a broiler pan works well). Carefully fill the baking pan with warm water to a depth of about 1 inch.

PER SERVING	
Calories 298	Carbohydrates 66 g
Total Fat 0.5 g	Fiber 2 g
Saturated Fat 0.0 g	Sugar 59 g
Trans Fat 0.0 g	Protein 7 g
Polyunsaturated Fat 0.0 g	DIETARY EXCHANGES:
Monounsaturated Fat 0.0 g	4½ Other Carbohydrate
Cholesterol 5 mg	1 Very Lean Meat
Sodium 114 mg	

Bake for 40 to 45 minutes, or until a cake tester or wooden toothpick inserted in the center comes out clean. Carefully transfer the cake pan (without the water) to a cooling rack. Let the cake cool for 10 minutes. Carefully invert onto a cake plate or platter and remove the paper. Let cool for 15 minutes.

Meanwhile, in a small saucepan, melt the fruit spread over low heat, stirring occasionally.

Top the cake with a thin coating of the fruit spread, reserving some spread to serve with the cake. Sprinkle with half the raspberries.

To serve, spoon the reserved fruit spread onto 10 dessert plates. Cut the cake into 10 slices. Place on the fruit spread. Top with the remaining raspberries. Dust lightly with the confectioners' sugar.

lemon poppy seed cake

SERVES 10

Perfect with an afternoon cup of tea, this moist cake has a bold lemon flavor accented with the delicate crunch of poppy seeds.

    Cooking spray
 2 cups all-purpose flour
 ¾ cup sugar
 1 tablespoon poppy seeds
 2 teaspoons baking powder
 ¼ teaspoon baking soda
 ¼ teaspoon salt
 ¾ cup unsweetened applesauce
 1 teaspoon grated lemon zest
 ¼ cup fresh lemon juice
 2½ tablespoons canola or corn oil
 2 tablespoons light corn syrup
 1 teaspoon lemon extract
    Whites of 4 large eggs

Preheat the oven to 350° F. Lightly spray a 9-inch round cake pan with cooking spray.

In a medium bowl, stir together the flour, sugar, poppy seeds, baking powder, baking soda, and salt.

In another medium bowl, stir together the remaining ingredients except the egg whites. Stir into the flour mixture just until combined.

In a large stainless steel or glass mixing bowl, with an electric mixer on high speed, beat the egg whites until stiff peaks form (the peaks don't fall when the beaters are lifted).

PER SERVING

Calories 214	Carbohydrates 40 g
Total Fat 4.0 g	Fiber 1 g
Saturated Fat 0.5 g	Sugar 18 g
Trans Fat 0.0 g	Protein 4 g
Polyunsaturated Fat 1.5 g	DIETARY EXCHANGES:
Monounsaturated Fat 2.0 g	2½ Other Carbohydrate
Cholesterol 0 mg	1 Fat
Sodium 196 mg	

Using a rubber scraper, gently fold the batter into the beaten egg whites. Pour into the cake pan, lightly smoothing the top with the scraper.

Bake for 30 minutes, or until a cake tester or wooden toothpick inserted in the center comes out clean. Let cool in the pan for 10 minutes. Loosen the sides of the cake with a thin metal spatula. Invert the cake onto a cooling rack. Serve warm, at room temperature, or chilled.

COOK'S TIP on Poppy Seeds and Sesame Seeds

You can intensify the flavor of both poppy and sesame seeds by dry-roasting. Store these popular seeds in the refrigerator. Otherwise, the oil in the seeds may turn rancid.

pumpkin-carrot cake

SERVES 8

You don't even need a mixer for this from-scratch cake!

> Cooking spray
> 1 cup shredded carrots
> ½ cup canned solid-pack pumpkin (not pie filling)
> ½ cup egg substitute
> 1 tablespoon canola or corn oil
> 1 teaspoon vanilla extract
> 1 cup all-purpose flour
> ¾ cup sugar
> ¼ cup chopped walnuts
> 1 teaspoon ground cinnamon
> ½ teaspoon baking soda
> 2 tablespoons confectioners' sugar
> ½ teaspoon ground allspice or ground nutmeg

Preheat the oven to 350° F. Lightly spray a 9-inch square metal baking pan with cooking spray.

In a medium bowl, whisk together the carrots, pumpkin, egg substitute, oil, and vanilla.

In a small bowl, stir together the flour, sugar, walnuts, cinnamon, and baking soda. Stir into the carrot mixture just until combined. Pour into the baking pan.

Bake for 25 to 30 minutes, or until a cake tester or wooden toothpick inserted in the center comes out clean. Transfer to a cooling rack and let cool for at least 15 minutes.

To serve, cut the cake into 8 pieces. Sift the confectioners' sugar over the cake. Sprinkle with the allspice.

PER SERVING	
Calories 197	Carbohydrates 36 g
Total Fat 4.5 g	Fiber 2 g
Saturated Fat 0.5 g	Sugar 22 g
Trans Fat 0.0 g	Protein 4 g
Polyunsaturated Fat 2.5 g	DIETARY EXCHANGES:
Monounsaturated Fat 1.5 g	2½ Other Carbohydrate
Cholesterol 0 mg	1 Fat
Sodium 121 mg	

orange angel food cake

SERVES 12

Light and refreshing, this dessert is also pretty and festive. It makes a perfect finish for a rich meal. The best surprise is how easy it is to make.

2 envelopes unflavored gelatin (2 tablespoons total)

½ cup cold water

1 cup boiling water

1 cup sugar

1 6-ounce can frozen orange juice concentrate, thawed

1 10-inch angel food cake

4 11-ounce cans mandarin oranges in water or juice, drained, divided use

8 ounces frozen fat-free whipped topping, thawed in refrigerator

In a large bowl, stir together the gelatin and cold water until dissolved. Stir in the boiling water, sugar, and orange juice. Let the mixture cool, but do not let it set.

Meanwhile, cut the cake into 2-inch cubes. Pack the cake cubes and 3 cans drained mandarin oranges into a $13 \times 9 \times 2$-inch glass baking dish.

Fold the whipped topping into the cooled gelatin mixture. Pour over the cake and mandarin oranges, allowing the mixture to run down between the cubes. Top with the remaining 1 can mandarin oranges. Cover and refrigerate until set. Cut into 12 squares.

COOK'S TIP

To avoid the trans fat and sodium often found in commercial baked products and mixes, try making your angel food cake from scratch. There's no better way to be sure the treat you're serving is heart healthy as well as delicious.

PER SERVING

Calories 289	Carbohydrates 68 g
Total Fat 0.0 g	Fiber 1 g
Saturated Fat 0.0 g	Sugar 48 g
Trans Fat 0.0 g	Protein 5 g
Polyunsaturated Fat 0.0 g	DIETARY EXCHANGES:
Monounsaturated Fat 0.0 g	4½ Other Carbohydrate
Cholesterol 0 mg	
Sodium 272 mg	

chocolate
mini-cheesecakes

These mini-cheesecakes are pure bliss in a small package! Enjoy them plain or dress up each serving with a few blueberries or raspberries or one perfect strawberry.

¼ cup plus 2 tablespoons chocolate graham cracker crumbs

4 ounces low-fat cream cheese, softened

4 ounces fat-free cream cheese, softened

½ cup sugar

½ cup fat-free sour cream

½ cup egg substitute

2 tablespoons unsweetened cocoa powder

1 teaspoon vanilla extract

Preheat the oven to 325° F.

Line a 12-cup muffin pan with foil or paper bake cups. Sprinkle 1½ teaspoons crumbs into each.

In a large mixing bowl, with an electric mixer on medium-high speed, beat the cream cheeses, sugar, and sour cream until light and fluffy, about 3 minutes.

Add the egg substitute, cocoa powder, and vanilla. Beat on medium speed until blended. Fill the bake cups with the mixture (an ice cream scoop works well for this).

Bake for 18 to 20 minutes, or until the center is set (doesn't jiggle when gently shaken). Transfer the pan to a cooling rack and let cool for 15 to 20 minutes. Cover the pan and refrigerate for at least 30 minutes, or until completely cooled, before serving.

PER SERVING

Calories 96	Carbohydrates 14 g
Total Fat 2.0 g	Fiber 0 g
Saturated Fat 1.0 g	Sugar 10 g
Trans Fat 0.0 g	Protein 4 g
Polyunsaturated Fat 0.0 g	DIETARY EXCHANGES:
Monounsaturated Fat 0.5 g	1 Other Carbohydrate
Cholesterol 9 mg	½ Fat
Sodium 122 mg	

apple-rhubarb crisp

SERVES 8

The apples give sweetness and the rhubarb contributes tartness to this fruit crisp.

Cooking spray

Filling

2 cups sliced fresh or frozen unsweetened rhubarb, thawed and drained if frozen

2 cups peeled and sliced cooking apples, such as Rome Beauty, Winesap, or Granny Smith

½ cup sugar

1 tablespoon cornstarch

Topping

⅔ cup uncooked old-fashioned or quick-cooking rolled oats

½ cup all-purpose flour

¼ cup firmly packed light brown sugar

3½ tablespoons light tub margarine

Lightly spray an 8-inch square glass baking dish or 1-quart glass casserole dish with cooking spray. Put the filling ingredients in the dish and stir together. Let stand for 1 hour.

Preheat the oven to 375° F.

In a medium bowl, stir together the oats, flour, and brown sugar.

Using a pastry blender, cut the margarine into the topping mixture until it resembles coarse crumbs. Sprinkle over the filling.

Bake for 30 to 40 minutes, or until the topping is light brown. Transfer to a cooling rack and let cool for about 20 minutes before serving.

PER SERVING	
Calories 171	Carbohydrates 36 g
Total Fat 2.5 g	Fiber 2 g
Saturated Fat 0.0 g	Sugar 23 g
Trans Fat 0.0 g	Protein 2 g
Polyunsaturated Fat 0.5 g	DIETARY EXCHANGES:
Monounsaturated Fat 1.0 g	2½ Other Carbohydrate
Cholesterol 0 mg	½ Fat
Sodium 44 mg	

peach-raspberry cobbler

SERVES 8

Cobbler gets its name from the cobbled or bumpy appearance of the biscuitlike topping that bakes over a bubbly fruit filling. What a great way to get in a serving of fruit!

Filling

3 cups fresh or frozen unsweetened sliced peaches or nectarines

3 cups fresh or frozen raspberries

3 tablespoons water

½ cup sugar

2 tablespoons all-purpose flour

½ teaspoon ground ginger

Topping

⅓ cup all-purpose flour

¼ cup whole-wheat flour

2 tablespoons light brown sugar

1 tablespoon wheat germ

1 teaspoon baking powder

2 tablespoons light tub margarine, chilled

¼ cup egg substitute

2 tablespoons fat-free milk

Preheat the oven to 400° F.

In a large saucepan, bring the peaches, raspberries, and water to a boil over high heat. Reduce the heat and simmer, covered, for 5 minutes, or until soft, stirring often.

PER SERVING	
Calories 179	Carbohydrates 37 g
Total Fat 2.0 g	Fiber 5 g
Saturated Fat 0.0 g	Sugar 24 g
Trans Fat 0.0 g	Protein 6 g
Polyunsaturated Fat 0.5 g	DIETARY EXCHANGES:
Monounsaturated Fat 0.5 g	2½ Other Carbohydrate
Cholesterol 0 mg	½ Fat
Sodium 139 mg	

Meanwhile, in a small bowl, stir together the sugar, 2 tablespoons flour, and the ginger. Stir into the cooked fruit mixture. Cook until thickened and bubbly, stirring constantly. With the heat on low, keep the filling hot while you make the topping.

In a medium bowl, stir together the flours, brown sugar, wheat germ, and baking powder.

Using a pastry blender, cut in the margarine until the mixture resembles coarse crumbs. Make a well in the center.

In a small bowl, stir together the egg substitute and milk. Pour into the well. Using a fork, stir into the topping mixture just until moistened.

Pour the hot filling into a 1½-quart glass baking dish. Immediately spoon small mounds of the topping onto the hot filling.

Bake for 20 to 25 minutes, or until a cake tester or wooden toothpick inserted in one of the biscuit mounds comes out clean. Serve warm.

key lime tart
with tropical fruit

SERVES 8

Serve this tropical treat after a spicy meal to cool down the heat.

　　　　Cooking spray
1¼ cups low-fat graham cracker crumbs
¼ cup unsweetened applesauce
1 14-ounce can fat-free sweetened condensed milk
3 ounces low-fat cream cheese, softened
1 teaspoon grated lime zest
½ cup fresh or bottled Key lime juice or fresh lime juice
¼ teaspoon almond extract
2 cups fat-free frozen whipped topping, thawed in refrigerator
1 medium mango, sliced
1 medium banana, thinly sliced
½ cup fresh or canned pineapple chunks, in their own juice if canned

Preheat the oven to 350° F. Lightly spray a 9-inch pie pan with cooking spray.

In a medium bowl, stir together the graham cracker crumbs and applesauce. Transfer to the pie pan. Lay a piece of plastic wrap on top to keep the crumbs from sticking to your hands. Press the mixture onto the bottom and up the sides of the pie pan. Discard the plastic wrap.

Bake for 8 minutes, or until toasted. Let cool completely on a cooling rack.

In a large bowl, whisk together the condensed milk, cream cheese, lime zest, lime juice, and almond extract until smooth. Fold in the whipped topping until well blended. Spoon into the crust, smoothing the top. Cover and refrigerate for at least 1 hour, or until the filling is thickened. Arrange the fruit in a decorative pattern on top.

PER SERVING	
Calories 288	Carbohydrates 59 g
Total Fat 2.5 g	Fiber 2 g
Saturated Fat 1.0 g	Sugar 44 g
Trans Fat 0.0 g	Protein 6 g
Polyunsaturated Fat 0.0 g	DIETARY EXCHANGES:
Monounsaturated Fat 1.0 g	4 Other Carbohydrate
Cholesterol 12 mg	½ Fat
Sodium 153 mg	

gingersnap and graham cracker crust

MAKES ONE 9-INCH PIECRUST

You can either fill this crust and bake it along with the filling or bake the crust before filling it. It's so good either way, plus it's extremely low in harmful fats and contains no cholesterol.

¾ cup low-fat graham cracker crumbs

¾ cup low-fat gingersnap crumbs

2 tablespoons light corn syrup

2 tablespoons unsweetened apple juice

In a medium bowl, stir together all the ingredients. Using your fingers, press the mixture onto the bottom and up the sides of a 9-inch pie pan.

The crust is ready to fill and bake. If you need a prebaked crust, bake it at 350° F for 10 minutes, then let cool before filling.

PER SERVING (based on ⅛ of pie crust)

Calories 77	Carbohydrates 16 g
Total Fat 1.0 g	Fiber 0 g
Saturated Fat 0.0 g	Sugar 7 g
Trans Fat 0.0 g	Protein 1 g
Polyunsaturated Fat 0.0 g	DIETARY EXCHANGES:
Monounsaturated Fat 0.5 g	1 Other Carbohydrate
Cholesterol 0 mg	
Sodium 66 mg	

mock baklava

SERVES 12

Traditional baklava is usually full of butter and therefore loaded with saturated fat. Through the wonders of modern technology—in the form of butter-flavor cooking spray—here is a revamped and no-guilt version of this Greek sweet.

¾ cup raisins

⅔ cup finely chopped pecans or walnuts, dry-roasted

Butter-flavor cooking spray

8 sheets frozen phyllo dough, thawed

½ cup honey

2 teaspoons ground cinnamon

Preheat the oven to 350° F.

In a small bowl, combine the raisins and nuts.

Lightly spraying every other phyllo sheet with cooking spray, stack the sheets. Spread the raisin-nut mixture over the top sheet, leaving a 1-inch border on all sides.

Drizzle with the honey and sprinkle with the cinnamon.

Starting on a long side, roll lengthwise, jelly-roll style. Tucking the ends of the roll under, place with the seam side down on a nonstick baking sheet. Lightly spray the top with cooking spray. Cut shallow slashes through the pastry to the raisin-nut mixture at 1½-inch intervals so steam can escape during baking.

Bake for 20 to 30 minutes, or until light golden brown. Cut into 12 slices using the vent lines as guides.

PER SERVING

Calories 169	Carbohydrates 31 g
Total Fat 5.0 g	Fiber 2 g
Saturated Fat 0.5 g	Sugar 18 g
Trans Fat 0.0 g	Protein 2 g
Polyunsaturated Fat 1.5 g	DIETARY EXCHANGES:
Monounsaturated Fat 3.0 g	2 Other Carbohydrate
Cholesterol 0 mg	1 Fat
Sodium 63 mg	

COOK'S TIP

This dish freezes well. Prepare as directed but omit spraying the top and baking. (Do cut the steam vents.) Freeze overnight on a baking sheet, then wrap in freezer paper or aluminum foil for freezing. To bake, place the frozen baklava on a nonstick baking sheet, lightly spray with butter-flavor cooking spray, and bake at 350° F for 35 to 45 minutes, or until golden brown.

triple-chocolate brownies

SERVES 16

This super-rich-tasting brownie is the ultimate chocolate fix. To save time and more than 70 calories, you can dust the brownies with sifted confectioners' sugar instead of frosting them.

Cooking spray

Brownies

1 14-ounce can fat-free sweetened condensed milk

½ cup fat-free chocolate syrup

½ cup egg substitute

1½ teaspoons vanilla extract

⅔ cup all-purpose flour

½ cup unsweetened cocoa powder

1 teaspoon baking powder

⅓ cup mini semisweet chocolate chips

¼ cup chopped pecans

Frosting (optional)

2 cups confectioners' sugar

3 tablespoons unsweetened cocoa powder

2 tablespoons coffee liqueur or strong coffee

2 tablespoons fat-free chocolate syrup

½ teaspoon vanilla extract

1 to 2 tablespoons fat-free milk (as needed for consistency)

✻ ✻ ✻

Confectioners' sugar for dusting (if not using frosting)

PER SERVING	
Calories 162	Carbohydrates 30 g
Total Fat 2.5 g	Fiber 1 g
Saturated Fat 1.0 g	Sugar 22 g
Trans Fat 0.0 g	Protein 4 g
Polyunsaturated Fat 0.5 g	DIETARY EXCHANGES:
Monounsaturated Fat 1.0 g	2 Other Carbohydrate
Cholesterol 3 mg	½ Fat
Sodium 73 mg	

PER SERVING (with frosting)	
Calories 240	Carbohydrates 48 g
Total Fat 3.0 g	Fiber 1 g
Saturated Fat 1.0 g	Sugar 38 g
Trans Fat 0.0 g	Protein 4 g
Polyunsaturated Fat 0.5 g	DIETARY EXCHANGES:
Monounsaturated Fat 1.0 g	3 Other Carbohydrate
Cholesterol 3 mg	½ Fat
Sodium 75 mg	

Preheat the oven to 350° F. Lightly spray a 13 × 9 × 2-inch metal baking pan with cooking spray.

In a large mixing bowl, with an electric mixer on medium speed, beat the condensed milk, chocolate syrup, egg substitute, and vanilla for 2 minutes, or until creamy.

Reduce the speed to low. Gradually add the flour, cocoa, and baking powder, beating after each addition and scraping the sides as needed. Increase the speed to medium and beat for 2 minutes.

Reduce the speed to low. Add the chocolate chips and pecans, beating for 10 seconds, or until distributed throughout the batter. Spoon into the pan.

Bake for 18 to 20 minutes, or until a cake tester or wooden toothpick inserted in the center comes out almost clean. Transfer to a cooling rack and let cool for about 30 minutes before preparing the frosting.

In a medium mixing bowl, with the mixer on low speed, beat all the frosting ingredients except the milk until smooth, gradually adding the milk until the desired consistency. Spread on the brownies.

If not using frosting, sift confectioners' sugar over the cooled brownies.

streusel-topped blueberry bars

SERVES 12

This cookie will satisfy your craving for blueberry pie without all the work or all the saturated and trans fats.

1 cup fresh or frozen blueberries, thawed if frozen

¼ cup sugar

1 tablespoon cornstarch

1 teaspoon grated lemon zest

1 tablespoon fresh lemon juice

1 teaspoon vanilla extract

   Cooking spray

¾ cup all-purpose flour

¾ cup uncooked old-fashioned or quick-cooking rolled oats

½ cup sugar

¼ cup firmly packed light brown sugar

⅓ cup low-fat buttermilk

   White of 1 large egg

In a small saucepan, stir together the blueberries, ¼ cup sugar, cornstarch, lemon zest, lemon juice, and vanilla. Bring to a simmer over medium-high heat. Reduce the heat and simmer for 5 minutes, or until the blueberries are tender and the mixture is thickened, gently stirring occasionally if you want a chunky texture (no need to be gentle if you want the blueberries more mashed). Remove from the heat. Set aside.

Preheat the oven to 350° F. Lightly spray a 9-inch square metal baking pan with cooking spray.

PER SERVING	
Calories 128	Carbohydrates 29 g
Total Fat 0.5 g	Fiber 1 g
Saturated Fat 0.0 g	Sugar 19 g
Trans Fat 0.0 g	Protein 2 g
Polyunsaturated Fat 0.0 g	DIETARY EXCHANGES:
Monounsaturated Fat 0.0 g	2 Other Carbohydrate
Cholesterol 0 mg	
Sodium 14 mg	

In a medium bowl, stir together the flour, oats, ½ cup sugar, and the brown sugar.

Whisk in the buttermilk and egg white just until combined. Don't overmix; the batter should be lumpy. Reserve ½ cup mixture for topping.

To assemble, spread the remaining mixture in the baking pan. Spread the blueberry mixture on top. Spoon the reserved topping mixture in teaspoon-size dollops over the blueberry mixture.

Bake for 23 to 25 minutes, or until the center is set (doesn't jiggle when gently shaken). Transfer to a cooling rack and let cool for 15 minutes before cutting into 12 bars.

cocoa-almond meringue kisses

SERVES 14

These meringues are crisp on the outside and chewy on the inside.

Cooking spray

Whites of 3 large eggs

⅛ teaspoon cream of tartar

¾ cup sugar

3 tablespoons unsweetened cocoa powder

½ teaspoon vanilla extract

¼ cup sliced almonds

Preheat the oven to 325° F. Lightly spray two large baking sheets with cooking spray.

In a large stainless steel or glass mixing bowl, with an electric mixer on high speed, beat the egg whites and cream of tartar until stiff peaks form (the peaks don't fall when the beaters are lifted).

Add the sugar, 2 tablespoons at a time, beating well after each addition. (The meringue shouldn't feel grainy when rubbed between your fingers.)

Add the cocoa and vanilla, beating well to blend.

Fold in the almonds. Drop by tablespoonfuls onto the baking sheets.

Bake for 25 minutes, or until crisp on the outside. Remove the cookies immediately from the baking sheets and let cool on cooling racks. Store in an airtight container.

PER SERVING

Calories 60	Carbohydrates 12 g
Total Fat 1.0 g	Fiber 0 g
Saturated Fat 0.0 g	Sugar 11 g
Trans Fat 0.0 g	Protein 1 g
Polyunsaturated Fat 0.0 g	DIETARY EXCHANGES:
Monounsaturated Fat 0.5 g	1 Other Carbohydrate
Cholesterol 0 mg	
Sodium 12 mg	

coconut cornflake cookies

Cookies for breakfast? The thought will be tempting when you try these crunchy, fruity cookies. They'll please kids and parents alike.

Cooking spray	3 cups all-purpose flour
1 cup sugar	1 teaspoon baking powder
⅔ cup light tub margarine, at room temperature	½ teaspoon baking soda
½ cup egg substitute	1 cup dried mixed fruit bits
1 teaspoon vanilla extract	2 cups coarsely crushed cornflake cereal
1 teaspoon coconut extract	

Preheat the oven to 375° F. Lightly spray two baking sheets with cooking spray.

In a large bowl, stir together the sugar, margarine, egg substitute, and vanilla and coconut extracts until smooth.

In a small bowl, combine the flour, baking powder, and baking soda. Using a spoon, gradually stir into the sugar mixture until the flour is incorporated (the dough will be slightly sticky).

Gently stir in the fruit bits to distribute throughout the dough.

Put the cornflakes in a shallow bowl or on a large platter. Drop a teaspoon of dough onto the cornflakes and roll to coat. Place the cookie on a baking sheet and flatten slightly with the bottom of a glass. Repeat with the remaining dough, leaving 2 inches between cookies.

Bake for 10 to 11 minutes, or until the cookies feel slightly soft when lightly pressed in the center. Transfer the cookies to cooling racks. Let cool completely, about 30 minutes.

PER SERVING

Calories 118	Carbohydrates 23 g
Total Fat 1.5 g	Fiber 1 g
Saturated Fat 0.0 g	Sugar 10 g
Trans Fat 0.0 g	Protein 2 g
Polyunsaturated Fat 0.5 g	DIETARY EXCHANGES:
Monounsaturated Fat 1.0 g	1½ Other Carbohydrate
Cholesterol 0 mg	½ Fat
Sodium 109 mg	

bavarian custard parfaits

SERVES 8

Simple to prepare yet elegant in appearance, this dessert is perfect to serve at your next dinner party. Almost any fresh fruits except melons and citrus fruit work well in this recipe, so feel free to make substitutions.

1 1-ounce package fat-free, sugar-free instant vanilla pudding mix

1 cup fat-free milk

1 cup fat-free sour cream

1 cup fat-free vanilla yogurt

1 teaspoon vanilla extract

½ cup fat-free frozen whipped topping, thawed in refrigerator

¼ cup all-fruit strawberry spread

1½ cups fresh blueberries

1½ cups sliced fresh hulled strawberries

2 tablespoons plus 2 teaspoons sliced almonds, dry-roasted if desired

In a medium bowl, whisk together the pudding mix and milk until smooth.

Whisk in the sour cream, yogurt, and vanilla until smooth and slightly thickened.

In a small bowl, using a rubber scraper, gently fold together the whipped topping and strawberry spread.

In each of eight parfait or wine glasses, layer the mixtures in the following order: scant ¼ cup pudding mixture, scant ¼ cup blueberries, scant ¼ cup pudding mixture, scant ¼ cup strawberries. Top each serving with about 1 tablespoon whipped topping mixture and 1 teaspoon almonds.

PER SERVING

Calories 197	Carbohydrates 37 g
Total Fat 2.0 g	Fiber 2 g
Saturated Fat 0.0 g	Sugar 24 g
Trans Fat 0.0 g	Protein 7 g
Polyunsaturated Fat 0.5 g	DIETARY EXCHANGES:
Monounsaturated Fat 1.0 g	½ Fruit
Cholesterol 8 mg	2 Other Carbohydrate
Sodium 280 mg	½ Fat

chocolate soufflé
with vanilla sauce

SERVES 6

This wonderful soufflé uses cocoa instead of chocolate. You'll think this classic dessert tastes just like its high-fat counterpart.

Cooking spray

⅓ cup fresh orange juice

⅓ cup sugar

Whites of 4 large eggs

¼ cup unsweetened cocoa powder (Dutch-process preferred)

2 tablespoons orange liqueur

¾ cup fat-free vanilla ice cream or frozen yogurt, softened

Preheat the oven to 300° F. Lightly spray six 5-ounce custard cups with cooking spray. Set aside.

In a small saucepan, stir together the orange juice and sugar. Cook over medium-high heat for 3 to 4 minutes, or until the mixture is syrupy, stirring occasionally. Remove from the heat.

In a large stainless steel or glass mixing bowl, with an electric mixer on high speed, beat the egg whites until stiff, but stop before dry peaks form.

Pour the syrup over the egg whites. Beat for 2 minutes.

Add the cocoa and liqueur. Beat just until well mixed. Pour into the custard cups.

Bake for 12 minutes, or until the soufflés have puffed. Do not overbake or the soufflés will become tough.

To serve, spoon 2 tablespoons softened ice cream into the center of each soufflé. Serve immediately.

PER SERVING	
Calories 117	Carbohydrates 23 g
Total Fat 0.5 g	Fiber 1 g
Saturated Fat 0.0 g	Sugar 18 g
Trans Fat 0.0 g	Protein 4 g
Polyunsaturated Fat 0.0 g	DIETARY EXCHANGES:
Monounsaturated Fat 0.0 g	1½ Other Carbohydrate
Cholesterol 0 mg	
Sodium 54 mg	

mango brûlée
with pine nuts

SERVES 4

Easy, elegant, and fast, this very special dessert requires only four ingredients.

> 2 cups cubed fresh mango, papaya, or peaches
>
> ⅔ cup fat-free sour cream
>
> 2 tablespoons pine nuts
>
> 2 tablespoons dark brown sugar

Preheat the broiler.

Place the fruit in a single layer in a 9-inch pie pan.

Stir the sour cream and dollop over the fruit. Spread the sour cream evenly.

Sprinkle with the pine nuts and brown sugar.

Broil 4 to 6 inches from the heat for 1 to 2 minutes, or until the sugar melts and the pine nuts toast. Watch carefully so the nuts don't burn. Serve immediately.

COOK'S TIP

If fresh fruit is out of season, you can use frozen unsweetened fruit that's been thawed, fruit in a jar, or fruit canned in unsweetened juice.

PER SERVING

Calories 139	Carbohydrates 28 g
Total Fat 2.5 g	Fiber 2 g
Saturated Fat 0.5 g	Sugar 22 g
Trans Fat 0.0 g	Protein 4 g
Polyunsaturated Fat 1.0 g	DIETARY EXCHANGES:
Monounsaturated Fat 1.0 g	1 Fruit
Cholesterol 7 mg	1 Other Carbohydrate
Sodium 38 mg	½ Fat

honey-baked pecan peaches

SERVES 8

Self-made delectability—luscious fruit is cut in half, baked upside down over honey and pecans, then flipped and served in the sauce it makes as it cooks.

Cooking spray

2 tablespoons honey

¼ cup finely chopped pecans

4 large peaches or nectarines (about 6 ounces each), peeled if desired and halved

¼ teaspoon ground cinnamon

2 tablespoons light tub margarine

¼ teaspoon vanilla extract

Preheat the oven to 350° F.

Lightly spray a 9-inch round cake or pie pan with cooking spray. Pour the honey into the pan and heat in the oven for 2 minutes, or until the consistency of pancake syrup. Remove the pan from the oven and swirl to coat the bottom.

Sprinkle the pecans over the honey.

Sprinkle the cut sides of the peaches with the cinnamon. Place with the cut side down on the pecans. Using a fork, pierce each peach half several times for faster cooking.

Bake for 20 minutes, or until tender. Leaving the syrup in the pan, transfer the peaches with the cut side up to a platter.

Add the margarine and vanilla to the syrup, stirring until the margarine melts. Spoon over the peaches. Let stand for 10 minutes to absorb flavors. Serve warm or at room temperature.

PER SERVING	
Calories 82	Carbohydrates 12 g
Total Fat 4.0 g	Fiber 2 g
Saturated Fat 0.0 g	Sugar 11 g
Trans Fat 0.0 g	Protein 1 g
Polyunsaturated Fat 1.0 g	DIETARY EXCHANGES:
Monounsaturated Fat 2.0 g	1 Other Carbohydrate
Cholesterol 0 mg	1 Fat
Sodium 23 mg	

apple-raisin sauce

Save lots of time, effort, and fat grams by serving this delectable fruit sauce over fat-free vanilla ice cream or frozen yogurt instead of making apple strudel à la mode.

3 medium apples

2 cups unsweetened apple juice

¼ cup raisins or dried cranberries

1 teaspoon ground cinnamon

1 tablespoon cornstarch

2 tablespoons cold water

Peel the apples if desired. Chop coarsely.

In a large saucepan, bring the apples, juice, raisins, and cinnamon to a boil over medium-high heat. Reduce the heat and simmer for 15 minutes, or until the apples are tender.

Meanwhile, put the cornstarch in a cup. Add the water, stirring to dissolve. Stir the cornstarch mixture into the cooked apple mixture. Cook for 1 to 2 minutes, or until thick and smooth, stirring constantly.

Serve warm.

PER SERVING

Calories 96	Carbohydrates 25 mg
Total Fat 0.0 g	Fiber 1 g
Saturated Fat 0.0 g	Sugar 20 g
Trans Fat 0.0 g	Protein 1 g
Polyunsaturated Fat 0.0 g	DIETARY EXCHANGES:
Monounsaturated Fat 0.0 g	1½ Fruit
Cholesterol 0 mg	
Sodium 4 mg	

bananas foster plus

This 1950s specialty of Brennan's restaurant in New Orleans has been updated with a pretty trio of fruit and significantly less saturated fat.

2 tablespoons light tub margarine

3 tablespoons light brown sugar

¼ teaspoon ground cinnamon

⅛ teaspoon ground nutmeg

2 medium bananas, cut into ½-inch slices

2 kiwifruit, peeled and cut into ½-inch slices

1 medium peach, peeled, or nectarine, peeled if desired, cut into ½-inch slices, or ½ cup drained canned sliced peaches in juice

1 tablespoon dark rum or ¼ teaspoon rum extract

2 cups fat-free vanilla frozen yogurt or ice cream

In a medium skillet, melt the margarine over medium heat.

Stir in the brown sugar, cinnamon, and nutmeg. Cook for 3 to 5 minutes, or until the sugar melts and the mixture is the desired consistency, stirring constantly.

Gently stir in the bananas, kiwifruit, and peach. Cook for 1 minute, or until heated through, gently stirring constantly.

Stir in the rum. Cook for 1 minute, gently stirring constantly.

Scoop the frozen yogurt into four bowls. Spoon the banana mixture on top.

PER SERVING

Calories 233	Carbohydrates 50 g
Total Fat 2.5 g	Fiber 3 g
Saturated Fat 0.0 g	Sugar 40 g
Trans Fat 0.0 g	Protein 4 g
Polyunsaturated Fat 0.5 g	DIETARY EXCHANGES:
Monounsaturated Fat 1.5 g	1½ Fruit
Cholesterol 0 mg	2 Other Carbohydrate
Sodium 91 mg	½ Fat

strawberries romanoff

SERVES 6

This dreamy dessert can also be served as a breakfast treat; just leave out the liqueur and top with crunchy whole-grain cereal. For flavor variety, try substituting other fruits and complementary liqueurs. Plan enough time for the yogurt cheese to thicken and become creamy—and, yes, it is worth the wait!

Sauce

1 cup Yogurt Cheese (recipe on page 329)

¼ cup firmly packed light brown sugar

2 tablespoons fruit-flavored liqueur, such as orange or strawberry (optional)

1 teaspoon vanilla extract

½ teaspoon ground cinnamon

❊ ❊ ❊

2 pints fresh strawberries

2 tablespoons finely chopped pecans, dry-roasted

In a small bowl, whisk together the sauce ingredients until thoroughly combined. Cover and refrigerate for at least 1 hour, or until slightly firm.

Meanwhile, discard the stems from the strawberries. Cut the strawberries into bite-size pieces.

To serve, spoon the berries onto six dessert dishes. Top each serving with the sauce and a sprinkling of pecans.

PER SERVING	
Calories 114	Carbohydrates 21 g
Total Fat 2.0 g	Fiber 2 g
Saturated Fat 0.0 g	Sugar 18 g
Trans Fat 0.0 g	Protein 4 g
Polyunsaturated Fat 0.5 g	DIETARY EXCHANGES:
Monounsaturated Fat 1.0 g	½ Fruit
Cholesterol 1 mg	1 Other Carbohydrate
Sodium 33 mg	½ Fat

yogurt cheese

MAKES ABOUT 1 CUP

2 8-ounce containers fat-free plain yogurt without gelatin

Place a double-thick layer of fine-mesh cheesecloth or paper coffee filters inside a rustproof colander. Put the colander in a bowl, leaving enough space for about 1 cup of whey (watery liquid) to drain out of the colander. (The collected whey shouldn't touch the bottom of the colander.) Pour the yogurt into the colander, cover loosely with plastic wrap, and refrigerate for 8 hours. This will yield about 1 cup firm yogurt cheese and 1 cup drained whey (you can discard this or save for another use).

COOK'S TIP

You can use yogurt cheese almost anywhere a recipe calls for plain yogurt or sour cream. Make a double batch so you have enough to use for the strawberries and as a base for any number of dips and sauces, both savory and sweet.

very berry sorbet

SERVES 2

To freeze or not to freeze, that is the question. With this slightly tart dessert, either answer is correct. Try both ways and see which you prefer.

1½ cups frozen unsweetened blackberries, slightly thawed

2 teaspoons water

1 teaspoon frozen orange juice concentrate

1 teaspoon brandy or Cognac (optional)

Fresh mint sprigs (optional)

In a food processor or blender, process all the ingredients except the mint until smooth.

If serving immediately, spoon into two dessert bowls and garnish with the mint sprigs; to serve later, spoon without the mint into an airtight freezer container and freeze. Remove from the freezer about 15 minutes before serving to soften.

PER SERVING

Calories 77	Carbohydrates 19 g
Total Fat 0.5 g	Fiber 6 g
Saturated Fat 0.0 g	Sugar 13 g
Trans Fat 0.0 g	Protein 1 g
Polyunsaturated Fat 0.5 g	DIETARY EXCHANGES:
Monounsaturated Fat 0.0 g	1½ Fruit
Cholesterol 0 mg	
Sodium 1 mg	

strawberry margarita ice

SERVES 6

This frosty dessert takes its key ingredients from the popular frozen margarita. You can adjust the level of sugar depending on the sweetness of your strawberries and how tart you like your "margaritas."

2 cups fresh or frozen unsweetened strawberries, hulled if fresh, thawed if frozen

⅔ cup fresh lime juice

½ to ⅔ cup sugar

1 tablespoon tequila or fresh lime juice

1 tablespoon orange liqueur or fresh orange juice

In a food processor or blender, process all the ingredients until smooth. Pour into a 9 × 5 × 3-inch loaf pan. Cover and freeze for 4 hours, or until firm but not frozen solid.

Meanwhile, put a large mixing bowl in the refrigerator to chill.

When the mixture is firm, break it into chunks and put them in the chilled bowl. Using an electric mixer, beat until smooth but not melted. Serve immediately or return the mixture to the loaf pan, cover, and freeze until serving time. To serve when frozen, scrape across the surface with a spoon and mound the shavings in dessert dishes.

COOK'S TIP

If you leave the strawberry mixture in the freezer until it becomes frozen solid, let it stand at room temperature for about 15 minutes before breaking it into chunks and beating as directed.

PER SERVING	
Calories 111	Carbohydrates 26 g
Total Fat 0.0 g	Fiber 1 g
Saturated Fat 0.0 g	Sugar 23 g
Trans Fat 0.0 g	Protein 0 g
Polyunsaturated Fat 0.0 g	DIETARY EXCHANGES:
Monounsaturated Fat 0.0 g	2 Other Carbohydrate
Cholesterol 0 mg	
Sodium 1 mg	

Appendix A
healthy shopping strategies

To make good choices as you stock your pantry, it's important to take the time to know what you are buying. The best way to find the best foods is to compare product labels and key words on packaging. It's easy to identify the products that contain saturated fat, trans fat, cholesterol, and sodium and find others that you can substitute to help your heart. The labeling on packaged foods gives you all the information you need to put together delicious meals that will help you manage your fat intake and lower your cholesterol.

Read Nutrition Labels

The U.S. Food and Drug Administration (FDA) requires that all U.S. food manufacturers put a nutrition label on their products. This label states how much total fat, saturated fat, trans fat, cholesterol, sodium, carbohydrate, fiber, sugar, and protein each serving contains. The information shown is based on a daily intake of 2,000 calories. You may need to consume a different calorie level depending on your age, gender, and activity level and whether you're trying to lose, gain, or maintain your weight. (To determine how many daily calories are right for you, see "Manage Your Weight," page 8.)

Focus on these important nutrient values:

- **Fats and cholesterol.** The lower the amounts of saturated fat, trans fat, and cholesterol, the better. See "Follow a Heart-Healthy Diet" on page 4 for information on how to know what amount of fat is right for you.

- **Sodium.** The less sodium a food contains, the better. Lower amounts will help you keep your total daily intake at or below 2,300 mg. (Some people, such as middle-aged or older adults, African Americans, or those with high blood pressure, should keep their sodium intake even lower. See "Limit Sodium Intake" on page 6.)

- **Carbohydrates.** When checking the carbohydrate value, also consider the dietary fiber. Soluble fiber can help reduce levels of LDL cholesterol, so look for high-fiber carbohydrates. Examples are whole-grain foods, dried beans, peas, vegetables, and fruits.

- **Protein.** In this case, more is not always better. When you check labels, remember that you should aim for a daily maximum of 5 ounces of cooked lean meat, poultry, or seafood.

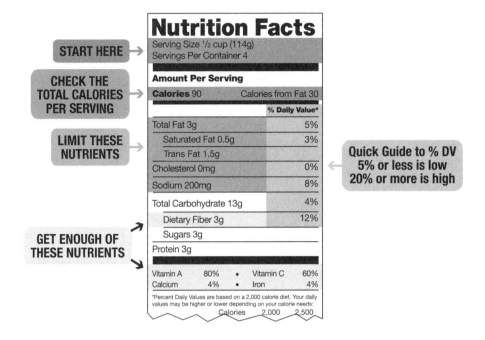

Nutrition Facts

START HERE →

Serving Size ½ cup (114g)
Servings Per Container 4

CHECK THE
TOTAL CALORIES
PER SERVING →

Amount Per Serving

Calories 90   Calories from Fat 30

	% Daily Value*
Total Fat 3g	5%
Saturated Fat 0.5g	3%
Trans Fat 1.5g	
Cholesterol 0mg	0%
Sodium 200mg	8%
Total Carbohydrate 13g	4%
Dietary Fiber 3g	12%
Sugars 3g	
Protein 3g	

LIMIT THESE
NUTRIENTS →

Quick Guide to % DV
5% or less is low
20% or more is high

GET ENOUGH OF
THESE NUTRIENTS

Vitamin A	80%	•	Vitamin C	60%
Calcium	4%	•	Iron	4%

*Percent Daily Values are based on a 2,000 calorie diet. Your daily values may be higher or lower depending on your calorie needs:

Calories   2,000   2,500

Check total calories per serving. Look at the serving size and determine how many servings you're really consuming. If you eat double the servings, you also double the calories and nutrients. Think about how eating the food will affect your calorie balance, keeping in mind that for a 2,000-calorie diet:

- 40 calories per serving is considered low;
- 100 calories per serving is considered moderate; and
- 400 calories or more per serving is considered high.

Limit certain nutrients. If you are trying to lower your cholesterol, you need to be especially careful to limit your saturated fat, trans fat, and cholesterol.

Get enough of other nutrients. Make sure you get 100 percent of the fiber, vitamins, and other nutrients you need every day.

Understand % DV. The % DV (daily value) section tells you the percentage of each nutrient in a single serving, in terms of the daily recommended amount. As a guide, if you want to consume less of a nutrient, such as saturated fat, cholesterol, or sodium, choose foods with a lower % DV (5 percent or less is considered low). If you want to consume more of a nutrient, such as fiber, look for foods with a higher % DV (20 percent or more is considered high).

Identify Sources of Saturated Fat, Trans Fat, and Cholesterol

When reading food labels, also look at the ingredients. They are listed in descending order, with the greatest amount first and the least amount last. When checking on saturated and trans fats and cholesterol in foods, watch for the ingredients in the table below. Be aware that the term "vegetable oil" can mean coconut, palm, or palm kernel oil, each of which is high in saturated fat. Look instead for products that list a specific polyunsaturated or monounsaturated vegetable oil, such as olive, canola, or corn oil. Trace amounts of trans fat occurs naturally in foods such as meat and whole milk. However, by eating less meat and poultry each day and using fat-free or low-fat dairy products, you can easily stay within the recommended limit for trans fat and saturated fat combined.

High in Saturated Fat and Cholesterol	High in Saturated Fat	High in Trans Fat
• Animal fats (bacon, beef, chicken, lamb, pork, turkey)	• Cocoa butter	• Partially hydrogenated vegetable oil
• Butter	• Coconut	• Vegetable shortening
• Cheese	• Coconut oil	
• Cream	• Palm kernel oil	
• Egg and egg yolk solids	• Palm oil	
• Lard	• "Vegetable oil" made from coconut, palm, or palm kernel oil	
• Whole-milk products		

Be careful with foods that are advertised as "cholesterol-free." Even if a food contains no cholesterol, it can contain saturated fat, such as coconut and palm oils, and/or trans fat, such as stick margarine and shortening. Saturated and trans fats raise LDL cholesterol levels in the blood and increase the risk of developing heart disease.

Understand Key Words on Food Packaging

The Food and Drug Administration has guidelines for the descriptors (see the chart below) that food manufacturers are allowed to put on their packages. Whether you're reducing your blood cholesterol level, watching your weight, or both, it pays to read these descriptors carefully.

Key Words	Per Serving
Fat-free	Less than 0.5 g fat
Low-saturated-fat	1 g or less
Low-fat	3 g or less
Reduced-fat	At least 25 percent less fat than the regular version
Light	Half the fat of the regular version
Low-cholesterol	20 mg or less, and 2 g or less of saturated fat
Low-sodium	140 mg sodium or less
Lean	Less than 10 g fat, 4.5 g or less saturated fat, and less than 95 mg cholesterol
Extra lean	Less than 5 g fat and less than 95 mg cholesterol

Use the Heart-check Mark

Look to the American Heart Association Food Certification Program for additional help in food selection. The program's heart-check mark is an easy, reliable tool you can use to quickly identify products that are heart healthy. The heart-check mark on a food package means the product has been screened and verified to meet American Heart Association food criteria for being low in saturated fat and cholesterol for healthy people over age two.

For a list of certified products, visit heartcheckmark.org. Use the free, online "My Grocery List" builder to create a customized, heart-healthy grocery shopping list. Save your list for future use and print or download it anytime from your Web-enabled mobile phone or PDA.

 American Heart Association

Products displaying the heart-check mark meet American Heart Association food criteria for saturated fat and cholesterol for healthy people over age 2.

heartcheckmark.org

Appendix B
healthy cooking strategies

As you prepare the recipes in this book, your time in the kitchen will be well spent. With each satisfying meal, you will be helping your heart. To create these heart-healthy dishes, we rely on certain principles that allow us to cut back on saturated fat, trans fat, cholesterol, and sodium without losing flavor and appeal. You can apply the same techniques to all the foods you cook at home.

High-Flavor, Low-Fat Preparation

You can avoid a great deal of saturated fat by grilling, baking, roasting, or steaming instead of deep-fat frying or pan-frying. You'll find that these lower-fat cooking methods result in dishes that are just as tasty as their higher-fat counterparts.

Help-Your-Heart Cooking Techniques

As you prepare meals, use nonstick cookware, cooking spray, or a bit of unsaturated oil instead of butter or margarine to keep foods from sticking as they cook. You can follow this heart-healthy practice with most recipes and most of the cooking techniques below, which are the ones you'll see most frequently in this cookbook.

Braising or Stewing. Braising (for a pot roast with vegetables, for example) and stewing (for stews and chilis) are similar slow-cooking methods that are great ways to tenderize tougher cuts of meat. Lightly spray a pan with cooking spray or use a small amount of olive or canola oil, then brown the food on all sides. (This step intensifies the flavor and adds color to the meat or chicken, but it can be left out if you wish.) Pour off any fat. Simmer the food in a tightly covered pot on the stovetop or in the oven, using a small amount of flavorful liquid if braising and enough to cover the food if stewing. Because braising or stewing meat or poultry cooks the fat out into the sauce, begin a day ahead if possible. Prepare the dish, then refrigerate it overnight. The extra time lets the flavors blend and causes the chilled fat to rise to the top and harden, making it easy to remove. Braising is also a good method for cooking firm vegetables, and stewing is good for some fresh fruits, such as plums and cherries, and for dried fruits. Braising and stewing are not recommended for tender cuts of meat.

Grilling or Broiling. Interchangeable in many recipes, grilling (cooking over direct heat) and broiling (cooking under direct heat) usually provide a crisp, browned crust and a moist, tender interior. While the food cooks, the fat drips away into the grill or the broiler pan, but the flavor remains. Both methods work well with lean, tender, fairly thin foods, such as fish steaks or fillets, thin steaks, chicken breasts, and hamburgers, that can be cooked relatively quickly over high heat. Trim all visible fat before grilling or broiling; doing so will not only cut down on the amount of "bad" fat but also help prevent flare-ups. Marinades provide extra flavor, but use a minimum amount of oil in them as another way to help prevent flare-ups. Vegetables and fruit also taste great when grilled or broiled. One important note about broiling: If your recipe says, for example, to broil about 4 inches from the heat, that means 4 inches from the heat element to the top of the food you are broiling, not to the top of the broiling rack.

Microwave Cooking. Fast and easy, microwave cooking uses moist heat, making it an especially healthy way to cook vegetables and fruits. That's because very little liquid is needed, so nutrients are retained. Foods don't stick, so you don't need much added fat, if any, and cleanup is easy. To adapt a recipe for the microwave oven, try to find a similar microwave recipe to use as a guide. Cut the cooking time of the conventional recipe to one-fourth to one-third of the time it recommends. If the food isn't done, gradually increase the cooking time until it is. Also, reduce the amount of liquid used in most foods by about one-third because less liquid evaporates in microwave cooking.

microwave cooking tips

- Choose foods that cook well in moist heat: chicken, fish, ground meat, vegetables, sauces, and soups.
- Choose a microwaveable container slightly larger than the dish required for cooking the recipe in a conventional oven.
- Choose pieces that are about equal in size and shape; they will cook more uniformly.
- Add fat-free or low-fat cheese and other toppings near the end of cooking to keep the top of your food from becoming tough or soggy.

Poaching. Poaching is an excellent way to prepare delicate foods, such as seafood, chicken, and fruit. To poach food, immerse it in a pan of almost-simmering well-seasoned liquid (the bubbles should not break the surface of the liquid), and cook it without a cover. Although you can use water as the liquid, some more-flavorful choices are fruit juice, wine, and fat-free, low-sodium broth. After the food is cooked, remove it from the pan and reduce the remaining liquid (decrease the volume by boiling the liquid rapidly) to make a delicious sauce.

Steaming. Steaming is appropriate for almost any food that can be boiled or simmered, including chicken breasts and vegetables. The food is cooked in a basket over simmering water and covered, thus retaining the natural flavor, color, and nutrients. To add flavor to the finished dish, put herbs in the steaming liquid, usually water or broth. Be sure the liquid does not touch the bottom of the basket.

Stir-Frying. Quickly stirring food in a minimum of hot oil seals in the natural juices of meats and seafood and preserves the texture and color of vegetables. Stir-frying is typically done in a wok, although a large skillet also works well. The high temperature and the constant movement of the food keep it from sticking and burning. Once you actually start stir-frying, everything moves quickly, so slice or dice each ingredient into uniform pieces (for more even cooking) and prepare any sauces before you begin.

Roasting or Baking. Both roasting and baking use the dry heat of an oven. The line between the two methods is blurry, but roasting is usually done without a cover and at higher heat, whereas baking may or may not use a cover and usually is at somewhat lower heat. Some sources consider meats and poultry (especially large cuts and whole birds) to be roasted and breads, desserts, and casseroles to be baked. You can use either method for firm fruits and vegetables. When roasting meat, discard the visible fat and place the meat on a rack in a roasting pan to prevent the meat from sitting in its fat drippings. If needed, baste with fat-free liquids, such as wine, fruit juice, or fat-free, low-sodium broth. Plan on removing the meat from the oven 15 to 20 minutes before serving. Letting the meat "rest" makes it easier to carve. For whole birds, discard as much fat as you can before roasting, but leave the skin on until the poultry is cooked. Discard the skin before serving the poultry. Roasting also works well for a number of fruits, such as peaches and bananas, and vegetables from asparagus to zucchini, but not green, leafy vegetables.

Help-Your-Heart Cooking Tips

Here are some tips for heart-smart cooking as well as ways to help trim saturated fat, cholesterol, sodium, and calories from your home-cooked dishes—without trimming taste:

Meats, Poultry, and Seafood

- Remove all visible fat before cooking meat or poultry.

- After you roast or braise meat or poultry, refrigerate it with its liquid, then discard the drippings after the fat has risen to the top and hardened. Save the defatted liquid to use as gravy for meat or poultry or in stews, sauces, and soups.

- If you're using leftover marinade for basting or in a sauce, take precautions—be sure to boil the marinade for at least 5 minutes before using it to kill any harmful bacteria that the raw food might transmit.

- Before cooking most chicken dishes, discard the skin and all visible fat. (See the tip on page 137 for how-to pointers.) Be sure to scrub the cutting surface and utensils well with hot, sudsy water after preparing poultry for cooking. If you're roasting a chicken, leave the skin on to prevent the chicken from drying out. Discard the skin before serving the chicken.

- Baste meats and poultry with fat-free, low-sodium broth, wine, or fruit juice instead of melted butter or other liquids high in fat.

- Buy turkeys that are not self-basting. Self-basting turkeys are high in saturated fat and sodium.

- Try grilling or broiling fish, either directly on the grill or broiler pan or wrapped in aluminum foil. Using a few herbs and some citrus juice as seasoning will let you enjoy the wonderful flavor of the fish itself instead of tasting batter and frying oil.

Vegetables

- To retain natural juices, wrap food in aluminum foil before grilling or baking. Also try wrapping food in edible pouches made of steamed lettuce or cabbage leaves. No need for heavy sauces!

- Cook vegetables just long enough to make them tender-crisp. Overcooked vegetables lose both flavor and important nutrients. With more natural flavor, there's less temptation to use butter or rich sauces.

- Cut down on cholesterol by using more vegetables and less poultry, seafood, or meats in soups, stews, and casseroles. Finely chopped vegetables also are great for stretching ground poultry or meat.

- Use small amounts of lean meats instead of salt pork or fatback to flavor vegetables.

- When you make stuffing, substitute chopped vegetables for some of the bread.

Soups, Sauces, and Gravies

- After making soups and sauces, refrigerate them and skim the hardened fat off the top.
- Instead of using a butter-flour mixture or eggs to thicken soups, stews, and sauces, use pureed cooked vegetables or a tablespoon of cornstarch or flour blended with a cup of fat-free, low-sodium broth or water. Add the blended liquid and simmer until the dish thickens.

In General

- Substitute herbs, spices, and salt-free seasonings for salt as you cook and at the table.
- Substitute onion or garlic flakes or powder for onion or garlic salt.
- Add a drop of lemon juice to the water you cook pasta in, and eliminate the salt and oil.
- Reduce or omit salt in baking recipes that don't use yeast.
- Since most recipes that include sugar call for more of it than necessary, you can usually use one-fourth to one-third less than specified.
- Use wheat germ, bran, whole-wheat bread crumbs, panko, or matzo meal in place of buttered crumbs to top casseroles.
- Instead of croutons, fried bacon, or fried onion rings in salads and casseroles, try nuts, water chestnuts, or wheat berry sprouts for added crunch.

Adapting Recipes

If you're afraid you'll have to give up your favorite recipes to eat heart-healthy, don't worry. You can still enjoy most of those dishes simply by making a few easy substitutions to cut back on saturated fat, trans fat, cholesterol, and sodium.

When Your Recipe Calls For	Use Instead
Regular broth or bouillon	Fat-free, low-sodium broths, either homemade or commercially prepared; low-sodium bouillon granules or cubes, reconstituted according to package directions.
Butter or hard margarine	When possible, use fat-free spray margarine or fat-free or light tub margarine. However, if the type of fat is critical to the recipe, especially in baked goods, you may need to use stick margarine. Choose the product that is lowest in saturated and trans fats.
Butter or hard margarine for sautéing	Vegetable oil or cooking spray; fat-free, low-sodium broth; wine; fruit or vegetable juice.
Cream	Fat-free half-and-half; fat-free nondairy creamer; fat-free evaporated milk.
Eggs	Cholesterol-free egg substitutes; 2 egg whites for 1 whole egg.
Evaporated milk	Fat-free evaporated milk.
Flavored salts, such as onion salt, garlic salt, and celery salt	Onion powder, garlic powder, celery seeds or flakes. Use about one-fourth the amount of flavored salt indicated in the recipe.
Ice cream	Fat-free, low-fat, or light ice cream; fat-free or low-fat frozen yogurt; sorbet; sherbet; gelato.
Oil in baking	Unsweetened applesauce.
Table salt	No-salt-added seasoning blends.
Tomato juice	No-salt-added tomato juice.
Tomato sauce	No-salt-added tomato sauce; 6-ounce can of no-salt-added tomato paste diluted with 1 can of water.
Whipping cream	Fat-free whipped topping; fat-free evaporated milk (thoroughly chilled before whipping).
Whole milk	Fat-free milk.

Appendix C
healthy dining out strategies

If you're like most other Americans, you often don't make dinner—you make reservations or you head out for a quick bite more than half the time. Instead of feeling guilty and worrying about how restaurant food will affect your heart, learn how to eat out with your heart in mind.

Smart Strategies Every Day

What are you in the mood for today? Whether you eat out a lot or only once in a while, these tips will help you make better choices of what to eat.

Know Before You Go

- Visit Web sites of fast-food and casual dining restaurants and print out the nutritional information for their meal choices. Keep the printouts where you can refer to them when you make food selections.
- Avoid all-you-can-eat buffets. It's very hard not to overeat.

Order with Your Heart in Mind

- In general, try to eat a small amount of meat and lots of vegetables.
- Request smaller portions or plan to share entrées. Ask for a to-go box and plan to take home a part of your meal.
- Select foods with less cheese and sauce, or ask for those extras on the side. That way you can control how much of them you eat.
- When you order side dishes, ask the kitchen to omit any sauces, margarine, or butter.
- Feel free to ask about ingredients or how a dish is prepared. Don't hesitate to request substitutions or a specially prepared dish. Most chefs are eager to please.
- Choose broiled, baked, grilled, steamed, or poached entrées over the high-fat fried ones.
- Order potatoes baked, boiled, or roasted—not fried. Then leave off the butter and margarine. Try fat-free or low-fat sour cream, pepper, and chives instead. Salsa also is an excellent potato topper.

- Order salad dressings on the side so you can control your portions. Better yet, try a squeeze of lemon instead of rich dressings.
- Ask for whole-grain breads and rolls when available. Another good choice is melba toast. Use olive oil or soft margarine instead of butter or stick margarine.
- Drink water or fat-free or low-fat milk instead of sugar-laden soda and juice drinks.
- For dessert, choose something light, such as fresh fruit or sorbet.

Smart Strategies by Cuisine

No matter where you are, use your head to make wise choices for your heart. Here are specific strategies geared to several popular restaurant types:

Fast Food

- Pass up the "value size" meal options, and avoid double meat. That's almost certainly much more than the recommended serving size of 2 to 3 ounces.
- Order salad for your main dish, and choose grilled or broiled chicken breast options without breading.
- Avoid mayonnaise and other high-calorie dressings and sauces. Onions, lettuce, and tomato add flavor without the fat. Use pickles and ketchup sparingly because of their high sodium content.
- Have a side salad instead of the usual french fries.
- Skip the bacon on your sandwich or salad.

Asian

- Choose a steamed or poached main dish or try a stir-fried chicken or seafood and vegetable dish.
- Ask the chef to use a minimal amount of oil and leave out the soy sauce, MSG, and salt.
- Choose entrées with lots of vegetables.
- Instead of tempura-style vegetables, ask for steamed or stir-fried vegetables.
- Ask for brown rice instead of white and steamed instead of fried.
- Avoid the crisp fried noodles usually served as an appetizer.

Italian

- Opt for pasta with a small amount of olive oil or with marinara or marsala sauce instead of pasta with a cream sauce, such as Alfredo.
- Try a seafood selection or meatless pasta in place of an entrée with sausage or meatballs.
- If you order pizza, choose one with a thin crust. Opt for topping ingredients such as spinach, mushrooms, broccoli, and roasted peppers instead of sausage or pepperoni.
- Ask for plain Italian bread instead of buttery garlic bread.
- For dessert, choose an Italian ice.

Mexican

- Choose spicy grilled chicken or fish instead of a fried entrée.
- Ask your waiter to bring soft corn tortillas instead of the fried tortilla chips usually served as an appetizer.
- Choose corn tortillas rather than flour tortillas. The latter are high in sodium and may contain lard.
- Use salsa, pico de gallo, cilantro, and jalapeños for added flavor.
- If your entrée comes with sour cream, ask if fat-free or low-fat is available. If not, ask the kitchen to leave it off.
- Ask for a tomato-based sauce, such as ranchero, instead of a creamy or cheesy sauce, such as sour cream or queso.
- If you order a taco salad, don't eat the fried shell.

Appendix D
the science behind the recommendations

What happens in your body that turns foods that are supposed to help nourish into a potential threat instead? Here's a brief explanation of how the cholesterol in your body affects the well-being of your heart. This science forms the basis for our recommendations on how to eat better for better health.

How Cholesterol Affects Your Heart

Your body needs some cholesterol—a waxy fatlike substance—to strengthen cell walls and for other body functions, such as producing hormones. Your blood carries cholesterol and other fats through your body in distinct particles called *lipoproteins*. (Because lipids, or fats, do not mix with water, the body wraps them in protein to move them through the bloodstream.) Three types of lipoprotein make up the major part of your total blood cholesterol measurement: low-density lipoprotein (LDL), high-density lipoprotein (HDL), and very-low-density lipoprotein (VLDL).

Ongoing research continues to clarify how the different lipoproteins work in the body. LDL lipoproteins carry cholesterol to the inner walls of the arteries, where it can collect and contribute to the buildup of plaque. That process is called *atherosclerosis*. Plaque buildup narrows the artery walls and reduces the flow of blood. If a plaque ruptures, it triggers a blood clot to form. If the clot forms where the plaque is, it can block blood flow or break off and travel to another part of the body. If blood flow to an artery that feeds the heart is blocked, it causes a heart attack. If the blockage occurs in an artery that feeds the brain, it causes a stroke. On the other hand, HDL lipoproteins may prevent cholesterol from collecting by carrying it away from the arteries.

Low-Density Lipoprotein: The "Bad" Cholesterol

In most people, LDL cholesterol makes up 60 to 70 percent of total blood cholesterol. A very clear relationship exists between LDL cholesterol level and risk of heart disease: The higher the level, the greater the risk. This is why LDL cholesterol is the primary target of efforts to lower cholesterol.

The optimal level for LDL cholesterol is less than 100 milligrams per deciliter (mg/dL). Near optimal/above optimal is between 100 and 129 mg/dL. An LDL level between 130 and 159 mg/dL is considered a borderline high risk. If your

LDL cholesterol is between 160 and 189 mg/dL, you are at high risk for heart disease. LDL cholesterol that is 190 mg/dL or above is considered very high.

High-Density Lipoprotein: The "Good" Cholesterol

Typically, one-third to one-fourth of the cholesterol in your blood is carried in HDL cholesterol. HDL is considered the "good" cholesterol because an HDL cholesterol level of 60 mg/dL or higher may offer some protection against heart disease. The mean level of HDL cholesterol for American adults age 20 years and older is just over 51 mg/dL.

Strong evidence indicates that low HDL levels (less than 40 mg/dL for men, less than 50 mg/dL for women) are directly related to higher risk for heart disease. Low levels of HDL cholesterol can be caused by many factors. The most common are smoking, overweight and obesity, and lack of exercise. Fortunately, you can change all these factors to increase your HDL level and reduce your risk of heart disease.

VLDLs and Triglycerides

Another type of lipoprotein that carries blood cholesterol is very-low-density lipoprotein. VLDLs also carry most of the blood triglycerides. Triglycerides are other lipids found in the blood, as well as in the body's fat tissue. In fact, triglycerides make up most body fat. Fats found in foods—such as butter, margarine, and vegetable oil—are also triglycerides. As blood circulates, triglycerides are removed from VLDLs to be used for energy by cells or stored as body fat. The remaining lipoprotein particles are called VLDL remnants. These remnants can be taken up by the liver or transformed into low-density lipoprotein. Elevated VLDL cholesterol levels signal the potential need for cholesterol-lowering therapy.

High blood levels of triglycerides are associated with increased risk for heart disease. This is especially true when other risk factors, such as overweight and obesity, smoking, hypertension, diabetes, and low HDL cholesterol, are present.

Research Continues

Scientists continue to explore the complex biochemistry behind the relationship between diet and health. The American Heart Association funds important research that helps us all learn more about how diet impacts heart health. Thanks to the investment in this type of research over the years, the American Heart Association is able to make diet and lifestyle recommendations as a strategy to reduce the risk of cardiovascular diseases. As we publish the fourth edition of this cookbook, current studies are investigating topics such as the effects of various vitamin supplements in patients with stroke and heart failure, as well as how eating behaviors relate to risk factors such as obesity, high cholesterol, and high blood pressure. Other research projects are studying the mechanisms of how foods such as soy and fish might provide protection against risk, and how social interactions affect our eating behaviors. For more information on the latest findings in this constantly evolving field, visit americanheart.org.

Appendix E
risk factors for heart disease and stroke

Several conditions in addition to high blood cholesterol levels contribute to the risk for heart disease and stroke. Some are givens that cannot be changed. Others result from a combination of your habits and how your body reacts to those habits, and these are the factors you can change to reduce your risk.

Risk Factors You *Cannot* Change

- **Family History.** The tendency toward heart disease seems to run in families. Children of parents with heart disease are more likely to develop it themselves, particularly if heart disease was a cause of premature death in the parents or grandparents. Race is also a factor. Compared with whites, blacks develop high blood pressure earlier in life, and their average blood pressures are much higher. As a result, their risk of heart disease is greater.
- **Gender and Increasing Age.** Earlier in life, men have a greater risk of heart attack than women. Men tend to have higher levels of LDL cholesterol and lower levels of HDL cholesterol than women. However, women's death rate from heart disease increases after menopause. Most people who die of heart attack are age 65 or older. At older ages, women who have heart attacks are twice as likely as men to die within a few weeks of an attack.

Risk Factors You *Can* Change

- **High Blood Cholesterol.** "Fats, Cholesterol, and Heart Health" (pages 1–11) presents a complete discussion of how an elevated level of LDL or a reduced level of HDL cholesterol can increase the risk for heart disease and stroke. If you have high blood cholesterol, you can assess your risk and take steps to improve your cholesterol profile.
- **High Blood Pressure.** High blood pressure has no symptoms, which is why it's often called the "silent killer." High blood pressure increases the risk of stroke, heart attack, kidney failure, and congestive heart failure. Have your blood pressure checked regularly. A blood pressure

reading of 140/90 millimeters of mercury (mm Hg) or above is considered high and is referred to as hypertension. A blood pressure reading of 130/85 to 139/89 mm Hg is considered prehypertension. Lifestyle changes such as eating a healthy diet, limiting sodium intake, being physically active, losing weight, and quitting smoking can help prevent or postpone the onset of high blood pressure. Your doctor can help you control existing high blood pressure through these same lifestyle changes and medication, if needed.

- **Physical Inactivity.** Physical inactivity is another major risk factor for heart disease. Regular exercise can help control levels of harmful LDL cholesterol, raise levels of helpful HDL cholesterol, and lower blood pressure in some people. Lack of physical activity also increases the likelihood of overweight or obesity. Being physically active is an important part of lowering your risk for heart disease.

- **Overweight and Obesity.** In addition to being considered a disease itself, obesity also is a risk factor for heart attack, congestive heart failure, sudden cardiac death, and angina, or chest pain. It puts added strain on the heart, which can lead to other serious conditions, such as weakened heart muscle and irregular heart rhythms. Being overweight or obese can lead to high blood pressure, increased LDL cholesterol, decreased HDL cholesterol, and increased triglyceride levels, and the risk of developing diabetes is greater as well. For more information, see "Manage Your Weight," page 8.

- **Smoking.** A smoker's risk of dying from coronary heart disease is two to three times that of a nonsmoker. Smokers also have two to four times the risk of sudden cardiac death. Your risk of heart disease also increases if you breathe in secondhand smoke at home or at work. When you stop smoking, no matter how long or how much you have smoked, your risk of heart disease drops rapidly. Your risk for coronary heart disease, stroke, and peripheral vascular disease is reduced, and one to two years after you quit, your risk is reduced substantially.

- **Diabetes.** The 15 million Americans who have physician-diagnosed diabetes are major candidates for heart disease and stroke. Since the risk factors of having diabetes and being overweight often go hand in hand, it's especially important for diabetic patients to watch their diet and maintain a healthy weight. You can reduce your risk of developing diabetes—or if you have diabetes, you can help control it—by adopting the same recommendations that are good for your heart: Eat a healthy diet, be physically active, lose weight if needed, manage your blood pressure, stop smoking, and monitor your blood glucose levels.

The term *metabolic syndrome* refers to a combination of any three of the following risk factors: a waist measurement greater than 40 inches for men and greater than 35 inches for women; a triglyceride level of 150 mg/dL or higher; HDL less than 40 mg/dL for men and less than 50 mg/dL for women; systolic blood pressure of 130 mm Hg or higher or diastolic blood pressure of 85 mm Hg or higher; and a fasting glucose reading of 100 mg/dL or higher. With metabolic syndrome, the risk of heart disease that comes with high blood cholesterol is even greater.

Warning Signs of Heart Attack and Stroke

When you see the signs of heart attack or stroke symptoms, every second counts. *If you or someone near you experiences any of the symptoms listed in the boxes below, act immediately and call 911.* Be aware that not all signs occur in every heart attack or stroke.

heart attack warning signs

Some heart attacks are sudden and intense, but most start slowly, with mild pain or discomfort. Often people wait too long before getting help.

- **Chest discomfort.** Most heart attacks involve discomfort in the center of the chest that lasts more than a few minutes or that goes away and comes back. It can feel like uncomfortable pressure, squeezing, fullness, or pain.
- **Discomfort in other areas of the upper body.** Symptoms can include pain or discomfort in one or both arms, the back, neck, jaw, or stomach.
- **Shortness of breath.** This may occur with or without chest discomfort.
- **Other signs.** These may include breaking out in a cold sweat, nausea, or lightheadedness.

For both men and women, the most common heart attack symptom is chest pain or discomfort. However, women are somewhat more likely than men to experience some of the other common symptoms, particularly shortness of breath, nausea/vomiting, and back or jaw pain.

stroke warning signs

Act quickly if you or someone near you has one or more of these warning signs of stroke:

- Sudden numbness or weakness of the face, arm, or leg, especially on one side of the body
- Sudden confusion or trouble speaking or understanding
- Sudden trouble seeing in one or both eyes
- Sudden trouble walking, dizziness, or loss of balance or coordination
- Sudden, severe headache with no known cause

In cases of suspected stroke, immediately call 911 or the emergency medical services (EMS) number so an ambulance can be sent. If possible, check the time so you'll know when the first symptoms appeared. If given within three hours of the start of stroke symptoms, clot-busting drugs can stop some strokes in progress, reducing long-term disability and saving lives.

Appendix F
for more information from the American Heart Association

For the most up-to-date information from the American Heart Association or American Stroke Association, contact us directly.

- Call the American Heart Association at 1-800-AHA-USA1 (1-800-242-8721) or the American Stroke Association at 1-888-4STROKE (1-888-478-7653).

- Visit us at americanheart.org or strokeassociation.org. You will find recommendations on how to live a heart-healthy lifestyle, as well as in-depth information on cardiovascular diseases and stroke. You'll also find links to online interactive health tools, community and advocacy programs, and an extensive encyclopedia of medical and technical information.

- Write us at American Heart Association, National Center, 7272 Greenville Avenue, Dallas, Texas 75231-4596.

- To find out what's happening in your local area, contact your regional American Heart Association office at local.americanheart.org.

Index

oils, cooking
    best choices for, 19, 20
    heart-healthy substitutes,
        342
    high in saturated fats,
        335
    high in trans fats, 335
    serving size, 16
    servings per day, 16
    types of fat in, 19
    types to avoid, 19
    unsaturated, types
        of, 20
okra
    Gumbo with Greens and
        Ham, 62–63
    Red and Green Pilaf, 264
olive oil, fats in, 19
olive(s)
    Broiled Salmon with
        Pesto and Olives, 111
    Fresh Basil and Kalamata
        Hummus, 33
    Greek-Style Stewed
        Chicken, 163
    Moroccan Chicken,
        160–61
    Roasted Potato and
        Chicken Salad with
        Greek Dressing,
        84–85
    Slow-Cooker Tuscan
        Chicken, 154
    Spinach, Chickpea, and
        Olive Pasta, 221
    Tilapia with Roasted Red
        Bell Peppers and
        Olives, 124
    Tomato Bursts, 37
omega-3 fatty acids, 6–7,
    21
onions, weight and volume
    equivalents, 25
orange-flower water, cook's
    tip on, 69
orange(s)
    Beets in Orange Sauce,
        250–51
    Boston Citrus Salad, 69

Citrus Rice Salad, 76
Fresh Fruit Salad with
    Poppy Seed and
    Yogurt Dressing, 75
Orange Angel Food
    Cake, 307
Orange-Ginger Chicken
    Skewers, 46
Orange-Strawberry Froth,
    297
weight and volume
    equivalents, 25
Oven-Fried Green
    Tomatoes with Poppy
    Seeds, 273

P
palm kernel oil, fats in, 335
palm oil, fats in, 335
pancake(s)
    Dutch Baby, 288–89
    Gingerbread Pancakes
        with Apple-Berry
        Topping, 286–87
    Pan-Fried Pasta Pancake
        with Vegetables, 220
    Pan-Fried Pasta Pancake
        with Vegetables, 220
panko, cook's tip on, 257
paprika, smoked, cook's tip
    on, 31
Parmesan cheese
    Eggplant Parmigiana,
        240–41
    Parmesan-Peppercorn
        Ranch Dressing, 93
    Spinach Parmesan, 266
pasta
    Artichoke-Rotini Salad
        with Chicken, 86
    Broiled Vegetables, Orzo,
        and Tomatoes with
        Feta, 229
    Cajun Chicken Pasta,
        164–65
    Pan-Fried Pasta Pancake
        with Vegetables, 220

Penne and Cannellini
    Bean Casserole with
    Sun-Dried Tomatoes,
    216–17
Rustic Tomato Soup,
    54–55
Salmon and Rotini with
    Chipotle Cream, 113
Seafood Pasta Salad, 82
Spinach, Chickpea, and
    Olive Pasta, 221
Toasted Ravioli with
    Italian Salsa, 42–43
Triple-Pepper and White
    Bean Soup with Rotini,
    65
Tuna-Pasta Casserole,
    119
Turkey Tetrazzini, 173
Whole-Wheat Pasta with
    Vegetable Sauce,
    214–15
see also couscous;
    noodles
peach(es)
    Bananas Foster
        Plus, 327
    French Toast with Peach
        and Praline Topping,
        292
    Honey-Baked Pecan
        Peaches, 325
    Peach-Raspberry
        Cobbler, 310–11
    Summertime Soup, 50
peanut butter
    Crab Spring Rolls with
        Peanut Dipping Sauce,
        40–41
pears
    Seared Tuna with
        Mango-Pear Salsa,
        116–17
peas
    Chicken Ragout, 156–57
    Grilled Teriyaki Sirloin,
        178–79
    Ham and Rice Salad,
        88–89